Before the Normans

University of Pennsylvania Press
MIDDLE AGES SERIES
Edited by Edward Peters
Henry Charles Lea Professor
of Medieval History
University of Pennsylvania

A complete listing of the books in this series
appears at the back of this volume

Before the Normans

Southern Italy in the Ninth and Tenth Centuries

Barbara M. Kreutz

University of Pennsylvania Press

Philadelphia

First paperback printing 1996

Library of Congress Cataloging-in-Publication Data
Kreutz, Barbara M.
  Before the Normans : Southern Italy in the ninth and tenth centuries / Barbara M.
Kreutz.
      p.   cm.—(Middle Ages series)
  Includes bibliographical references and index.
  ISBN 0-8122-1587-7
  I. Italy, Southern—History—535–1268.   2. Italy, Southern—Social conditions.
I. Title.   II. Series.
DG827.K74   1992
945'.702—dc20   91-29118
                                                                                      CIP

*For I.W.K., of course, and for H.H. and S.H.,
who made of Rome a magnet, and enriched
Apulia.*

I may be wrong, but . . . I can find no admirable traits in the people of southern Italy during the long history of Norman-Swabian domination, nothing then to arouse my local pride, no reassuring patriotism, no *virtù*. For comfort, I must turn instead to the pre-Norman scene with all its diversity and contrasts, when the various peoples came to each other's aid and joined together for self-protection.

Benedetto Croce, *Storia del Regno di Napoli* (author's translation)

Contents

Acknowledgments

THIS BOOK has been many years on the way, and I have incurred many debts to many people. The list must certainly begin with the late Robert L. Reynolds of the University of Wisconsin, who long ago (despairing of luring me to Genoa) suggested a dissertation involving Norman southern Italy. An exceptional man, Robert Reynolds left his mark on all his students, and this study owes a great deal to him—not least his insistence that one come to know intimately the physical terrain of the region under study. In the end, however, I moved back in time, before the Normans, and I soon became deeply indebted to David Herlihy, who succeeded Robert Reynolds at Wisconsin. He wisely cautioned against excessive ambition with my dissertation ("do the big book later"); and his determined questioning of my evidence saved me from many egregious errors and taught me invaluable lessons for the future. Moreover, without his gentle prodding over the past twenty years, the "big book" might never have been completed.

In the 1970s, I began to plan a comprehensive treatment, making as many trips to Italy as circumstances permitted. In 1979–80, thanks to the support and encouragement of David Herlihy, Archibald Lewis, and A. L. Udovitch, I had the luxury of a year's Fellowship in History at Radcliffe's Bunting Institute. That made it possible to start shaping the book in earnest, and my debts escalated: to the Bunting Institute and my fellow Fellows, particularly the late Laila Zamuelis Gross; to the staff of Harvard's Widener Library (the best resource in this country for south Italian materials); and to Professor Ernst Kitzinger, who generously took time to aim me in the right art-historical direction, vital for my region.

In the 1980s, other duties delayed completion, but my debts went on mounting. Various notions were tested in papers at conferences, here and abroad; Bryn Mawr College helped make possible participation in two major foreign meetings. In Italy, scholarly contacts were, as always, stimulating and pleasurable, and I am grateful to those there who have helped keep me aware of new developments, and especially to the Centro di Cultura e Storia Amalfitana. In this country, new ideas came from many

sources. Early on, S. D. Goitein, whose magisterial studies illumined many
dark corners of the Mediterranean, had urged that I not overlook southern
Italy's Jewish communities; Maria Raina Fehl pointed me toward the
most recent investigations. Academic friends and acquaintances around the
country patiently answered scores of questions, and Petra Lent helped
speed my progress at some crucial moments. At Bryn Mawr, my colleagues
in many disciplines continuously sharpened my perceptions, as had, in the
previous decade, my multidisciplinary colleagues and friends at the University
of Wisconsin.

South Italian material is not easy to come by in this country, and time
at the Vatican Library has always rushed by too quickly. In recent years I
have therefore been fortunate in having the University of Pennsylvania's
libraries as a resource, as well as the New York Public Library Research
Division, the Morgan Library, and the Firestone Library at Princeton. But
I am especially indebted to the staff of the Bryn Mawr College libraries:
Eileen Markson of the Art and Archaeology Library and, in Canaday,
Charles Burke (Interlibrary Loan), Jane McGarry (Acquisitions), and Ann
Denlinger and Trudy Reed.

I need also to thank the two anonymous scholars who served as readers
for the manuscript of this study; their perceptive comments and suggestions
have unquestionably led to a better book. And I must thank as well
Yvonne Holman, who created the complex maps the book required.

Finally, this study would have been difficult to accomplish (and certainly
far less enjoyable) had I not, over the years, had generous help and
stimulation from others in this country who have ventured into medieval
southern Italy, particularly Robert P. Bergman, Robert Brentano, Armand
Citarella, Dorothy Glass, Margaret Frazer, Paul Mosher, Father Anthony
P. Via, Tom Walker, and Henry Willard. Some have now abandoned
southern Italy for other pursuits, but this book embodies my gratitude to
all of them.

It also carries with it my boundless gratitude to my family, who have
borne with exemplary patience and goodwill my decades-long preoccupation
with southern Italy. To my extraordinary husband, in particular, who
has helped in countless ways, I can only promise, for the future, time in that
splendid region with no note-taking and no waiting for the small boy to
find the old lady who knows the man who may have the key to the tenth-century
ruin.

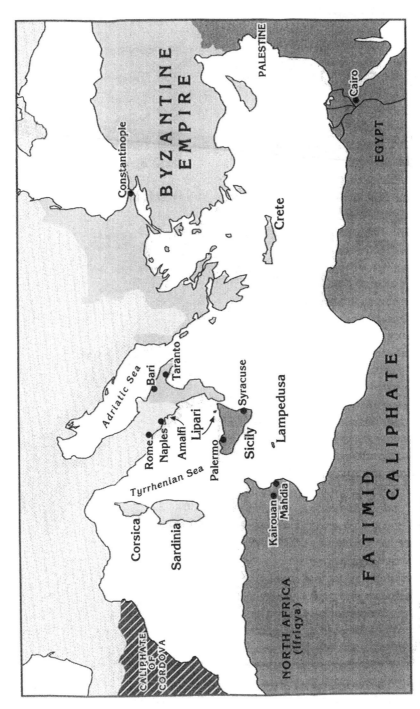

Map 1. The Mediterranean ca. 980 A.D.

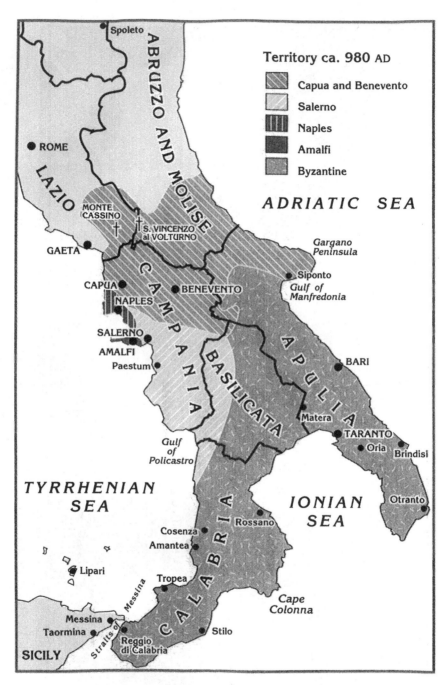

Map 2. The modern *regioni* of southern Italy.

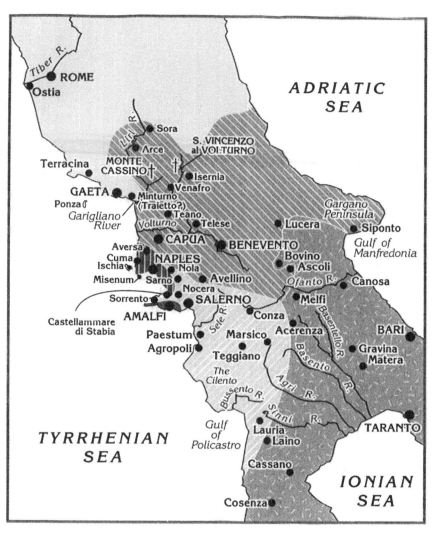

Map 3. The core area ca. 980 A.D.

Abbreviations

MGH	*Monumenta Germaniae Historica*
MGH Dipl. RIG	—— *Diplomata Regum et Imperatorum Germaniae: Die Urkunden der Könige und Kaiser* I, II
MGH Epist.	—— *Epistolae*
MGH SS	—— *Scriptores*
MGH SSrG	—— *Scriptores rerum Germanicarum*
MGH SSrL	—— *Scriptores rerum Langobardicarum et Italicarum*

Annal. Baren.	*Annales Barenses, MGH SS* V: 51–56.
Annal. Ben.	*Annales Beneventani, MGH SS* III: 173–85.
Annal. Bertin.	*Annales Bertiniani. Annales de Saint-Bertin*, ed. F. Grat, J. Viellard, and S. Clemencet (Paris, 1964).
Annal. Reg. Franc.	*Annales Regni Francorum*, ed. Kurze, *MGH in usum scholarum*(Hanover, 1895).
AS	*Acta Sanctorum*, ed. Bollandists (Antwerp, 1643–).
ASPN	*Archivio Storico per le Province Napoletane.*
Capasso, *Mon.*	Bartolommeo Capasso, *Monumenta ad neapolitani ducatus historiam pertinentia*, 2 vols. in 3 (Naples, 1881–92).
Cap. Reg. Franc.	*MGH Capitularia Regum Francorum* II, ed. Boretius and Krause (Hanover, 1897).
CDA	*Codice Diplomatico Amalfitano* I, ed. Riccardo Filangieri di Candida (Naples, 1917).
CDC	*Codex Diplomaticus Cavensis*, 8 vols., ed. M. Morcaldi, M. Schiani, and S. De Stefano (Naples, Milan, and Pisa, 1873–93).
Chron. Salern.	*Chronicon Salernitanum*, ed. Ulla Westerbergh (Stockholm, 1956).
Chron. S. Ben. Casin.	*Chronica Sancti Benedicti Casinensis, MGH SSrL*, pp. 468–78.

Chron. Vulturn.	*Chronicon Vulturnense*, ed. Vincenzo Federici, 3 vols. (Rome: Istituto Storico Italiano, 1925).
Cilento, *Sign. cap.*	Nicola Cilento, *Le origini della signoria capuana nella Longobardia minore* (Rome: Istituto Storico Italiano per il Medioevo, Studi Storici 69–70, 1966).
Cod. Carol.	*Codex Carolinus, MGH Epistolae* III.
De admin. imp.	Constantine Porphyrogenitus, *De administrando imperio*, ed. G. Moravcsik, trans. R. J. H. Jenkins (Budapest, 1949); Vol. II, *Commentary*, ed. R. J. H. Jenkins (London, 1962).
Divisio	*Radelgisi et Siginulfi Divisio Ducatus Beneventani, MGH Leges* IV: 221–25.
Erchempert	*Historia Langobardorum Beneventanorum, MGH SSrL*, pp. 231–64.
Falkenhausen, *Dominazione*	Vera von Falkenhausen, *La dominazione bizantina nell'Italia meridionale dal IX all'XI secolo* (Bari, 1978); trans. and partial rev. of *Untersuchungen über die byzantinische Herrschaft in Süditalien von 9. bis ims 11. Jahrhundert* (Wiesbaden, 1967).
Gay, *Ital. byz.*	Jules Gay, *L'Italie méridionale et l'empire byzantine depuis l'avènement de Basile I jusqu'à la prise de Bari par les Normands (867–1071)* (Paris, 1904); reprint, 2 vols. (New York, 1960).
Jaffé-Loew.	P. Jaffé, *Regesta Pontificum Romanorum*, 2d ed., revised by S. Loewenfeld, F. Kaltenbrunner, and P. Ewald (Leipzig, 1885).
John the Deacon	*Gesta Episcoporum Neapolitanorum, MGH SSrL*, pp. 424–36.
Leo Marsicanus	Leo Marsicanus [Leo of Ostia], *Chronica Monasterii Casinensis*, ed. Hartmut Hoffmann, *MGH SS* XXXIV (Hanover, 1980).
Liutprand, *Rel. Const.*	Liutprand, *Relatio de legatione constantinopolitana, MGH SSrG in usum scholarum*, ed. J. Becker (Hanover, 1915).
LP	*Le Liber Pontificalis*, 3 vols., ed. L. Duchesne (Paris, 1955).
Lupus Proto.	[Bari annals attributed to Lupus Protospatarius], *MGH SS* V: 51–63.

Paul the Deacon	Paul the Deacon, *Historia Langobardorum, MGH SS in usum scholarum*, ed. Waitz (Hanover, 1878).
PG	J. P. Migne, ed., *Patrologia Graeca (Patrologiae Cursus Completus, Series Graeca)*.
Poupardin, *Inst.*	René Poupardin, *Etude sur les institutions politique et administratives des principautés lombarde de l'Italie méridionale* (Paris, 1907).
Settimane	Settimane di studio [annual conferences] del Centro Italiano di Studi sull'Alto Medioevo, Spoleto.
Vita Athanasii	*Vita Athanasii Episcopi Neapolitani, MGH SSrL*, pp. 439–49.

Introduction

SOUTHERN ITALY has been largely ignored by most historians of medieval Europe. Since the region was both prominent and prosperous in antiquity, one might have expected more curiosity. In fact, however, most non-Italian historians have abandoned Italy altogether after the sixth century and the arrival of the Lombards, not to return (so to speak) until the eleventh or twelfth century. And even then they typically have glanced south only briefly, to consider the Normans, and thereafter have largely concentrated on developments from Rome northward.

This study focuses on mainland southern Italy in the centuries immediately preceding the Normans: in particular, the ninth and tenth centuries. We should know what the Normans encountered. But that is not the only reason for paying attention to the south. In this early medieval period, southern Italy was in effect a giant laboratory, one in which polities were tested and where Byzantium, the Lombards, the Islamic world, and the Latin West constantly intersected.

The politics and political misadventures of this region in Charlemagne's day, and on through the ninth century, have a particular fascination; we know many of the players from other settings. But tenth-century developments deserve consideration as well, for in the tenth century southern Italy's complex Mediterranean culture began genuinely to coalesce. And then, toward the end of that century, the region began to fall subject to the forces molding Europe.

If early medieval southern Italy has received scant attention from modern historians, that at least is not a new phenomenon. Until the eleventh century, medieval Europe seemed scarcely aware of the region. Even after 774, when northern Italy was absorbed within the Carolingian Empire, visitors to the south still seemed mainly restricted to the occasional caller at Monte Cassino, or to the occasional pilgrim bound for the Holy Land by way of south Italian ports.[1] Then in 1071 a Norman force under Robert Guiscard wrested Bari from its Byzantine defenders; in 1072, the Guiscard's brother Roger seized Palermo, capital of Muslim Sicily; and in

1077 the principality of Salerno, southern Italy's last Lombard enclave, fell to the Normans. Adventurers from Normandy had begun drifting down early in the eleventh century; now these dramatic achievements led the whole of western Europe to notice Italy below Rome. And contemporaries found much of interest there, particularly after Roger II linked the mainland and Sicily in a unified Norman *Regno*.

For twentieth-century historians, equally drawn to Roger's *Regno*, its greatest appeal lies in its commingling of pan-Mediterranean elements. The Normans' contemporaries also noted this, and the *Regno*'s affluence impressed them even more. Yet most chroniclers of the Norman era passed quickly over the preamble to this prosperous and unusual civilization. Like most modern historians (particularly in the English-speaking world), they seemingly assumed that everything of interest began only with the Normans.

Compounding this neglect, those modern historians who have investigated the Norman period have tended to concentrate on developments associated with Roger II's court at Palermo; they have virtually ignored peninsular southern Italy. Yet there has been one notable exception, the pioneering study by Evelyn Jamison on the feudal apportionment of the south Italian mainland.[2] Her investigation (and, earlier, Chalandon's monumental work) made plain that fiefs there were fiercely fought over, obviously viewed as prizes worth having.[3] This may seem surprising. Most medievalists know only that mainland southern Italy, largely poor today, was in addition fragmented when the Normans arrived, part claimed by Byzantium, the rest divided among a cluster of Lombard principalities (Capua, Benevento, Salerno) and the duchies of Naples and Amalfi. What could such a confused and confusing region have to offer?

No one would now make C. R. Beazley's assumption that it took "the spirit of an imperial race," "Northern blood," to "awaken commercial and maritime activity" in the Mediterranean.[4] Yet we do still retain other biases that may blind us to the facts. More than we may realize, we work within the shadow of those eminent nineteenth-century historians who thought big was better. Empires were more to be admired than kingdoms, kingdoms were interesting more or less in proportion to their size, and little worthy of notice could have occurred within small political entities with ill-defined boundaries and institutions.[5] In the nineteenth century, this attitude caused latter-day Ghibellines to deplore south Italian resistance to domination by the western emperors.[6] In the twentieth century, presumably the same bias has led the history of pre-Norman southern Italy to be investigated mainly by Byzantinists.

Byzantinists have produced some invaluable studies: first, in 1904, Jules Gay's magisterial *L'Italie méridionale et l'Empire byzantin depuis l'avènement de Basile I jusqu'à la prise de Bari par les Normands (867–1071)*, and in our own day (to cite only two examples) Vera von Falkenhausen's commanding analysis of Byzantine administration in southern Italy, and the many essays of André Guillou.[7] Much is missed, however, when this region is viewed only from a Byzantine perspective. The Macedonian dynasty did reassert Byzantine rights there at the end of the ninth century, and for the next two hundred years a significant portion of southern Italy was dominated by Byzantium. Yet an equally significant area remained free of Byzantine control, and it is in fact from that area that one learns most about life in the south before the Normans.

Jules Gay's contemporary, René Poupardin, describing the Lombard area, depicted an anarchic world: "L'histoire des principautés lombardes de l'Italie méridionale aux IXᵉ, Xᵉ, et XIᵉ siècles est un récit de luttes intestines aussi stérile qu'obscures."[8] But Poupardin derived this gloomy picture mainly from monastic narratives, hardly the work of dispassionate observers. If one makes use of a wider range of sources, and peels off the topmost layer of the society to examine the play of forces underneath, a very different picture comes into view. It is not necessarily a pretty scene; these were rough and violent times. Yet, if we look carefully, we find some developments well worth attention.

Over the past forty years, some distinguished Italian historians have taken fresh looks at early medieval southern Italy, and some important studies have been published. Unfortunately, however, this new historiography is insufficiently known outside Italy. The notion has persisted that the Normans conquered in southern Italy essentially undeveloped territory, a region that would acquire dynamic characteristics only under Norman tutelage. But we should remind ourselves that southern Italy did attract the Normans, a people not known for interest in cultivating the wilderness. There are conflicting legends about how the first wave of Normans happened to come south, but the most suggestive (if much embroidered) is that reported by Amatus of Monte Cassino. According to Amatus, in about the year 1000 a small group of Normans chanced to pass through Lombard Salerno just as Arabs arrived in the port seeking their annual tribute. Shocked by the Salernitans' readiness to pay up, the Normans drove the Arabs off, whereupon the astonished but delighted Salernitan ruler loaded his visitors with tantalizing local products as farewell gifts, hoping thus to lure more Normans to Salerno, to serve as resident protectors.[9] A rival

legend reports a southern Lombard encountering Normans on pilgrimage
at the celebrated shrine of St. Michael, on southern Italy's Adriatic coast,
and there recruiting them to help in freeing Apulia of Byzantine control.[10]

Both of these legends may be largely fanciful; one study of the Norman arrival favored a third alternative, involving calculated papal intervention.[11] Nonetheless, there are elements in both of the popular legends that
suggest at least some residue of truth, if not total historicity. However they
were recruited, the Normans must have thought significant rewards could
be theirs. Few Normans were altruists.

And in fact at least one portion of southern Italy had achieved considerable prosperity in the course of the tenth century: the core area of
Lombard domination, roughly equivalent to the *regione* or administrative
region of Campania. (Throughout this study, modern geographical terminology is used unless otherwise noted, and "southern Italy" refers chiefly to
the modern *regioni* of Campania, Calabria, Basilicata, and Apulia. Territory
on the upper edge, within Lazio, Molise, and Abruzzo, also figures occasionally. Map 2 shows the present-day boundaries of these regions; inevitably, there have been some changes in boundary or even name since classical
and/or medieval times. Campania, however, has altered only in size.)[12]

Significantly, Campania was the site of the first Norman fiefdom.
Moreover, Norman leaders quickly began intermarrying with Campania's
ruling families, including that of Salerno. And later in the eleventh century,
as the Normans increased in number and expanded their power, it was
Campania, and especially Lombard Salerno, upon which they drew for key
functionaries.

Fortunately, no area in southern Italy (with the possible exception of
Monte Cassino) has left sources so rich. For much of southern Italy we can
only guess at the texture of life in the ninth and tenth centuries. But if we
concentrate on Campania, and for the tenth century take a particularly close
look at the Lombard principality of Salerno and its neighboring city-state,
Amalfi, we can begin to sense what attracted the Normans. We also can
detect the distinctive flavor of early medieval southern Italy. This was a
Mediterranean society, at the confluence of four civilizations: Romanic,
Lombard, Byzantine, and Islamic.[13] Everywhere, but surely especially in
Campania, there was some fusion of all of these elements. The result was an
unusual culture and an economy stimulated by pan-Mediterranean contacts.

The primary aim of this book is to convey the feel of south Italian
society in the ninth and tenth centuries and to probe its underlying struc-

tures. The book's shape reflects that aim. Since political developments were crucial in establishing the context, they dominate the earlier, ninth-century chapters. I have made no attempt to recount every minor shift and change, but we do need to track the move toward internal stability and also (from the late ninth century on) the move toward an uneasy equilibrium between Byzantine and non-Byzantine southern Italy. Moreover, interactions with the western emperors, and with the papacy and Byzantium and the Arab world, were important in forming southern Italy; this aspect of the story has therefore received considerable attention. In the later chapters, however, readers will notice a change in approach. By the tenth century the political configuration was set; in the best documented areas we see an improving economy and encounter only a few major events or disruptions. Thus, although the political background remains important, it does not dominate the later chapters. There we can concentrate far more on the multifaceted characteristics of south Italian society.

In effect, the book's structure attempts to mirror the actual world of southern Italy. All evidence suggests that in the tenth century, at least in the autonomous areas, the population was less focused on events and crises than in the ninth century, and more focused on internal development. This study follows the same pattern.

One other point needs to be noted here. In this book, the chief emphasis is on southern Italy's autonomous areas, particularly the Lombard principalities and the duchies of Naples and Amalfi. These supply the richest sources, and it was there, to Campania, that the first Normans came, inevitably to be influenced by what they found. Nonetheless, one premise here is at variance with traditional treatments. The sharp distinction customarily made between "Byzantine" and "Lombard" southern Italy, with the implication that "Byzantine" and "Lombard" constituted totally separate spheres, has long stood in the way of a proper view. For example, the city-state of Amalfi and the principality of Salerno (primary vantage points for Chapters 5 and 6) have usually been characterized, respectively, as "Byzantine" and "Lombard," and treated as completely separate, inherently hostile entities. Yet in fact throughout most of the period under consideration Amalfi and Salerno had a symbiotic relationship. Moreover, the Amalfitans hardly viewed themselves as Byzantine subjects in a modern sense, and the Salernitans found much in Byzantine culture attractive. There is also the example of Apulia, on the eastern side of the peninsula. In the late ninth century, Apulia was assertively reclaimed by Byzantium, but its population remained predominantly, even defiantly, Lombard.

All in all, we find sociocultural trends washing across southern Italy without much regard to boundaries. We also find a common preoccupation with the Islamic world, which—with the Muslim conquest of Sicily in the ninth century—came to be increasingly close to southern Italy in every sense. Inevitably then, at least to some degree, this book represents a consideration of the whole of southern Italy in the two centuries preceding the Norman incursion.

Anyone embarking today on an overview of early medieval southern Italy must be profoundly grateful for all the work done over the past thirty or forty years by scholars from many disciplines. The notes attempt to recognize this debt, but it cannot be overstated. Despite the absence of any new, overall treatment, neglect has certainly not been universal. Significant contributions have been made not only by historians in Italy, but also by an international array of art historians, archaeologists, and Monte Cassino specialists.

The contrast with the situation of a generation ago is especially striking. For scholars, early medieval southern Italy was then something of a morass; there was a plethora of sources but many of them were problematic. Today, however, most pieces of the south Italian mosaic are well defined. Pratilli forgeries that had contaminated even the *Monumenta*, and here and there the work of Amari (even, in one or two instances, that of Jules Gay), were masterfully dealt with by the late Nicola Cilento.[14] Cilento also unscrambled the history of Lombard Capua and illuminated the unusual society of pre-Norman Naples. There has been much new work on Amalfi, too, and on Salerno: many valuable studies, and Ulla Westerbergh's edition of the *Chronicon Salernitanum*. Hartmut Hoffmann has reedited the Monte Cassino chronicle of Leo Marsicanus ("Leo of Ostia"); and Herbert Bloch, Father Tommaso Leccisotti, and others have clarified many issues relating to Monte Cassino. The only other major monastery, San Vincenzo al Volturno, has also received interdisciplinary attention.

In sum, much of the south Italian evidence has been resifted over the past forty years, and in a manner informed by new perspectives. Indeed, so much has been done that no single book—nor any single bibliography—can reflect it all. Those interested in particular topics will thus want to use the studies cited in the notes as guides to further material.

Here, however, something more does need to be said about the primary sources most important to my own analysis. For although I am greatly indebted to the labors and insights of others, as the notes demonstrate, nonetheless my own view of early medieval southern Italy has been primarily shaped through work, over nearly three decades, with the contemporaneous documentation.

Sources from ninth-century southern Italy are exceptionally rich. In addition to miscellaneous charters, there are two ninth-century Monte Cassino chronicles (that of Erchempert, and the *Chronica Sancti Benedicti Casinensis*) and also two narratives from Naples (John the Deacon's *Gesta Episcoporum Neapolitanorum* and the *Vita Athanasii*); all four range quite broadly across the contemporary scene. There is, as well, a rich trove of late eighth-century and ninth-century papal letters bearing on southern Italy, and there is also the *Liber Pontificalis*.

For the tenth century, the situation is very different, and this too has influenced the form of this book. We have only one major chronicle for the tenth century, the *Chronicon Salernitanum*, and almost no papal documentation. But many charters have survived, especially (but not solely) from Salerno. The tenth century would in any case seem appropriate for considering south Italian society; the charters make it especially suitable. Also, for the tenth century we can draw on an array of supplementary documentation: scattered references in Arab narratives, reports by Liutprand, some Byzantine evidence, one Hebrew narrative concerning south Italian Jews, and hagiographies devoted to the Byzantine hermit-saints of southern Italy.

Overall, plainly, there are ample sources, if not homogeneous records suitable for quantification. And fortunately most have been soundly edited (or in some cases reedited). Fortunately, too, given my meager Greek and lack of Arabic, most of the Greek and Arabic narratives have been translated. (Many of the Greek hagiographies, for example, can be found in Latin translation; and there are modern translations, predominantly French, of most of the Arabic narratives.) With charters, of course, one cannot rely on translations. But the few surviving Greek charters have already been thoroughly combed by Byzantinists, and I have therefore been able to concentrate on the Latin charters, which are especially numerous for the Salerno region. The principal source for the latter is the *Codex Diplomaticus Cavensis*, a nineteenth-century multivolume edition of Salerno area charters for the ninth and tenth centuries (and through to 1065); the edition is sufficiently reliable (with some few, recently identified exceptions) to permit working with these charters in their published form.[15] But I have also briefly examined some of the original charter rolls, to satisfy myself on certain points.

Anyone working with ninth- and tenth-century south Italian materials must be prepared for often eccentric Latin. Oddities in spelling, case, and syntax are reminders that this was not only a language in transition but also a language affected by Greek and other pan-Mediterranean influences.[16] Yet, despite the frustrations, these are highly rewarding sources. Lively and unselfconscious, they convey a vivid sense of time and place. For my narrative sources I have therefore used contemporary local chronicles to the greatest extent possible, relying only occasionally on later works such as the late eleventh-century Monte Cassino chronicle of Leo Marsicanus and the twelfth-century *Chronicon Vulturnense*. I have generally also been wary of annalists or chroniclers far from the scene, although occasionally these do furnish valuable information.

It need hardly be said that one cannot believe everything reported in the chronicles, contemporary or not. Nor can one accept at face value everything seemingly agreed to in the charters. Yet it seems wrong to suspect every charter of dissimulation. In this period, at least in the regions from which most of the documentation comes, most contracts were drafted by rather unsophisticated scribes or notaries; as with embellishments in chronicles, there are usually inadvertent but unmistakable clues when a charter is masking something.

Local charters involving land conveyance demonstrate this lack of sophistication. In these south Italian contracts, by and large we do not encounter the terminology apparently by then in common use in the north of Italy. Even large estates are often described merely as "terra," and contemporary leases contain no stock phrases such as "ad livellum." I too have therefore avoided such terms, not wishing to imply a degree of standardization that in fact did not yet prevail in the south. Variation in terminology—and approach—is a hallmark of these contracts, one of their most interesting and revealing features.

Altogether, in my use of the sources I have attempted to convey their spirit as well as their substance. I have sought in them not only evidence of the shaping of southern Italy in the ninth and tenth centuries but also the special flavor of this region.

The degree to which southern Italy differed from the rest of Europe in this period must ultimately be left for experts on other areas to judge; some south Italian practices seem unique, some not. In one respect, however, we can be confident of similarity. As one would expect in the early Middle Ages, borders between political entities were fluid. Fringe territory constantly changed hands (just as jurisdictional power grew weaker the further one got from the center). Thus, in relation to the political divisions, Map 2 can give only proximate indications, based on fragmentary evidence and applicable only to one point in time, and it also shows only the *modern* outlines of the various *regioni*.

Finally, something must be said about the notes and the Bibliography. Citations in the notes are limited to author, title, and date. Full information is supplied in the Bibliography, including, for sources, the particular editions used. It should also be noted that the Bibliography lists only sources and studies actually cited in the text and notes. This has meant leaving out many studies (and older works) from which I have benefited over the years. I have, however, attempted to cite all major recent treatments, and these can point to works not mentioned directly.

1. The Beginnings

AS JULES GAY NOTED LONG AGO, the lower half of the Italian peninsula, the portion lying below Rome, first became a separate and distinct geopolitical region in 774, with the Carolingian conquest of northern Italy.[1] It is true that it was not politically unified until the late eleventh century, under the Normans. From 774 on, however, southern Italy mostly pursued its own separate destiny, and indeed, as the Kingdom of Naples, it continued to do so until the unification of Italy in the nineteenth century.

The events of 774 not only drew a new boundary and set southern Italy apart; they also altered the dynamics of the ethnic and political forces within that region. There, for the next three centuries, Byzantium and the southern Lombards, both now restricted to the lower half of the peninsula, would confront each other. Moreover, both would be profoundly affected, if in different ways, by the shrinking of the distance between Italy and the Islamic world in the ninth century as a result of the Arab conquest of Sicily. Interaction with the Islamic world would have major significance for southern Italy over the course of three centuries. In time, for at least a portion of the region, it would mean growing prosperity. But the Arab factor would also make southern Italy the graveyard of papal, Carolingian, and Ottonian ambitions in the south.

This study concentrates on the ninth and tenth centuries, the period which largely formed the southern Italy the Normans entered. To set the stage, however, it is necessary first to review the main developments of the preceding centuries. We can then consider the scene at the end of the eighth and the beginning of the ninth century.

The Sixth to Eighth Centuries

Southern Italy had been devastated by the troubles of the sixth century, when Justinian's armies battled the Ostrogoths for control of Italy and then plague and the invading Lombards ravaged the survivors. Grim times leave few records, but we know a bit about the fate of Naples, which can serve as a symbol of the whole.

The entire area around the Bay of Naples had signified prosperity and pleasure in the Roman era. Local tradition stressed the Greek roots of civilization in that region, a matter of great local pride. Local tradition also emphasized associations with Aeneas and the founding of Rome, and with St. Peter and the introduction of Christianity to Italy. (According to a local legend, St. Peter had come first to Naples, before going on to Rome, and had founded there his first church on Italian soil.)[2] Despite these associations, however, Naples had readily come to terms first with Odoacer and then with Theodoric. And, for a time, this policy of accommodation had paid.[3] Cassiodorus, in the early sixth century, described Naples as still a delightful and populous place.[4] But then came Belisarius and the Byzantine campaign of reconquest, beginning in 535; Naples held out against him and was terribly punished for its resistance.[5] The city was taken by the Byzantines at great cost to its defenders, and the surrounding area was then ravaged alternately by the Ostrogothic and Byzantine armies until the Ostrogoths (under Teias, Totila's successor) were conclusively defeated at the foot of Mount Vesuvius. By the time of Gregory the Great, only a generation later, Naples' glories were dimmed. There are references to internal disorders, and in 581 had come the first of the Lombard attacks from which Naples was to suffer intermittently throughout the early medieval period.[6] Over the next two centuries, Naples continued nominally Byzantine, and there was some consistency of communication with Constantinople. Yet at best the city was a beleaguered outpost, cut off from overland communication with the Byzantine exarch at Ravenna and to a considerable degree reduced to living, marginally, on its memories.

For the Lombards now dominated southern as well as northern Italy. In 571, only two years after they had swept down into the Italian peninsula, the Lombards had established a southern Lombard duchy centered on Benevento. Benevento itself was a venerable Roman city, strategically located in the high interior of the peninsula, at the junction of the Via Appia and the Via Appia-Traiana, and thus midway between the city of Rome and the key Adriatic seaports of Bari and Brindisi.[7] Because of its distance from the main center of Lombard power in the north, the duchy of Benevento soon became virtually autonomous. Its Lombards soon also began to demonstrate great destructive force, moving quickly to wipe out virtually all vestiges of Byzantine control over the south Italian land area, and plundering churches and monasteries. Even Monte Cassino was sacked, in about 580. Its monks fled, and for the next century and a half the site stood abandoned. In many cases, as bishoprics fell vacant, new bishops seem not to have been appointed. To the extent that major Roman landowners had survived in southern Italy to witness the Lombard arrival, they now presumably became tributaries of the invaders.[8] In fact, however, the entire population must have been drastically reduced. In the latter seventh century, roughly a hundred years after the Lombards had come, the Lombard duke of Benevento allowed a number of Bulgarians to settle on Beneventan lands "quae usque ad illud tempus deserta erant."[9]

In 663, a Byzantine emperor did make one attempt to reassert Byzantine supremacy in southern Italy. In that year, Constans II landed with a large army at Taranto, the major port on the instep of the Italian boot. Moving northward, his army apparently met with considerable success until it neared the core area of Beneventan Lombard strength. But there Constans proved unable to take the crucial hill-town of Acerenza (Roman Acerentium), roughly halfway between Taranto and the city of Benevento. And shortly thereafter he abandoned his campaign entirely when Benevento also proved impossible to storm.[10]

It is instructive to note what happened subsequently with Constans and his army. After giving up his attempt to crush the southern Lombards, Constans had gone on to Rome (where he stripped off the Pantheon's copper roof as booty) and then, heading south again, he had called at Naples, that Byzantine outpost. He was warmly welcomed there, as one might expect, but what is interesting is that, next, he and his army apparently proceeded overland, without interference, all the way down the Tyrrhenian coast to Reggio before crossing over to Sicily. In theory, most of the territory between Naples and Reggio was then held by the Beneventan Lombards. Perhaps at that time it was so underpopulated, seemed such unpromising country, that the Lombards had no interest in defending it. Or perhaps this unhindered journey should simply remind us that "sovereignty," throughout the early medieval period, had very limited implications. It certainly never implied all-encompassing control and supervision. For south Italian land areas well away from the core centers, sovereignty, as such, must have been irrelevant much of the time. This appears to have been the case in Constans' day and, indeed, would continue to be true for several more centuries.

In practical terms, "sovereignty" mainly then meant, for rulers, the ability to extract taxes. (This may seem an obvious statement, but the sharpness of focus on revenue is striking. In the tenth century, Constantine

Porphyrogenitus would note the significance of southern Italy to Byzantium primarily in terms of payments into the imperial fisc.)[11] For the upper layer of a ruler's subjects, sovereignty also meant access to mechanisms for the adjudication of disputes. But for the populace as a whole, particularly those eking out an existence at any distance from the major fortified centers, sovereignty meant little; certainly it offered virtually no hope of protection in time of trouble. The acknowledged ruler of a region usually fought only to defend key *castra*, fortified towns; enemy forces typically moved across rural areas almost without opposition.

Of course, this state of affairs was not peculiar to southern Italy; it was typical of the whole of western Christendom in the early medieval period. Thus we find the French monk Bernard, when traveling through Arab Egypt and Palestine in the late ninth century, quite astonished at the degree of law and order he found there, even—and he stresses this—in the countryside.[12]

Furthermore, in the early medieval period sovereignty was often confidently asserted without any real basis in fact. Byzantium, throughout the ninth and tenth centuries, continued to describe as part of the Byzantine Empire some areas of southern Italy which in reality had had no meaningful subordination to Byzantium for a very long time. Twentieth-century historians have not always recognized the illusory nature of some of these Byzantine claims, and this is an issue to which we will revert. Meanwhile, however, it is well to bear in mind the situation in relation to rural areas, which often constituted, at best, a sort of no-man's-land.

Moreover, even in the tenth century, and in a part of southern Italy unquestionably subject to Byzantine authority, Byzantium sometimes had difficulty in enforcing order. In one celebrated example, at Rossano in Calabria in the latter tenth century, the local populace refused to obey Byzantine officials when ordered to fit out ships for the Byzantine fleet— even though that fleet was to be used in part for their own protection. Not only did they refuse (probably fearing Arab reprisals), but they proceeded to burn the ships and kill the ships' officers. This story is told in the contemporary *Life* of the hermit-monk St. Nilus, which goes on to report the nervous citizens of Rossano then turning to Nilus, whom they plainly viewed as a more reliable protector. (And through what must certainly be counted a major miracle, he persuaded the Byzantine commander not to punish the offenders).[13] The hagiographer had undoubtedly embellished this tale, but clearly the inhabitants of towns like Rossano were often ambivalent about Byzantine authority.

From the sixth century on, the Lombards were continuously on the scene, so Lombard sovereignty had at least been consistently manifested. Yet in their case, too, we should surely suspect only limited effectiveness in the more isolated parts of their territory. If, in the tenth century, sovereignty would often prove more rhetoric than reality, this must have been doubly true earlier.

Nonetheless, control of key ports and *castra* always did matter, and by the early part of the eighth century the Beneventan Lombards once again held Taranto and Brindisi, on either side of the heel of the peninsula.[14] They had also pushed the northern limits of their duchy to within fifty or sixty miles of Rome itself by taking a string of small settlements in the Liri River valley.[15] Thus, in the eighth century, the Lombards could claim almost the whole of southern Italy, excepting only three fringe areas: most of a narrow strip along the Tyrrhenian coast, with Gaeta at one end, the Amalfitan peninsula at the other, and Naples in the middle; lower Calabria (the toe of the boot); and the Otranto region, at the tip of the heel.[16] Constans' reconquest, limited in any case, had been almost entirely nullified.

Indeed, in the middle of the eighth century the Beneventan Lombards' position in southern Italy looked extraordinarily secure. Byzantium, wracked now by internal struggles over iconoclasm, was obviously no threat. In northern Italy, the Lombard kingdom was at its zenith, and the Lombard ruler appears to have treated his duke of Benevento more as ally than subordinate.

Arichis and Charlemagne

In 758, Arichis II became Duke of Benevento; in every respect a remarkable man, he married the daughter of the Lombard king Desiderius and with her presided over a cultivated ducal court that included such figures as Paul the Deacon. By now, all of the Lombards had come to terms with orthodoxy and the Church even if they were sometimes at odds with the papacy. At the northern edge of the duchy of Benevento, the monastery at Monte Cassino had been resettled about 718, and both it and the burgeoning monastic complex of San Vincenzo al Volturno (by tortuous modern roads, some fifty kilometers northeast of Monte Cassino) were richly patronized by Beneventan Lombards. At Monte Cassino, a close relative of Arichis became abbot in the late eighth century, and he devoted the twenty-one years of his abbacy to an ambitious building program. Arichis himself also erected a splendid ducal church at Benevento and named it Sancta Sophia in deliberate imitation of Justinian's great foundation.[17]

Yet by 787, the year of Arichis's death, the Beneventan position appeared seriously threatened. Some thirteen years earlier, the Lombard kingdom in the north had abruptly vanished, absorbed within the Carolingian Empire. Arichis's son and heir, Grimoald, had been taken north by Charlemagne as hostage for Beneventan good behavior. Arichis's brother-in-law, heir to Desiderius and brother to Adalperga, Arichis's wife, was a refugee in Constantinople, trying to enlist Byzantine support for an attempted restoration of the Lombard throne. The only positive developments in which the dying Arichis could take comfort were that he had, so far, forestalled any absolute Carolingian takeover of his duchy, and in addition he had established a second (and strongly fortified) Beneventan capital, at Salerno, on the Tyrrhenian coast south of Naples.

Given the assertiveness of the papacy under Pope Hadrian I, who enjoyed the military backing of the Franks and was certainly no friend to the Lombards, the creation of a base farther from Rome must have seemed highly desirable. In addition, both Thomas Hodgkin and Jules Gay believed that Arichis valued Salerno because it provided a Tyrrhenian port. Hodgkin speculated that Arichis wanted an entry point through which a Byzantine force might come to his aid in the event of a Carolingian attack. Gay thought Arichis had the more aggressive aim of placing his Lombards in position to dominate the Tyrrhenian littoral, including Byzantine Naples.[18] This last does in fact seem the more likely motive, for Arichis II was an exceedingly forceful ruler. Hodgkin called him "in some respects the finest specimen of a ruler whom the Lombard race produced," and his virtues certainly included a sharply honed sense of the value of strategic offense.[19]

Fortunately for the Beneventan Lombards, Arichis's widow Adalperga appears also to have been an impressive individual. Paul the Deacon paid tribute to her intellectual attainments in dedicating to her his history of the Roman Empire, and she was to prove as adept as her late husband at saving Benevento from Carolingian domination. In 787, her first task was to persuade Charlemagne to free Arichis's heir Grimoald so that he could come home to govern what had now become the "principality" of Benevento; after the fall of Desiderius, Arichis had begun to style himself Prince of Benevento (rather than duke), in recognition of the fact that there was no longer any other Lombard ruler. Given that demonstration of Lombard ambition, one might have expected Charlemagne to refuse Adalperga's request; certainly some of his advisers (and, most vociferously, Pope Hadrian) urged him not to surrender Grimoald.[20] But Charlemagne chose to disregard the advice. He may have been influenced by Paul the Deacon, who had moved on to the Carolingian court but retained strong personal ties to the Beneventan dynasty. Perhaps Paul the Deacon (now back at Monte Cassino) argued that a strong but loyal principality in the south of Italy would keep Byzantium in check.

In any case, Grimoald was released. In return, the Beneventans were to recognize Carolingian hegemony on their coinage and in the indictions of their charters—and to shave in the manner of the Franks.[21] This last touch appears to have been Charlemagne's response to one of Hadrian's most recent salvos. The previous year, just before Arichis's death, Charlemagne had led a force south as far as Capua with the aim of extracting submission from Arichis. The latter, however, had refused to come to Capua; instead, he had merely sent hostages (including Grimoald) together with the promise of an annual tribute of 7,000 *solidi*. Somewhat uncharacteristically, Charlemagne had not made an issue of this act of defiance.[22] But no sooner had he returned north (reported the ever-vigilant Hadrian) than the Beneventans demonstrated their contempt for him and their lack of good faith by seeking Byzantine aid and—most outrageous, in Hadrian's view—promising to adopt Byzantine-style dress and hairstyles.[23] Charlemagne's new agreement with Grimoald therefore committed the Beneventans to personal and visible demonstration of their loyalty to the Franks. Charlemagne had seemingly been persuaded by Hadrian's superior knowledge of the south Italian scene; the new agreement recognized the importance of tangible symbols in a region where Byzantium, however weakened temporarily, still generally set the aesthetic and sartorial standard.

Soon after Grimoald's return home, he had occasion to demonstrate his loyalty. His uncle, claimant to the Lombard throne, invaded Italy with a combined Byzantine-Lombard force, and Grimoald, surely disappointing his uncle, helped the Franks repel the invasion.[24] Thereafter, however, the principality of Benevento gradually drifted back to its independent ways. All references to Charlemagne soon disappeared from charters and coinage; doubtless the Frankish style in barbering was abandoned equally quickly.[25]

In other words, as Pope Hadrian had endlessly warned Charlemagne, the Beneventan Lombards were not to be trusted. They would be deferential when necessary, but never reliably subservient. One of Hadrian's most indignant reports of Lombard perfidy concerned a plot purportedly hatched at the very moment Charlemagne was debating whether to free Grimoald. According to Hadrian, four Frankish legates, journeying toward Salerno to meet with Arichis's widow, learned something that sent them scurrying back north to safety. Allegedly, some Salernitan Lombards had persuaded neighboring Naples and its then-dependencies, Sorrento and Amalfi, to help in disposing of the envoys. Apparently, Naples, Sorrento, and Amalfi were prepared to forget the Lombard attacks they had suffered over time, in the greater cause of keeping outsiders from the region. The conspirators, however, counted on awareness of the long-standing enmity between the Lombards and their neighbors. According to Hadrian, it was planned that, after the legates had finished their discussions with Adalperga and gone down to the seafront outside the city walls, some Lombards would rush at them from one side while a group of Neapolitans, Amalfitans, and Sorrentans attacked from the other; then, after the envoys had been killed, each side would say that unfortunately the envoys had been thought part of the other's hostile force.[26]

This was a devilishly ingenious plan, if true, but prophetic of the way things were to go over the next two centuries. Time and time again in southern Italy in the ninth and tenth centuries, local enmities and ethnic or political divisions would be forgotten in the face of external threat.[27]

Thereafter, Hadrian and others continued to complain about the wicked southern Lombards. But Charlemagne was now preoccupied with problems in the north and he made no significant response to appeals for disciplinary action. The southern Lombards seem never to have been called to account for their abandonment of visible deference or for any other alleged misdeeds. Pippin waged one or two minor campaigns in an effort to enforce Beneventan subordination, but (with obvious Lombard pride) the ninth-century Monte Cassino chronicler Erchempert reported Grimoald's defiant response: "I was born free, and, God willing, I shall remain free forever!"[28] In 812, when Charlemagne and the Byzantine Emperor Michael I reached an accord, as an apparently related development there was a new Beneventan promise of annual tribute to the Franks.[29] But Benevento's essential autonomy seems not to have been in question, and after Charlemagne's death in 814, his heir, Louis the Pious, paid even less attention to that part of the world, so far from the Carolingian heartland. Louis may well have shared Alcuin's view that southern Italy could offer nothing good, only noxious air.[30]

Furthermore, Pope Hadrian's immediate successors proved in the main not to share Hadrian's passionate interest in the aggrandizement of papal territory, which had had much to do with his continual rage at the expansionist Lombards. Recent scholarship has tended to support the authenticity of the *Ludovicianum*, that extraordinary document of 817 or thereabouts in which Louis the Pious seemingly confirmed papal title not only to some long-disputed areas at the northern edge of Beneventan territory but also to purported papal patrimony deep within southern Italy. As Thomas Noble has noted, however, the south Italian clauses of the *Ludovicianum* are surely best understood as representing only an ideal.[31] Certainly neither Charlemagne, who may originally have made this generous gesture of confirming lands he in no way controlled, nor Louis the Pious, who was seemingly repeating his father's move, ever made any effort to help the papacy to actual possesssion of these areas. Moreover, whereas Hadrian clearly had hoped for something more than empty words, his successors appeared content with a handsome document.

Thus, early in the ninth century, southern Italy found itself, once again, more or less on its own. The Carolingian and papal threats had receded. Byzantium now held only what Jules Gay described as small bits ("des morceaux épars") of south Italian territory; Constantinople's interests were centered elsewhere.[32] The Lombards, with their double capitals at Benevento and Salerno, were unquestionably the dominant force on the scene.

Southern Italy in the Early Ninth Century

Keeping this background in mind, we can now consider the general characteristics of southern Italy and its population at the start of the ninth century. How, for example, would southern Italy have looked to a visitor?

Physically, one of the most pronounced features would surely have been omnipresent reminders of Roman civilization in the form of Roman buildings and monuments. The south had constituted a vitally important part of Roman Italy. Countless major figures in Roman history had come from that region or possessed estates there. Many of the most significant events in the Roman era had taken place in the south: the final defeat of Hannibal in Italy and the great slave revolt led by Spartacus, to name only two of the most dramatic. The Via Appia and the Via Appia-Traiana traversed the region to reach Rome's major ports on the Adriatic. On and around the Bay of Naples, Rome had its western naval port, at Misenum, and its favorite pleasure resorts. Even today, one still encounters in southern Italy a few reminders of what would have been visible in the ninth century. Here and there, in the rural areas, one can still walk overgrown stretches of the Via Appia.[33] The great Roman amphitheater at Capua and the arch of Trajan at Benevento are still to be seen. There survive now only ruined remnants of Roman Baiae and Puteoli (modern Baia and Pozzuoli) along the shore of the Bay of Naples. But in the ninth century much more of Roman Baiae and Puteoli must have been in evidence, particularly their celebrated baths, since in the 860s the Emperor Louis II and his wife, Engelberga, made a point of stopping to bathe there.[34]

Altogether, what remains today only hints at the Roman echoes that must have dominated the landscape in the ninth century. Moreover, although many Roman towns had been virtually abandoned and the population of all urban areas had declined drastically, the urban topography was still basically Roman at the start of the ninth century; certainly the Lombards had not created new towns.[35] Indeed, in the eighth century, the more cultivated Lombards had even adopted Roman-style geographical archaisms; Paul the Deacon consistently referred to the Duke of Benevento as the Duke of the Samnites.[36]

One major development of the ninth and tenth centuries would be a gradual but unmistakable change from looking backward to moving forward. In the tenth century, of the two most prosperous centers on the Tyrrhenian side, one (Salerno) had comparatively little importance in the Roman era; the other (Amalfi) seems not to have existed at all as a town under Rome. Nonetheless, the quantity of *spolia* (Roman stonework, Roman columns) cannibalized for new construction from the ninth to the twelfth centuries tells us that Roman buildings (and Roman ruins) remained for a long time a significant feature throughout southern Italy. Certainly classical Rome still constituted a living presence at the start of the ninth century.

Ecclesiastically, too, southern Italy at the beginning of the ninth century reflected considerable continuity with the past. Today little remains of what must once have been a large number of early Christian churches. But if the fifth-century church or baptistery of Santa Maria Maggiore (on the outskirts of Nocera Superiore, between Naples and Salerno) is in any way typical, some of these early churches must have been impressive; and surely many were still standing at the start of the ninth century. Moreover, the administrative patterns, in terms of bishoprics, had remained essentially unchanged; significant ecclesiastical-administrative restructuring was to begin only in the eleventh century. Nonetheless, when the Lombards were at their most rapacious in the seventh century, many bishoprics had fallen vacant. At the beginning of the ninth century, bishops were certainly in place in all of the late-Roman sees in Campania. But in the deeper south, while most of the traditional sees continued to be listed, there was apparently still some ecclesiastical disorder and it is by no means clear that bishops were everywhere being appointed.

It is possible, too, that one ecclesiastical change had taken place, affecting one portion of southern Italy. In the second quarter of the eighth century, the Byzantine emperor Leo III had decreed that ecclesiastical provinces in Calabria hitherto overseen by Rome should thenceforth be under the patriarch of Constantinople. How effective this decree was, and indeed the extent of control exercised by either pope or patriarch over the more remote areas, are matters for debate.[37] In the late tenth century (as we shall see in Chapter 7) both pope and patriarch would claim authority to appoint bishops to various sees in the south, in what may chiefly have been an exchange of rhetorical bullets.[38] In any case, in Calabria at the start of the ninth century, the situation would surely have been further complicated by the controversies raging over iconoclasm, especially if (as some have thought) iconodule monks were fleeing into southern Italy.[39]

Debate over this possible influx of iconodule monks has raged in scholarly circles for decades and can never be decisively settled for lack of substantial evidence. The controversy is interwoven with the wider issue of the ethnic composition of the Byzantine-held areas of southern Italy, also much debated. On this second issue, the consensus now appears to be that, in contrast with Sicily, southern Italy had lost almost all trace of hellenization during the Roman period, and a Greek-speaking population began to be reintroduced only in the sixth century with the encouragement of Justinian. Thereafter, apparently, sporadic in-migrations of Greek-speakers continued, for various reasons and from various corners of the Mediterranean. Yet the numbers were never great. Only part of modern Calabria, and the Otranto region in the heel of Apulia, seem to have been truly hellenized (or rehellenized) to any significant extent.[40] Indeed, most scholars now seem agreed that, overall, the Greek population in southern Italy was always far smaller than Jules Gay and others once hypothesized. For example, in the tenth century Byzantium would control most of Apulia. But aside from the Otranto area, this apparently meant only that in Apulia there were Byzantine functionaries and small garrisons in the midst of a predominantly Lombard (or Lombard and Romanic) population.

Yet even if there were comparatively few Byzantine Greeks, and even if few iconodule monks had actually come, nonetheless later in the ninth century, in the more sparsely populated regions of lower Italy, there began to be one notable Byzantine-Greek presence: small, isolated clusters of Greek-speaking ascetics or hermits. Many were refugees from Arab-dominated Sicily, and so more will be said about them in subsequent chapters. The phenomenon is particularly characteristic of the tenth century, the period of St. Nilus of Rossano; the interactions then, between these individualistic manifestations of Byzantine Christianity and the Latinate Christianity of the Lombard core areas, were illuminating. Meanwhile, however, these hermit-saints should be borne in mind as one envisions the peninsula at the start of the ninth century, for their settling in this particular region can remind us of the forbidding nature of the terrain in the more remote parts of southern Italy. Most of what we now know as Calabria, as well as much of the lower portion of modern Basilicata (above the instep of the boot), is mountainous, rugged country. In those days, it was densely forested as well. Current scholarship suggests that massive deforestation did not take place until the nineteenth century, and the forests of Calabria in particular had been legendary. In the sixth century, for example, Gregory the Great had asked Lombard help in getting timbers from Calabria to replace the roof beams of Roman churches.[41] This region was thus to provide an ideal setting for those seeking a solitary life of asceticism and prayer.

There is still today a marked contrast between the wilder, mountainous regions of southern Italy and the areas of open plain. The Appenines extend down the center of the peninsula, forming a rugged spine, and then veer off into Calabria as if pointing toward Sicily. Yet on the western, Tyrrhenian side of the Appenines there is the fertile plain known as the Terra di Lavoro, extending more or less from Capua down to Naples, and renowned in Roman times for its exceptional productivity. Slightly farther south, there is also another, smaller plain on this western side, between Salerno and the coastal protuberance of the Cilento; here the imposing temples of the early Greek city of Paestum were still very much in evidence in the ninth century. (Below this region, one entered the formidable territory of Calabria, already described.) On the other, Adriatic side of the peninsula, the Appenines open to the southeast onto the great rolling plains of Apulia, notable grain country in the later Middle Ages. Even Apulia is not without variation in altitude; here and there, the land rears up into more rugged terrain and only the heel of the boot is mostly flat. Nonetheless, Apulia does provide greater stretches of arable land than any other section of southern Italy, and it had therefore been grain country in the Roman era as well. Whereas vineyards had flourished in the volcanic soil around Naples, the Romans had found Apulia admirably suited to great latifundia.

It is not possible to say with certainty what agricultural use was being made of Apulia at the start of the ninth century because there is virtually no documentation. In addition to field crops, however, Apulia had once had many olive plantations, and it appears that by now the olive had virtually disappeared from southern Italy, the trees presumably destroyed during the bad times of the sixth, seventh, and early eighth centuries.[42] On the opposite side of the peninsula, in Campania, agriculture had also suffered severely during that same period. Its revival there, the bringing back into cultivation of much of the land, was to be one of the most striking features of the ninth and especially the tenth centuries. But the dire situation in Campania before this revival began is indicated in a letter from Pope Hadrian to Charlemagne in 776 in which he reported inhabitants of the Campanian littoral so desperate with hunger that they were volunteering for enslavement when "Greek" slavers appeared offshore.[43]

Indeed, all over southern Italy in this period the level of existence for most of the population must have been abysmally low.[44] Jules Gay described the southern Lombards in the late eighth century as enjoying "une courte période d'éclatante prospérité" as a result of the remarkable achievements of Arichis II; and it is true that Arichis seems to have had large sums of money at his command.[45] Yet any wealth was surely concentrated in the hands of a very few people. Otherwise, one does not sense even modest prosperity, even in Campania, until the tenth century. Moreover, even Arichis's wealth was undoubtedly relative; as Robert Lopez once wisely warned, we should never make too much of contemporary reports of great riches in the early Middle Ages.[46]

For that matter, certainly at the start of the ninth century but also throughout the ninth and tenth centuries, everything was on a markedly small scale.[47] At Monte Cassino, where an aggressive building program began about 800, the new basilica at the foot of the mount is estimated to have measured 36.4 by 19 meters, an impressive size for that period but obviously modest by Roman or later medieval standards.[48] Giuseppe Galasso once calculated the circumference of the walls of the city of Salerno, as late as the twelfth century, as no more than 2.6 kilometers, and this would have encompassed gardens and orchards as well as habitations.[49] And on the opposite side of the peninsula one can still discern today the comparatively tiny areas that comprised Bari and Taranto in the ninth and tenth centuries.[50]

Traveling through southern Italy at the start of the ninth century, one would therefore have encountered mostly underpopulated and underdeveloped lands, with the surviving Roman monuments dwarfing contemporary buildings. Many of the chief cities had shrunk to small towns or now functioned now only in a military sense as fortified *castra*. Considering this scene, Galasso insisted we must ackowledge an absolute break in urban continuity. Only in the course of the ninth or perhaps even in the tenth century, according to Galasso, can we properly begin again to speak of south Italian cities in the sense of urban areas with a vital life of their own.[51]

And what of the composition of the population, overall? Plainly, the whole of southern Italy was still sparsely populated, as a result of three centuries of disaster, natural and man-made. Moreover, Greek-speaking Byzantines were relatively few in number, and mainly restricted to two or three isolated areas. In Campania, of course, there were many inhabitants of Gaeta and Naples who could speak and read Greek; those cities had had a Byzantine connection for centuries, and indeed the population of Naples and Gaeta must have included a good many individuals who were Byzantine-Greek in ancestry. In the tenth century, at both Naples and Gaeta, some would still sign their names in Greek letters, even though documents there were almost always drawn in Latin and Latin was the language commonly used.

But what was the ethnic composition of "Lombard" southern Italy? To what extent had the invading Lombards filled all available space, replacing the inhabitants they encountered? That a seventh-century duke of Benevento had welcomed refugee Bulgarians to "empty land" is ominously suggestive of the fate of earlier inhabitants. Yet surely there must have continued to be some substructure of non-Lombard peoples on the lowest rung of society. Perhaps, indeed, those Campanian "Lombards" whom Pope Hadrian described walking onto slave ships of their own volition were not ethnic Lombards but merely Lombard subjects. In and around the ports, too, there must have always been at least some individuals who had originally come from other parts of the Mediterranean. And there certainly were Jewish colonies in early medieval southern Italy; more will be said about this in Chapter 5. Altogether, then, when we envision "Lombard" southern Italy we should not envision total ethnic homogeneity.

Finally, we must review the local political situation at the start of the ninth century. Byzantium by then controlled only parts of Calabria, and the

area around Otranto at the tip of the heel. Only there might one have encountered resident Byzantine officials. Large areas of southern Italy that
Constantinople had once genuinely held, certainly including most of the
major ports in Apulia, were now in Lombard hands. But what of the region
around Naples, so hospitable to the Emperor Constans in the seventh
century?

At the start of the ninth century, the duchy of Naples, stretching around
the Bay of Naples (and somewhat inland to the northeast), still also counted
Sorrento and Amalfi, far out on the Amalfitan peninsula, as dependencies. In
addition, Naples at this point exercised some indeterminate degree of authority over Gaeta, well to the north along the Tyrrhenian coast.

Ostensibly, as the ninth century began, Naples and its dependencies
were all linked to Byzantium, attached administratively to Byzantium's
Sicilian patriciate. In fact, however, Naples and its dependencies were all
moving toward autonomy. Gaeta, close to papal territory and a potential
papal target, seems to have clung as long as possible to some semblance of
relationship with Byzantium, and because of its location Gaeta must have
seemed especially useful to Constantinople as a listening post. Yet even
Gaeta was by now essentially self-governing.[52] The chief political residue of
Gaeta's Byzantine connection was its rather loose tie to Naples, which
would persist for three or four more decades.

And at Naples, not only were there no resident Byzantine officials, but
changes in ruler now took place totally without Byzantine involvement. Of
course the position of Naples had always been somewhat anomalous. Its
ancient Greek and Roman-Imperial traditions predisposed Naples toward
attachment to Byzantium, but there also were close ties to the Roman
church. At the start of the ninth century we therefore find powerful members of the laity pro-Byzantine in sentiment, and the clergy generally pro-
papal and anti-Byzantine—but we also find both factions united in a
commitment to Naples' independence.[53] A familiarity with Graeco-Byzan-
tine culture did continue, for a long time, to represent a sort of caste mark at
Naples; for the citizens of Naples this plainly represented a way to set
themselves apart from the upstart Lombards. In the latter ninth century, it
would still be a matter of local pride that laity and clergy alike were
comfortable in both Greek and Latin, with a mid-ninth-century ruler
"eruditus" in both languages.[54] In practical terms, however, there was little
to be gained now from a Byzantine connection. Constantinople was currently in no position to help Naples with the threat from the ever more
powerful southern Lombards.

And at the beginning of the ninth century the Lombards appeared once again to be on the verge of taking over every last corner of southern Italy, including, this time, even the Naples region. Not only did Byzantium seem unlikely to stop them but, at least for the moment, the Carolingians seemed to have written off Italy below Rome. Meanwhile, the Lombards now had three major bases surrounding Naples: the traditional southern Lombard capital of Benevento, strategically situated on its high inland plateau; their new second capital on the coast at Salerno, just below the Amalfitan peninsula; and finally, an important Lombard gastaldate centered on the venerable Roman city of Capua, north of Naples on the route to Rome.

Elsewhere in southern Italy, in Basilicata and Apulia, Lombard gastalds were also strategically deployed, serving as local military governors and supervisors of tax and tribute collection. The records are sparse for the beginning of the ninth century, but at midcentury we find approximately thirty-one gastaldates, including some centered on each of the vital, formerly Byzantine ports in Apulia, such as Brindisi and Bari.[55] The extent of control exercised by these gastalds may have been somewhat uneven. Nonetheless, at the start of the ninth century, Lombard dominance of most of southern Italy seems to have been unquestioned.

Moreover, Arichis II had established for his southern Lombards a tradition of strong rule. He had constantly toured his territory, alert to any sign of disorder, and it was always clear that gastalds served only at his pleasure and subject to effective performance. Given continued strong rulership, Benevento and its southern Lombards seemed well on the way to increased dominance.

Yet the ninth century was to witness recurrent threats to Lombard power. The first came as a direct result of Lombard aggression, which led to Arab mercenaries coming into southern Italy. This then attracted the attention of both the papacy and the western emperors. The most significant political development, however, coming at the very end of the ninth century, would be the reappearance of Byzantium on the scene. It is therefore in order to end this chapter with one final comment on the place or role of Byzantium at the start of the century.

By the beginning of the ninth century the Byzantine emperors had lost physical control of most of southern Italy, and Naples, for example, was minting a coinage lacking any reference to the *basileus*.[56] Nonetheless, the aura of Byzantium did continue to glow, even if now more faintly. We sense this even in the Lombard regions of southern Italy. After all, Charlemagne had received his imperial crown only in 800; it would be a long time before the Carolingian crown acquired a patina comparable to Byzantium's. Constantinople's current ecclesiastical policies may have seemed eccentric, or worse. Furthermore, for the time being, Byzantium was plainly not to be counted upon, or feared, militarily. Yet the Byzantine Empire represented continuity with the grandest traditions of the past, with a historic Mediterranean world with which southern Italy still felt linked. Thus, even in a period in which there was no tangible Byzantine presence, Byzantium continued to figure in the consciousness of southern Italy. Byzantine artifacts, for example, continued to be greatly valued. Byzantium remained a powerful symbol, representing a standard of grandeur. One must not confuse this symbolic importance with political reality, as some have done. At the same time, however, we must not forget the persistence of this glow in the East.

2. The First Arab Impact

DURING THE FIRST HALF of the ninth century, southern Italy, almost entirely free of any Byzantine presence and seemingly more or less forgotten by the Carolingians, began to slide within the orbit of Islam. The real role of the Arabs in south Italian history has had little attention. General histories of medieval Europe, hurrying on from Charlemagne to the twelfth century, typically treat the Arab impact in the ninth and tenth centuries as the Mediterranean equivalent of Viking incursions in the north and the Magyar thrust farther east. Sometimes there is a map, with arrows, depicting Europe as a sort of allegorical St. Sebastian, an innocent and passive figure assailed by Arab, Viking, and Magyar arrows of violence, destruction, and death.

In fact, however, the Arab impact on southern Italy was far more complex than any such visual aid suggests. (Ethnically, too, the Arab situation was complex; the "Arabs" were by no means all ethnic Arabs. Yet "Saracen," although often used in contemporary sources, now carries too many literary connotations. Therefore, in this study, "Arab" serves as the general term.) The Arab impact was in fact very different from that of the Vikings and the Magyars. Unquestionably, Arab raids caused violence, destruction, and death; they were devastating in their effect on many parts of southern Italy, particularly in the ninth century but also, in some sections, on into the early eleventh century. And yet in southern Italy raids were by no means the only element in the Arab impact. Throughout this period, in cultural splendor and affluence the Islamic Mediterranean world vied with, and in some respects surpassed, Byzantium. Despite the raids, over time the south Italian relationship with the Islamic sphere brought increased prosperity, at least to much of Campania. And there were other effects as well.

The first notable change related to the Arab factor came in 849: a political reconfiguration of the Lombard regions.[1] It was preceded by the Arab raid on Rome in 846, which centuries later was still remembered as one of the dramatic crisis points in papal history. The background of both these midcentury events warrants exploration.

The Road to Arab Mercenaries

At the start of the ninth century, the southern Lombards dominated most of lower Italy, including most of Campania. Their ruler, styling himself "Prince of the Beneventans," or sometimes "Prince of the Lombard peoples," governed from two capitals: the old, traditional capital at Benevento, with its evocation of Lombard magnificence in its public monuments, and the new, second capital on the coast at Salerno, a town the Lombards had apparently held since the seventh century but that had only achieved enhanced status and fortification under Arichis II.[2] Within Campania, only the duchy of Naples and its dependencies still resisted Lombard dominance. The Lombards had nibbled away at Naples' territory to the north and east of the city, so that less now remained beyond the coastal strip along the bay.[3] That coastal strip did, however, extend down to include the Amalfitan peninsula (the southern arm of the Bay of Naples) and thus Sorrento and Amalfi, on either side of that peninsula, were still satellites of Naples. Altogether, Naples and her dependencies constituted a tempting target for the Lombards.

The two rulers who successively held the southern Lombard throne from the death of Arichis II in 787 to 817, Grimoald III and Grimoald IV, were presumably kept busy solidifying their control over the rest of southern Italy. Neither seems to have proved particularly threatening to Naples. In 817, however, perhaps because Grimoald IV was an ineffective ruler, or perhaps because the revenues now coming in from so large a land area made the southern Lombard throne an increasingly attractive prize, he was assassinated and replaced as prince by an ambitious relative, Sico, the erstwhile gastald of Acerenza.[4] (Acerenza, perched on a peak on the upland plateau of Basilicata, is now merely an impoverished hill-town, but it had been a reasonably important center in the Roman era and its strategic location kept it important on into the Norman period.) The pace of events in southern Italy now quickened.

Sico and his son Sicard ruled successively from 817 to 839. The ninth-century Monte Cassino chronicler Erchempert and the tenth-century *Chronicon Salernitanum* describe both as strong and ruthless rulers, draining church treasuries and evincing an especially keen interest in tax collection throughout their extensive territory (including, of course, regions once held or claimed by Byzantium). The sources say, for example, that the Muslim invasion of Sicily in the 820s distressed Sico chiefly because it lowered his Calabrian revenues by keeping Sicilian merchants from coming there. And we are told that Sicard regularly sent his *referendarius*, with many men, to collect taxes all over Calabria and Apulia.[5]

The late eleventh-century Monte Cassino chronicler Leo Marsicanus described Sicard as a man given to every carnal vice but, above all, consumed by greed.[6] We can guess that Sicard was not above extortions from monasteries. Nonetheless, Sicard's interest in economic matters had its positive side; he seems to have restored the value of the principality's coinage, which apparently had declined since Arichis's day. Much later in the century, his gold coinage, like that of Arichis, was still frequently stipulated in sale contracts, and some of his coins have survived until today.[7] In addition, however, Sicard unquestionably believed in territorial expansion. Thus, during his reign, Naples was increasingly pressured. Under Sico, a Lombard raiding party had gone so far as to steal, temporarily, the body of Naples' patron saint, Januarius (the San Gennaro whom Naples still honors).[8] Now Sicard, even more aggressive, seemed determined to swallow the whole of the duchy of Naples.

And so in 835 the Neapolitans hired Arab mercenaries to help defend their city-state.[9] Some twenty years earlier, Arabs had been reported cruising the waters around southern Italy, making hit-and-run raids. Indeed, in 812, the island of Ischia just off Naples had been attacked, and both people and treasure taken.[10] The Neapolitans thus had every reason to be wary of turning to the Arabs for help. Possibly they counted on the fact that "their" Arabs were different. In the case of the raid on Ischia, the raiding party had been "Mauri," very likely from among a group of dissident Spanish Ommayids then living as somewhat unwelcome refugees in Egypt and seemingly supporting themselves through raids and piracy.[11] These Ommayids, however, had conquered Crete in 827, and therefore for the time being were not troubling Italy. The Arabs whom Naples hired were apparently from Sicily, which North African Aghlabids were now in the process of wresting from the Byzantines.[12]

The *Pactum Sicardi*

Briefly, Naples had reason to hope that its problems had been solved with the aid of these new defenders. On July 4, 836, roughly a year after the arrival of the Arab mercenaries, Sicard signed with Naples a multi-clause treaty that seemed aimed at removing all possible causes of friction. Known to us as the *Pactum Sicardi*, the document took the form of a declaration on

Sicard's part, with the Lombards as "we" and the Neapolitans as "you."[13]
Sicard was thus asserting his status as the dominant ruler in the region,
granting concessions to lesser folk. Yet in fact both sides made concessions.
It is true that some clauses particularly restricted Naples, such as the one that
prohibited Naples in future from trading in, or selling overseas, any Lombards. (In the late eighth century, Pope Hadrian had reported "Greek"
slavers operating off the Campanian coast; whether or not those "Greeks"
had been from Byzantine-connected Naples, as some have surmised, in 836
the Neapolitans were obviously believed to be involved in the slave trade.)[14]
On the other hand, both sides agreed to extradite murderers, not to shelter
known rogues or each other's enemies, to return unharmed any slaves (*servos*
or *ancillas*) fleeing or taken from each other's territory, and not to impose
unreasonable duties on each other's merchandise. Further, Sicard promised not to impede merchants crossing the rivers near Capua (presumably important for merchants going overland to Rome) and also gave
assurance that traveling merchants and their merchandise would be protected from seizure or injury in the event of a mischance such as shipwreck.
Finally, some clauses—of which only the titles remain—attempted to settle
territorial conflicts along the border between Naples and Lombard territory. Altogether, the pact strikes a modern reader as an exceptionally
sensible and practical document, resolving a variety of disputes and providing clear-cut mechanisms for addressing the most commonly encountered
problems.

The marked emphasis on mercantile concerns is a particularly interesting feature of the *Pactum Sicardi*. Moreover, although this is not yet the
place to discuss Amalfi at length, it is important to note that one clause (of
which only the title survives) apparently dealt specifically with the Amalfitans as traders. In the preamble to the pact, Amalfi, along with Sorrento,
was cited as subject to Naples; thus the protections guaranteed to merchants in general would presumably have covered Amalfitan merchants. Yet
there was, in addition, this special clause entitled "de Amalfitanis qualiter
peragantur," which can be loosely translated as "concerning the Amalfitans,
wherever they may travel." Some twenty-odd years earlier, there had been
the first clear evidence that Amalfitans were active seafarers; after the Arab
hit-and-run raid on Ischia in 812, Amalfitan ships (along with ships from
Gaeta) had apparently pursued the raiders all the way to the island of
Lampedusa, between Sicily and North Africa.[15] Thus the missing clause of
the *Pactum Sicardi* very likely dealt specifically with Amalfitan seafaring,
perhaps with issues particularly related to wide-ranging trading; in the

absence of the clause itself, we can only surmise. In any case, however, the fact that Amalfi had a clause all to itself demonstrates Campanian recognition that Amalfi already played a distinctive role.

We must assume that the development which led to the *Pactum Sicardi* was the strengthening of Naples' position through the acquisition of Arab mercenaries. That action must have come as a shock, not only to the Lombards but to everyone observing the south Italian scene. Yet anyone watching closely over the past quarter-century might not have been totally surprised. When that band of "Mauri" had raided Ischia in 812, and Amalfitan and Gaetan ships had pursued the raiders, the Amalfitans and Gaetans had been responding to an appeal for naval help from the Byzantine *patricius* of Sicily. As guardian now of Byzantine interests in the central Mediterranean, the latter was concerned because not only Ischia but islands all the way from Ponza to Sicily had been hit. His call for help had gone to Naples as well. Yet Naples had not responded, even though Naples was, at least in theory, a Byzantine dependency, and even though Ischia was within sight of Naples and apparently populated by Neapolitans.[16]

Naples' non-response seemed an early example of the ambivalent attitude toward confrontation with the Arabs that Naples was to demonstrate throughout the ninth century. Of course, there may have been some other, internal political explanation. Naples had already begun to act less deferential toward Byzantium in many ways, no longer, for example, recognizing Byzantine sovereignty on the local coinage.[17] Nonetheless, this refusal to become involved in 812 hinted at the way Naples would often behave over the rest of the century whenever attacks on Arabs were proposed.

In other ways, too, Naples was pursuing an idiosyncratic course. One example was reflected in the preamble of the *Pactum Sicardi*; representing the *ducatum* of Naples we find not only the *magister militum* (a common alternative title for Naples' duke) but also the bishop. Everywhere in southern Italy in the ninth and tenth centuries, as indeed throughout the Christian world in that period, key bishoprics were often held by a relative of the local ruler. But at Naples in the ninth century the relationship tended to be even closer; bishop and ruler were, more often than not, brothers (or uncle and nephew), and they appear to have shared temporal governance to an unusual degree. In the last quarter of the ninth century, a bishop-brother would in due course become duke himself and thereafter wear both hats.[18] The Beneventan Lombards viewed the church as a valuable instrument for patronage as well as a handy source for forced loans; but at Benevento there was little day-to-day overlap between the two spheres. At Naples, in contrast, ecclesiastical and secular authority appeared to be regarded as more or less interchangeable. No deeply felt theological principles seemed to underlie this arrangement; apparently the Neapolitans simply found it comfortable and practical. And—particularly interesting—most of the time, as we shall see, the key role played by the bishop at Naples does not seem to have stood in the way of accommodation with the Muslim world.

The *Pactum Sicardi*, according to its preamble, was to remain in force for five years. In setting a five-year limit, those who drew it up were presumably recognizing the fluidity of events in Campania, and attempting to be realistic. Events were to prove them overly sanguine. The first breach of the pact occurred within two years. And between the year of the pact's signing, 836, and the midpoint of the ninth century, so many changes took place within Campania, so many external developments affected the region, that the *Pactum Sicardi* was soon forgotten by everyone but archivists.

We are mainly dependent for information about local happenings in these years on an array of local chronicles, ecclesiastical in origin. These are sometimes inconsistent in chronology and detail, and also sometimes scant the very developments we would like to know more about. However, the major political events were quite widely reported, and we sense now a quickening of pace and a general feeling of crisis. The next significant happening, the first open breach of the *Pactum*, came in late 838. From their second capital at Salerno, the Lombards had begun to cast a covetous eye at Amalfi, nominally subject to Naples but geographically much closer to Salerno. At this early date, Amalfitan ships were perhaps not venturing much beyond Italian and Sicilian waters, but Amalfi nonetheless offered interesting possibilities and would represent an attractive addition to Lombard territory. And so Sicard attacked Amalfi, apparently in collusion with an Amalfitan faction, and carried off to Salerno a sizable number of seemingly willing Amalfitan citizens.[19] The very next year, 839, Sicard was assassinated, and the transplanted Amalfitans fled home. But Amalfi was soon contacted by Salernitans loyal to Sicard; unwilling to recognize the successor proclaimed at Benevento, one Radelchis, they wanted instead to install Sicard's brother Sikenolf on the throne, and they needed Amalfitan help. A group of Salernitans and Amalfitans thereupon sailed all the way to Taranto, where Sikenolf was being held captive; presumably pretending to be merely Amalfitan merchants, they located and rescued Sikenolf, bringing him safely back to Salerno. And almost immediately Salerno, under Sikenolf's leadership, began a bloody civil war with Benevento.[20]

Fragmentation: Naples and Amalfi, Benevento and Salerno

Because the Lombards now controlled almost all of southern Italy, the conflict between Benevento and Salerno had ramifications throughout the lower Italian peninsula. And in Campania itself the events of 839 had an interesting (and apparently related) side effect. From that point, when for the first time Amalfitans had become directly involved in Lombard politics, Amalfi's relationship with Naples changed. Amalfi no longer appeared to recognize Neapolitan sovereignty but instead acted as an autonomous political entity.[21] It is noteworthy, however, that Amalfi apparently made an effort to stay clear of further entanglement in local Campanian infighting, a course made easier because of Amalfi's isolated position out on its precipitous peninsula. Thenceforth, in any case, Amalfi in the main pursued its own special interests, while at the same time managing (usually) to remain on good terms with both Naples and Salerno.

Amalfi's separation from Naples proved eventually to have been a significant development for southern Italy. At the time, however, as the chronicles make clear, all attention was focused on the fierce and bitter conflict now underway between Lombard Salerno and Lombard Benevento. That fragmentation so deplored by most historians of the south Italian scene had commenced. Moreover, the level of violence was about to rise, markedly. Altogether, from the 840s on through the rest of the ninth century, southern Italy hardly presents a pretty picture. Yet in the course of those decades the area did witness a dazzling international procession of characters: countless Arabs; the doggedly conscientious but hapless Carolingian ruler Louis II; perhaps the most interesting pope of the ninth century, John VIII; and, finally, that great Byzantine general, Nicephorus Phocas. Not again until the Norman era was southern Italy to be so focal a point of interest for so many contending forces.

Many of the happenings of the ninth century make exceptionally vivid the character of life and politics in southern Italy in this period. Moreover, interspersed with grim events there were moments of what can only be called high comedy as the wily south Italians worked at fending off outside interference.

The first significant development of the 840s was a veritable explosion in the number of Arabs on the south Italian scene. For more than twenty-five years after the Ischia raid of 812 (and one the following year at Civitavecchia) there were no reports of Arab attacks threatening mainland Italy.

True, in the 820s the Arabs had begun their conquest of Sicily. Also, the
Annales Regni Francorum tell of "pirates" in the year 820 seizing merchant
ships en route from Sardinia to the Italian mainland.[22] Although those
particular pirates may or may not have been Muslim, Arabs undoubtedly
were among those taking advantage of the anarchic maritime situation in
this period. Nonetheless, for nearly a generation no mention is made of
Arab land raids. The only Arab threat seemingly came from the mercenaries
that had been imported by Naples in 835. Then suddenly, in 838, Arabs
apparently coming from Sicily sacked Brindisi, a key port on the Adriatic
now held by the Lombards. Roughly two years later, others briefly occupied Taranto, in the heel; this must have occurred just after Sikenolf had
been rescued from the Beneventan Lombard loyalists holding the city. And
then, in late 840 or early 841, the major Adriatic port of Bari was briefly
occupied and plundered.

All of this was sufficiently shocking to cause Byzantium to turn its
attention to Italy again, if only to ask Venice to send a fleet south toward
Taranto. Constantinople viewed Bari, Brindisi, and Taranto as still very
much part of the Byzantine Empire, only temporarily in Lombard hands.
Clearly, Byzantium's chances of eventually reasserting dominion in southern Italy would be far poorer if the Arabs were allowed to ravage un-
checked. The Venetians did therefore send two successive fleets; both,
however, were mauled, and the victorious Arabs responded by commencing to raid much farther north along the Adriatic coast than ever before.[23]

Meanwhile, on the other side of the Italian peninsula, there were
equally alarming developments. In 842 or thereabouts, "multorum naves
Saracenorum" landed at Ponza, an island off Gaeta; the Arabs seemingly
planned to make Ponza a permanent raiding base. Although up to that
point Naples had not appeared alarmed by the growth of Arab power, the
Neapolitans plainly did not relish the prospect of a major Arab base so near
at hand. Duke Sergius of Naples therefore decided to take action, in alliance
with the other major coastal towns; a combined fleet from Naples, Gaeta,
Amalfi and Sorrento attacked Ponza, drove the Arabs off, and then apparently won a further victory off Point Licosa, just below the site of the
ancient Greek city of Paestum.[24] That settled matters for the moment. Yet
further Arab attacks all along the Tyrrhenian coast surely could be anticipated. The inhabitants of Ostia and Portus, at the mouth of the Tiber
downstream from Rome, appealed to Pope Gregory IV for help in improving their defenses.[25]

846: The Arab Sack of Rome

Everywhere from Rome south there must have been a sense now of the Arabs closing in, moving to take over the whole of the central Mediterranean. The Byzantine hold on Sicily was crumbling. Palermo, and indeed virtually all of western Sicily, had already fallen to the North African Aghlabids, and in 842 a massive Aghlabid force assaulted Messina at the northeastern tip of that island, one of the few major Sicilian towns still in Byzantine hands.[26] (Interestingly, it was reported that some Neapolitans at Messina, presumably merchants, sided with the Muslim attackers.)[27] And then within Campania, at roughly the same time, both Radelchis of Benevento and Sikenolf of Salerno hired Arab mercenaries to fight in their civil war.[28]

This move on the part of Benevento and Salerno soon caused untold misery for much of southern Italy, but it might not have attracted attention far from the scene had there not occurred, four years later, a highly dramatic event. In August 846, Arab raiders arrived at Ostia and Portus, with what was said to be eleven thousand men and five hundred horses in seventy-three ships.[29] These raiders seem to have had no connection with the Beneventan and Salernitan mercenaries. They had set sail from Campania, however; a Naples source reported that the Aghlabid leaders in Sicily had sent this huge force direct from Palermo and that the attackers had begun their operation by capturing the "castellum" at Misenum, site of the imperial Roman naval base at the outer tip of the Bay of Naples.[30]

This time, the raiders' target seemed unquestionably to be the Holy City itself. In a desperate attempt to hold them off, a makeshift army of Saxons, Frisians, and Franks was recruited from student and pilgrim hostels at Rome and dispatched toward Ostia, accompanied by some sort of Roman militia. For two or three days, this motley collection of amateur warriors ranged around the countryside but encountered few Arabs; the raiders kept out of sight, biding their time. Something, however, alarmed the Roman detachment and suddenly they rushed back to their city and the relative safety of the Aurelian walls, leaving behind the Saxons, Frisians, and Franks. The Arabs then struck. The hapless foreign recruits were slaughtered, and the raiders raced unimpeded up along the Tiber to Rome.[31]

They were heading toward extraordinary treasures, as they seem to have known. Over the past half-century, rejoicing in the stability now seemingly guaranteed by the Carolingian presence in Italy, successive popes had been enthusiastically engaged in embellishing Rome's churches. Many of the most impressive of these churches, certainly including St. Peter's and the basilicas dedicated to St. Paul and St. Lawrence, were outside the Aurelian walls and thus easy targets for the raiders. And these, like all of Rome's churches, were now filled to overflowing with rich liturgical vessels and with jeweled reliquaries housing all of the relics recently amassed.[32] It is no wonder that the raiders were said to have desecrated all the very holiest shrines, even the high altar over St. Peter's grave. European contemporaries cited this desecration as a calculated demonstration of Muslim contempt for Christianity. But probably the raiders' actions only proved that they had done sound intelligence work and knew exactly where to look for the most valuable treasures.

The best contemporary narrative of the Arab sack of Rome, apparently written by someone who actually experienced it, is that in the *Liber Pontificalis*. Unhappily, the manuscript of the Life of Pope Sergius II breaks off, the manuscript mutilated, at the most dramatic point, just when the citizenry of Rome is gathered to resist the approaching invaders at "the field of Nero" (presumably the area once known as the circus of Nero, outside the Aurelian walls between the Tiber and St. Peter's). We do learn, however, from other sources that the raiders essentially got what they wanted at Rome.[33] Most then headed south along the Appian Way, and in November met with their ships near Gaeta and sailed off. A Carolingian force, doubtless patched together within northern Italy, had apparently pursued and confronted them near Gaeta, but was crushed. And there was also one final, particularly interesting report. It appears that a combined Neapolitan-Amalfitan-Gaetan force formed at Gaeta as the Arabs approached, but did not engage them. The south Italians confined their efforts to ensuring that Gaeta itself was not attacked.[34]

Lothar, Louis, and the 849 *Divisio*

The 846 raid on Rome had wide-ranging repercussions. Not only did it appall western Europe; it was also to affect southern Italy in many ways, in both the short and long terms. There was an immediate reaction in Carolingian circles. This was, after all, the first time that the Holy City had been attacked since the days of Alaric and Gaiseric in the fifth century, and they at least had respected shrines and churches. A genuinely horrified Emperor Lothar quickly arranged for troops to be sent south. He also ordered a levy, throughout the empire, to fund walls with which Pope Leo IV could surround St. Peter's and the papal enclave—the Leonine walls, in other words.[35] The army was led by Lothar's twenty-two-year-old son, the future Louis II; he was to help shore up Rome's defenses, but clearly he was also instructed to see what else could be done to ensure that nothing like this ever happened again.

And indeed, if we may look ahead, when an Arab fleet did threaten again three years later, in 849, Rome and its protectors would prove ready. Pressure had successfully been applied even to Naples; Caesar, son of the Duke of Naples, was recruited to organize and lead a great Christian fleet. Not surprisingly, given Naples' history of consorting with Arabs, Pope Leo was somewhat dubious about Caesar's commitment; the latter had first to go to Rome and convince the pope that his intentions were pure.[36] But in fact Caesar did prove himself a valiant defender of the papal patrimony. Contemporary sources give him full credit for intercepting and defeating the Arab fleet in what came to be known as the Battle of Ostia. Indeed, Caesar's naval victory became legendary; in the early sixteenth century, he and it were commemorated in one of the monumental wall paintings done, to Raphael's design, for the papal chambers in the Vatican.[37] Only in a contemporary south Italian source do we find interesting additional information: the rumor that Caesar, even while driving off the Arab fleet, passed word to its commander that his ships could take refuge at Naples if they ran into bad weather fleeing south.[38] (As it happened, most of the Arab fleet was apparently lost in a storm before it could reach Naples.) Nevertheless, Rome was saved from attack in 849 and was never again directly threatened by an Arab army.

But the great "Battle of Ostia" was still nearly three years in the future when, in late 846, Louis and his Carolingian forces wended their way south, some months after the sack of Rome. Many of those accompanying Louis doubtless set off knowing only a few facts about the situation they faced. In sum, Arab raiders were a threat along both coasts of southern Italy, as indeed they now were virtually everywhere in the Mediterranean. They had sacked and even briefly held some of the region's key ports, cities well-known since Roman days. And, worst of all, the Arabs were not only pillaging the monasteries and churches of southern Italy and showing no mercy to monks or other peaceful individuals, but they had even dared to penetrate the holiest shrines of Rome itself, plundering and destroying.

Yet Louis himself obviously knew more than this. Contemporary south Italian monastic chronicles did not mince words about the role played by south Italian rulers in worsening the situation, and that message had clearly been passed to Lothar and Louis along the ecclesiastical network. The civil war between Lombard Benevento and Lombard Salerno had led first Radelchis of Benevento and then Sikenolf of Salerno to hire Arab mercenaries. Now, whenever these mercenaries were not attacking each other on behalf of their employers, they were raiding indiscriminately all over southern Italy. Moreover, and most shocking, the mercenaries' employers were paying them out of church and monastery treasuries. The *Chronicon Salernitanum* reports this in relation to local churches at both Benevento and Salerno, and two Monte Cassino chronicles list the irreplaceable treasures taken from Monte Cassino for this purpose by Sikenolf on at least six different occasions.[39]

That Lothar, and thus Louis, were fully aware of all these facts is revealed in the capitulary issued in October, apparently shortly before Louis set off. In that capitulary, Lothar not only proclaimed the need for funds for the Leonine walls, and announced Louis' expedition; he also reported that Guy of Spoleto was being dispatched to make peace between Benevento and Salerno as part of a multipronged effort to drive from Italy south of Rome its "Sarracenos et Mauros."[40]

Actually, Louis had heard earlier about the civil war between Benevento and Salerno, although at the time it may not have seemed particularly significant. In 844, as the Emperor Lothar's eldest son and heir apparent, Louis had come south to Rome to be crowned *rex langobardorum*. To Louis and his father, that title indicated de jure dominion over the southern Lombards as well as over Carolingian northern Italy. In fact, for the southern Lombards, Louis' title had little practical meaning; no Carolingian ruler had attempted to assert actual control over them since Charlemagne's day. Yet Louis' presence in Rome for this ceremony must have seemed to Sikenolf a splendid opportunity to gain support in his struggle for the Beneventan throne. And so Sikenolf had attended the coronation. Erchempert, the ninth-century Monte Cassino monk and chronicler, tells us that, in preparation, Sikenolf had paid Guy of Spoleto 50,000 gold *nummis* because Guy had asserted that only with his help could Louis be persuaded to endorse Sikenolf's claims.[41]

Guy of Spoleto was a Frank, who, as vassal to Lothar and Louis, held what had once been the Lombard duchy of Spoleto, northeast of Rome; clearly a wily entrepreneur, he was to make a good deal of money out of the Salerno-Benevento conflict. At least in this instance, however, Guy seems to have earned his pay. The *Liber Pontificalis*, while suggesting that Sikenolf came to Rome only because of his burning desire to see the pope and receive a papal blessing, refers to him as "Beneventorum princeps" and also notes, in passing, that Sikenolf obtained from Louis all he wished ("quidquid quesierat").[42] Presumably the papal biographer, so enthusiastic about Sikenolf, did not know that he had bribed Guy or that, just as when paying his Arab mercenaries, he had raised the money for the bribe by raiding church and monastery treasuries.[43]

In any case, despite Sikenolf's success at Rome in 844, at Benevento itself Radelchis had continued to be recognized as the rightful ruler. And so the civil war had raged on in the two years between Louis' coronation and the Arab attack on Rome. In fact, with each side continuing to employ Arab mercenaries, the war had become even more devastating. And the ecclesiastical institutions of southern Italy had continued to suffer in more ways than one, not only experiencing fearsome raids (for the mercenaries often raged out of control) but also forced to subsidize their tormentors.

It must have seemed ironic to knowledgeable churchmen that Radelchis of Benevento had been the first of the Lombard rulers to hire Arabs, thereby bringing so much grief to the region. For everything we know about Radelchis suggests a pious and conciliatory man, averse to violence. The *Chronicon Salernitanum*, that marvelous repository of south Italian gossip, reports Salernitans taunting the Beneventans that their ruler should be tonsured. The *Chronicon* also tells us that, as a youth, Radelchis's favorite occupation had been visiting the goldsmiths' workshops in Benevento to watch them at their craft.[44] Later, in 849, when through Louis' hard work the Benevento-Salerno conflict was resolved by formally splitting southern Lombard territory into two autonomous principalities, Radelchis would placate some leading Beneventans (who were losing lands as the result of partition) by compensating them from his own holdings. Altogether, it seems plain that Radelchis had hired mercenaries because he himself had no stomach for the fighting forced on him by the Salernitan rebellion.

Given his dislike of confrontation, it is not surprising that each of the two mercenary leaders who successively fought on Radelchis's behalf had come to exercise a virtual co-dominion with him over the territory Benevento still controlled. They freely used the city of Benevento as a base, venturing forth from there to raid, on one such expedition taking the *castrum* of Telese and then (moving in a wide arc) threatening Monte Cassino and sacking and pillaging from Isernia to Aquino and Arce.[45] Radelchis seems to have raised no objection; it would have been out of character. Indeed, the *Chronicon Salernitanum* tells one tale of Radelchis and his mercenaries which is so good that it must have been apocryphal; nonetheless, it certainly captures Radelchis's image in contemporary southern Italy. Guy of Spoleto (we read) at one point descended on Benevento to demand the surrender of Benevento's current Arab-mercenary leader, called "Apolaffar" in south Italian sources. Radelchis was ordered to go wake Apolaffar (who apparently was sleeping in a wing of the palace) in order to deliver him to Guy's troops. And what seemed most to distress Radelchis, for which he apologized profusely to Apolaffar, was that he could not even allow the mercenary time to find his shoes. (Apolaffar's understandable rejoinder was "Why are you worrying about my feet? What about my head!")[46] Radelchis, hating unpleasantness, clearly was singularly ill-suited to life in ninth-century southern Italy.

Sikenolf's relations with his Arab mercenaries were very different. He had promptly hired some (probably in 842) as soon as he heard that Radelchis had acquired an Arab force. So far as we know, Sikenolf made no objection to his Arabs engaging in random pillaging on their own whenever he did not need them, but there is every indication that he and his Salernitan supporters did in fact use their mercenaries almost constantly, and fought alongside them.[47] For Sikenolf, hiring Arab mercenaries was a means of enhancing his own military capabilities, certainly not a way to avoid personal involvement in combat. And with them, he had soon achieved notable success. These Arabs were obviously fierce fighters, and Sikenolf and his Salernitan Lombards seem to have been equally fierce and determined. Within five years, or by the time Louis arrived in southern Italy early in 847, Sikenolf had taken most of the major towns and *castra* within traditional Beneventan territory, leaving Radelchis in unquestioned control only of the city of Benevento, and of Siponto on the Gargano peninsula along the Adriatic coast.[48] Indeed, Radelchis, fearing that even Benevento might fall, at one point had sought help from the indefatigable Guy of Spoleto, always ready to provide services for a fee. Radelchis reportedly paid Guy 70,000 gold *nummis* to persuade Sikenolf not to attack Benevento.[49]

Louis thus arrived in southern Italy knowing he could not hope to stabilize the situation without expelling the Arabs and that he could not hope to do that without resolving the Lombard civil war. Although the Arab force that had struck Rome was not connected with the Arab bands operating within southern Italy, to some degree they all supported each other, if only by creating disruption on many fronts.

Unfortunately for Louis, his task in relation to the Arab presence had become more challenging even as he and his army marched south. There had been a new Arab attack on Bari, and this time that major Apulian port fell totally into Arab hands. For the next twenty-four years, from 847 to 871, Bari was to be the seat of a mini-emirate.[50] This emirate of Bari will receive more attention in Chapter 3. For the moment it is enough to know that in 847 Louis began his efforts by attempting, and failing, to retake Bari. Thereafter, the reports of his movements are so garbled and contradictory that it is not possible to track his campaign. But eventually, in what seems to have been May of 848 (and thus after more than a year of campaigning), he arrived at Radelchis's city of Benevento. And there he put to the sword one "Massar," the current leader of Benevento's Arab force, together with his mercenary followers.[51] Despite the attention this episode attracted, however, there is no evidence that, overall, Louis' campaign significantly decreased the number of Arabs in southern Italy. He did dispose of some of them permanently, but many of those he drove off simply found new lairs in other parts of the region.

The one truly important result of Louis' campaign was resolution of the Benevento-Salerno conflict. It would be very interesting to know exactly how this was achieved, for the settlement manifestly involved compromise. It must have called for deft diplomacy. Unfortunately, there is no clue in the sources; they do not even agree on who deserved credit for the settlement, with some naming Louis and others Guy of Spoleto. Nor do they agree about whether Louis was actually present at the formal signing.[52] Quite possibly, despite the testimony of Erchempert's usually reliable chronicle, Louis was in fact not there in person. And Guy of Spoleto very likely did do much of the negotiating and in that sense did deserve credit for the settlement; after all, Lothar's capitulary had specifically charged him with the peacemaking effort. Nonetheless, it seems obvious that Louis' presence in southern Italy and the resolution of the conflict were not merely coincidental.

The settlement treaty, usually dated to early 849, is informally known as the *Divisio*, an abbreviation for *Radelgisi et Siginulfi Divisio Ducatus Beneventani*.[53] Its wording defines it as a concession from Radelchis to Sikenolf, appropriate if one granted that Radelchis had the superior claim to authority over the southern Lombards. Perhaps that aspect of the treaty was therefore a gesture to enable Radelchis to save face (at least to some extent) as he parted with half of his territory. Otherwise, however, all evidence suggests that Sikenolf was the major victor. Jules Gay described the *Divisio* as marking, or foreordaining, the decline of Benevento. Nicola

Cilento contested this interpretation, insisting that Salerno's territorial share was not all that much better.[54] It is true that the divisions were roughly equal in size, and undeniably the comparative shift in importance between Benevento and Salerno, after the *Divisio*, was due to many factors. Nonetheless, the document as a whole conveys the sense of a beleaguered Benevento. For example, while the provisions regarding law and order and amity apply equally to both sides, only Benevento is singled out in the final compliance clause as liable to severe judgments (and ultimately an enormous penalty in gold) if the provisions were breached. All in all, assuming that Guy of Spoleto did play a crucial role in arranging the settlement, one might bear in mind that Guy was Sikenolf's brother-in-law and that Sikenolf had always rewarded Guy well for favors.

The *Divisio* split in half the principality of Benevento, which—with virtually no Byzantine presence now in Italy—had come to comprise almost the whole of southern Italy (excepting only Gaeta, Naples, Amalfi, and the extreme tips of the boot). The division was formally made in terms of gastaldates, the military and administrative districts through which the Lombard rulers governed and controlled their territory. The document names each of the gastaldates awarded to the new principality of Salerno; the total, including Salerno itself, comes to fifteen and a half. (The gastaldate of Acerenza was split between Benevento and Salerno, presumably because it straddled the natural boundary between what would now be two separate principalities.) Jules Gay and others have guessed at what gastaldates would have been left for Benevento, and that hypothetical tally comes to sixteen and a half.[55]

Notably, each of the principalities now theoretically included gastaldates based at erstwhile Byzantine port towns (Bari, Brindisi, and Taranto). Of these, Bari and Brindisi were apparently left to Benevento, while Taranto specifically appears on Salerno's list. Since both Bari and Taranto were at the moment in Arab hands, the new principality of Salerno and the truncated principality of Benevento thus appeared more or less equal in relation to currently nonproductive areas. Yet that aside, Salerno does appear to have had the best of the arrangement. The other gastaldates assigned to Salerno stretched from Capua in the north to Cosenza in the south; mostly on the western side of the peninsula, almost all of them (with the exception of Taranto) were traditionally Lombard and presumably would remain so. But Benevento's share, the eastern portion and the upper midsection of southern Italy, included not only places now held by the Arabs but also areas often claimed by the papacy, in the general vicinity of the monasteries of Monte Cassino and San Vincenzo al Volturno. Also, both of those great monasteries, with all of their lands, were specifically exempted from the division and placed under the protection of the Carolingian emperor. And—a further disdvantage—Byzantium at some point might attempt to reclaim much of the territory allocated to Benevento along the Adriatic coast; meanwhile, that area, with an Arab emirate established at Bari, was particularly vulnerable to Arab attack. In effect, then, Benevento's share was far less promising than Salerno's.

Several of the law-and-order provisions within the *Divisio* are reminiscent of the *Pactum Sicardi*. Neither side was to shelter murderers or troublemakers; both sides were to return fugitive *servos* and *ancillas* (and also, in this document, *aldiones*); safe passage across each other's territory was to be assured. (There is particular reference to safe passage through Beneventan territory to the great Lombard shrine of St. Michael on the Gargano peninsula.) Yet, in addition, there are clauses that make very clear the extent of the disturbances caused by the civil war. Monks, bishops and other clerics were now to be enabled freely to return to their monasteries or sees. And particular attention was paid to the Arab issue. The third clause stated that neither side in future was to league with Saracens or any other "generatione" in order to resume hostilities or cause depradations.[56] Clause 24 reverted to the Arab situation, stating that there was to be no seeking out of Saracens either for "adiutorium seu amicitiam." It then went on to say that all individual Saracens, except for those converted to Christianity in the days of Sico and Sicard (and not now apostate), were to be expelled; the implications of this last sentence will be discussed in the next chapter.

Although it is not clear that Louis himself was actually present at the signing of this momentous agreement, he must still have been near at hand, for in the document Radelchis declares that "before Louis leaves this land" he, Radelchis, will turn over to Salerno one of the surrendered gastaldates (Montella) and the promised half of the gastaldate of Acerenza.[57] And whether or not Louis was present, all of the leading Lombards of southern Italy certainly do appear to have attended the signing. The witness list rolls on for a full page, one resonant Lombard name after another.

There were to be several other significant developments in the next year or so. The hapless Radelchis died later in 849. (He was succeeded, at least briefly, by his inept son Radelgarius.) And toward the end of that same year Sikenolf of Salerno also died, having had only a few months to savor his triumph. His heir, called Sico after his grandfather, was only two, and so the governance of the new principality of Salerno was assumed by two regents, the little Sico's godfather Peter and the latter's son Ademar—cruel and ineffective rulers, events were to prove.

The rest of Europe took no notice of these changes of rule in distant southern Italy. The one event of 849 that attracted widespread attention was the great naval battle of Ostia, which had taken place in the spring. With that victory and Rome's new defensive walls, it could be hoped that the Holy City would be safe from any further raids. Emperor Lothar had reason to feel that his son Louis had done his work well. He had apparently pacified the contentious southern Lombards, and Carolingian standing in southern Italy had seemingly never been higher. And so, surely in part to reward this success in the south, Lothar now arranged to have Louis crowned co-emperor. The ceremony took place in Rome on Easter Sunday of 850.

3. A Carolingian Crusade

WITH THE LOMBARD CIVIL WAR settled by the *Divisio* and the Lombards' Arab mercenaries dispersed, Louis, in 849, must have gone back north with a genuine sense of accomplishment. A more stable southern Italy should offer less temptation to the Arabs.

He had, however, done little more than shift the locus of the threat—and only temporarily at that. There was still a hostile Arab presence in southern Italy, and it would become even more widely diffused (and even more threatening) over the next few decades. The rest of Europe, which tended to glance toward southern Italy only when there were major military actions involving northerners, would have reason to note two more campaigns in that region over the next seventy-five years. One would come in 871, when Louis was to make his final (and finally successful) effort to put an end to the Muslim emirate of Bari. The other would be the celebrated Garigliano campaign of 915, that massive combined operation to drive from their base near Gaeta an Arab band that was harassing papal territory.

Both of these campaigns (as well as the Arab actions that caused them) deserve attention, and Louis' expedition will figure prominently in this chapter and the Garigliano campaign in Chapter 5. At least for Campania, however, these were not the most significant happenings of the next three-quarters of a century. Transcending them in long-term significance—even transcending the pain and devastation engendered by Arab raids—was the beginning of a genuinely productive relationship between Campania and the Mediterranean Muslim world. The evolution of this relationship is only indirectly reflected in the chronicles; evidence for it must be gleaned from a wide variety of sources. Nonetheless, the evidence is there, in the background of the more visible events, as we shall see later in this study.

But for the period from 850 to 871, the focus of this chapter, we must continue to concentrate on the foreground, following the further adventures (and misadventures) of the conscientious but ill-starred Louis II, which led ultimately to the collapse of Carolingian hopes for southern Italy. And then we must look more closely at the Arabs who caused Louis so much grief.

Louis II: The Politics of Failure

The *Divisio* had disposed of the mercenary bands of Benevento and Salerno, but the emirate of Bari remained a major threat to south Italian peace and stability. Raiding parties swept west and northwest from Bari in a wide swath. In 852, only three years after the *Divisio*, Louis came south again in response to anguished pleas from the abbots of both Monte Cassino and San Vincenzo al Volturno. Once again, he tried to take Bari; once again he failed and went back north.[1] The only concrete accomplishment attributed to Louis on this trip south was one he would later have cause to regret. Peter and Ademar, the father and son who had been ruling Salerno as regents for the young Sico ever since Sikenolf's death in late 849, now wanted more formal recognition. Louis agreed to confirm them, and took little Sico back north with him to be groomed for eventual rule. The arrangement surely reflected naïveté on Louis' part and worked out badly for everyone concerned. Not only did Peter and Ademar prove to be abominable rulers, according to the local sources, but also, when some years later Sico ("ab omnibus diligebatur") was returning home to assume his princely responsibilities, Peter and Ademar had him assassinated.[2]

Of course, in 852 this unhappy ending lay far in the future. But Louis' 852 campaign had accomplished nothing toward halting Arab raids, and these continued. In 856, if a northern annalist was correct, territory in the vicinity of Naples was sacked.[3] According to south Italian sources, in 858 Conza and then parts of the Terra di Lavoro between Capua and Naples were ravaged; in 861, the fortified town of Ascoli was burned by Arab marauders, and the high valley of the Volturno, including Teano and the monastery of San Vincenzo, was raided; in 862, Conza was hit again, the *castrum* of Venafro taken at least temporarily, and the territory surrounding Monte Cassino scoured for loot.[4] Apparently at least once in this period, in 860, Louis came down again into southern Italy but again accomplished little in relation to the Arabs.[5]

Information about Arab actions in these years comes almost exclusively from Monte Cassino chronicles, and virtually all of the raids they report took place north of a hypothetical line drawn across Italy from Bari to Naples. Possibly the Bari Arabs did also raid deeper down in southern Italy, unbeknownst to the Monte Cassino chroniclers. Or it may be that the lower regions of the peninsula were left for Taranto's Arabs to pick clean. For Taranto was also in Arab hands by this time, its Arabs seemingly not connected with those at Bari but on friendly terms with them.[6]

In any case, it was the Bari emirate whose bands were now ravaging the areas of southern Italy nearest to Rome and papal territory, and plundering at will the rich monasteries of Monte Cassino and San Vincenzo. The monks of Monte Cassino and San Vincenzo had doubtless hoped that their special imperial status would bring with it imperial protection. Instead, they were forced to try to survive through any means at hand. In 862, a year of particularly severe raids, it was notable that Bari Muslims not only sacked huge stretches of Beneventan territory but also took Venafro, ideally situated for harassing both Monte Cassino and San Vincenzo; the former was only fifteen or twenty miles to the northwest, and the latter a similar distance to the northeast, up the valley of the Volturno. From Venafro, the raiders seem to have headed first for San Vincenzo, where they took all the portable treasures they could find and then extorted three thousand gold pieces ("tres milia aureos") in return for not burning the buildings. Next they went to Monte Cassino, where they were rewarded with a similar sum.[7]

Jules Gay exaggerated only slightly in saying that around 860 the Muslims seemed as strong in southern Italy, as surely on their way to total conquest there, as they were in Sicily.[8] The sources report comparatively little about events beyond the Lombard core areas, but what evidence there is suggests that deep in southern Italy the Arabs were scoring victory after victory. Not only did they hold Bari and Taranto, the two major Apulian ports. Some Arabs now also took Amantea, on Calabria's western coast. In addition, they were expanding their range of control everywhere in the interior. Apparently at about this time they captured the Apulian towns of Matera and Oria, thus acquiring some well-situated inland bases.

The Taranto Arabs were undoubtedly responsible for some of these conquests. Nonetheless, it was the increasingly aggressive emirate of Bari that now seemed most alarming. Other than its duration (847–71), we have little specific information about the Bari emirate. An Arab source provides only two major facts. Al-Balādhurī reports that Bari was conquered by a Muslim adventurer, described as a lowly *mirwah*, a former servant or perhaps freed slave of the Aghlabid emir of North Africa.[9] There is every indication that Kalfūn, this first emir of Bari, had acted entirely on his own. Arab chroniclers, aside from al-Balādhurī's brief reference, make no mention of what they apparently regarded as a conquest without importance, achieved by a Muslim without status. However, al-Balādhurī also says that Kalfūn's successor, the second emir of Bari, and then again "Sawdan," the third and last emir, sent requests to Baghdad for formal recognition of the emirate of Bari, and eventually recognition was granted.[10]

We have only three other scraps of news concerning Muslim Bari, but all three are interesting. At some point in the mid-860s, the Frankish monk Bernard, on his way to the Holy Land with two companions, came to Bari, "civitatem Sarracenorum." Bernard and his companions sought and received from Sawdan safe-conduct letters addressed to the "princes" of Baghdad and Jerusalem, letters they expected to find useful not only in the Holy Land but also en route, in Egypt.[11] The narrative of Bernard's journey suggests no shock that Bari, "formerly belonging to the Beneventans," was now in Muslim hands; Bernard and his companions received courteous treatment there and seem simply to have accepted the fact that Bari was no longer part of the Christian world. Next, they journeyed on deeper into southern Italy, to Taranto, also now Muslim-held, and there they embarked for Alexandria on an Arab ship carrying—and this they did deplore—Christian captives headed for the Egyptian slave markets.[12]

We get another glimpse of Muslim Bari in the somewhat problematic *Chronicle of Ahimaaz* (also sometimes known as the "Chronicle of Oria"), a Hebrew narrative of the eleventh century that provides a highly colored history of one eminent south Italian Jewish family.[13] Many of the anecdotes in this chronicle seem questionable, but it is noteworthy that Sawdan, the third and last emir of Bari, is memorialized in it as a wise and eminently civilized ruler. Sawdan, much the best known of the three Bari emirs, typically was pictured in the monastic chronicles as an arch-villain; "nequissimus ac sceleratissimus" were among the milder epithets.[14] This narrative, however, tells in glowing terms (and with obvious pride) of the honor and respect accorded by Sawdan over a six-month period to one Abu Aaron, described as a scholar famed throughout the Jewish communities of southern Italy. Sawdan, we are told, was deeply impressed by the wisdom of Abu Aaron and was desolate when the latter departed.[15] Doubtless much of this story was romantic fiction (even though there certainly were eminent scholars in southern Italy's Jewish communities). Yet it is interesting that the author, who did not mince words concerning the havoc wreaked by Arab raids (and on some key Jewish communities), nonetheless depicted Muslim Bari as a stable and well-governed city.

And indeed the emirate of Bari did endure for twenty-four years, nearly an entire generation. Both Bernard and (supposedly) Abu Aaron were there in what would prove to be its final years; nonetheless, at the time of their visits, Muslim rule must have seemed very much a settled fact of life. Other evidence shows that Bari under Muslim rule came to be accepted as simply another piece of the south Italian jigsaw puzzle, merely one more entity to be dealt with. At one point, a Spoletan in rebellion against Louis II apparently fled to Sawdan's Bari and remained there for some time.[16] And in the *Chronicon Salernitanum* we read that envoys ("legati") from Muslim Bari came to Salerno, where they were even lodged in the bishop's palace—to the rage of the bishop.[17]

But if some in southern Italy had come to accept Muslim Bari, for the guardians of ecclesiastical institutions (and their treasures) it signified a very real and continuous threat. Louis II, exercising sole responsibility in Italy since the death of Emperor Lothar in 855, could hardly view with equanimity the increasing consolidation of Arab power there. It is no wonder that he gradually became obsessed with the need to drive Sawdan and his fellow Muslims out of Bari.

The preparations for what Louis clearly hoped would be the decisive attempt began in 865, when he issued a capitulary calling up fighting men throughout northern Italy. They were to gather in the spring of the following year at Lucera, roughly seventy-five miles northeast of Bari.[18] Unhappily, the sources tell us nothing about what use was then made of this fighting force; possibly Louis did lead the army from Lucera to Bari in the spring of 866 but failed once again to take the city. In any event, by early summer of that year we find Louis approaching the Bari problem in a different way; accompanied (as always, since their marriage in 851) by his wife, Engelberga, he set off on a circular tour through Campania. Erchempert, a contemporary, reports that Louis' renewed attempt to take Bari had been strongly urged by the Lombard rulers of Benevento, Salerno and Capua.[19] Nonetheless, Louis by now had had twenty years' experience with the southern Lombard rulers and he knew that their internal rivalries and private ambitions could wreak havoc with any plans he made. Perhaps some new development that spring had made him freshly sensitive to this danger.

Louis and Engelberga began their tour, in June 866, at Monte Cassino, where Landolf, bishop of Capua and senior member of Capua's ruling clan, came to meet him. Five years earlier, in 860 or 861, Capua had broken free from Salerno (thus creating a third southern Lombard power center) and the Capuans were now making trouble everywhere in Campania. Bishop Landolf plainly hoped to gain Louis' favor by rushing to greet him, but the abbot of Monte Cassino apparently warned Louis that he was not to be trusted. Louis therefore rejected Landolf's overtures and proceeded to take Capua and install there, at least temporarily, a Spoletan overseer.[20] The taking of Capua must surely have involved some of the mobilized northerners; thereafter, however, during the rest of the tour through Campania, there was no further show of force.

After this, Louis and Engelberga journeyed further south, to Salerno, where there was now a strong new ruler, Guaifer, who had gained the throne by ousting the hated Ademar. Guaifer was to govern that principality with a very firm hand from 861 to 880, and he had already solidified his position in Campania through marriage alliances with both Capua and Amalfi. He apparently had also been quick to assure Louis of his allegiance, even before Louis' tour began, and he was careful to preserve the amenities as long as Louis remained in southern Italy.[21] Nonetheless, Louis undoubtedly thought it wise to see the situation there for himself.

From Salerno, Louis and Engelberga proceeded by ship to Amalfi, and then sailed on around the Amalfitan peninsula and up into the Bay of Naples, where they paused to enjoy the celebrated Roman baths at Pozzuoli (the Roman Puteoli).[22] Either for reasons of tact, given Byzantium's old claims to Naples, or because Naples in this period (despite the presence of a pro-Louis faction) was notorious for friendly relations with the Sicilian Muslims, Louis seems not to have ventured into the city of Naples. But the stay at Pozzuoli, on the outskirts, may have provided a good opportunity to assess the Neapolitan stance at close hand.[23] In any case, after Pozzuoli there were two more minor stops and then in December Louis and Engelberga finally ended their long tour at Benevento, where Radelchis's second son, Adelchis, now ruled.[24] Altogether, the disciplining of Capua and the Campanian tour had taken six months. Louis clearly wanted to be sure that nothing would interfere with his efforts to free Bari.

Roughly six months later, in the spring of 867, Louis, operating from Benevento, began his move. The capitulary of 865 had mobilized the northern forces for a year ("vestimenta . . . ad annum unum").[25] It was now more than a year since those called up had gathered at Lucera; it seems hard to believe that all of them had docilely remained all that time in southern Italy. Yet with what must have been a sizable army, Louis now marched on two of the newer Muslim strongholds: the towns of Matera and Oria, situated between Bari and Taranto. He captured both, and burned Matera.[26] Giosue Musca suggested that this cut the lines of communication between Bari and Taranto, but that surely overstates matters, given the rugged country and the military limitations of the period.[27] Nonetheless, the taking of Matera and Oria must have seemed a good omen. And Louis now also installed a garrison at Canosa, along the Appian Way about two-thirds of the distance from Benevento to Bari and thus in the Lombard-Arab frontier zone.

The following year, 868, a significant new factor entered the south Italian equation. Basil the Macedonian had seized power at Constantinople in September 867. Looking back today, we may wonder that so little attention was paid to this in contemporary south Italian sources, for the advent of the Macedonian dynasty was to have profound consequences for southern Italy. But we have the advantage of hindsight. At the time, it could hardly have been anticipated that this new dynasty would soon mean Byzantine forces and Byzantine governors in southern Italy once again. For nearly a century, Byzantium had seemed no more than a distant glow.

Moreover, farther north this had been true as well. From Charlemagne's day to the 860s, there had been comparatively little communication between Byzantium and either the Carolingian rulers or the papacy. In 842, in connection with an effort to gain Carolingian support for a joint anti-Muslim campaign, a Byzantine princess had apparently been offered as a bride for Louis, but negotiations had broken down and he had married Engelberga instead.[28] Thereafter, so far as we know, Louis had had no contact with Constantinople. And although there had recently been heightened contact on the ecclesiastical front, it had consisted mainly of acerbic battling between a determined Pope Nicholas I and an equally determined Patriarch Photius over ecclesiastical authority, with each convening rival councils and making angry counterclaims. Now, however, in 868, with Basil on the throne, Photius was at least temporarily in eclipse. Moreover, Pope Nicholas had died the preceding year, and the new pope, Hadrian II, seemed very anxious to achieve some degree of accord.[29]

This brings us, then, to Louis and his perception of the Byzantine situation and its potential for help with the south Italian Muslim problem. We have only circumstantial evidence for what took place between Louis and Basil in 868. But we know that Louis found Hadrian II congenial, so presumably he shared Hadrian's hopes for fruitful interaction with this new Byzantine emperor. Louis was at Benevento in March 868, still wrestling with the problem of how to take Bari.[30] It must have seemed obvious that a fleet attacking from the sea, in conjunction with the proposed land attack, could make a major difference to the chances for success. Louis apparently had no ships available, but Byzantium had notable naval resources. Did it occur to Louis that he would be running a terrible risk in seeking Byzantine aid for southern Italy? Apparently not. Probably by then he had become too obsessed with expelling the Muslims to look into the future. At any rate, the events of 869 and the succeeding two years provide convincing evidence that, as the *Chronicon Salernitanum* reported a century later, in the course of 868 Louis was in communication with Basil concerning naval help.[31] And it appears that, as a corollary, there was at least tentative agreement on a marriage alliance involving Louis' daughter and Basil's much loved oldest son, Constantine.[32]

The *Chronicon Salernitanum* says that Louis initiated this contact with Byzantium but in another place declares that Basil made the first overtures; the Byzantine version attributes the initial contact to Basil.[33] It hardly matters; plainly, some form of joint action was seen as mutually advantageous. For Louis, the perceived advantages were short term, related to the Arab situation in southern Italy. For Basil, however, a joint operation could mean help with several long-term aims. One of these, surely, was the revival of a Byzantine role in southern Italy; another, the most pressing need, was reestablishment of Byzantine control of the Adriatic. If Louis disposed of the Muslim enclave at Bari with only modest assistance from Basil, Byzantium would be freed of the need to accomplish that task itself. And with the Muslims driven from Bari, and thus from the Adriatic, Byzantium should find it much easier to protect the Dalmatian coast from raids—and thus also much easier to reassert Byzantine supremacy along that entire Dalmatian coast, incidentally disposing once and for all of Carolingian pretensions to any claim there. This might seem to be reading modern politico-military strategy into ninth-century events, but in fact Basil's grandson Constantine Porphyrogenitus, though not spelling it out in precisely these words, did connect the projected Basil-Louis alliance to the overall situation in the Adriatic.[34] And although Louis never seemed to realize the full implications of the enterprise, he too made at least indirect reference to Adriatic issues in the celebrated letter he sent to Basil three years later, in 871. This lengthy letter, reviewing most of the grievances accumulated over the preceding three years, is a prime source of information concerning the events of this period.[35]

Subsequent developments suggest that Louis expected the combined land-sea attack to take place in the late summer of 869. In June of that year, he was still at Benevento, with Engelberga, and so immersed in final preparations for the attack on Bari that his brother, Lothar II, had to come to Benevento in order to see him. Lothar, who had persuaded two German bishops to grant him a divorce some years earlier, had as a result become embroiled in a bitter battle with the papacy; he now hoped for Louis' assistance in arranging a reconciliation.[36] But even after journeying to Benevento, Lothar found Louis too preoccupied to help; instead, it was Engelberga who accompanied him to Monte Cassino where he was to meet with Pope Hadrian.[37]

As for Louis and his campaign, what actually happened later in 869 is controversial. The *Annales Bertiniani* reported that a Byzantine fleet of four hundred ships duly arrived off Bari, and indeed a Byzantine fleet apparently did come, although other reports indicate fewer ships. The annals go on to say that the fleet's commander (whom we know to have been Nicetas) expected to collect Louis' daughter, the promised bride, and send her back to Constantinople—but that "something happened" so that Louis was unwilling to surrender his daughter—and Nicetas in anger led the fleet away.[38] This abrupt departure suggests that Byzantium had viewed the plan for joint action as interrelated with a more significant agreement which the marriage would validate. Given that Louis had no male heir, could Basil have expected the marriage to transfer to Byzantium any Carolingian claims to southern Italy? If so, he would surely have been disappointed, for Louis' Carolingian relations would never have condoned that. It is nonetheless possible that this was his understanding.

In any case, Louis, too, appears to have had expectations that were not met; the "something" that had happened seems very likely to have been some impugning of Louis' status on Nicetas's part. For in the 871 letter Louis makes no mention of the marriage but does make a generalized, unspecific reference to Nicetas's arrogant and insulting behavior.[39] We can guess what that meant. The major portion of Louis' 871 letter consisted of a defiant assertion of his right to style himself not merely "emperor of the Franks" but Roman emperor; "Ludoguicus divina ordinante providencia imperator augustus Romanorum dilectissimo spiritualique fratri nostro Basilio gloriosissimo et piissimo eque imperatori nove Rome" is the letter's challenging commencement. Possibly, just before Nicetas arrived, or on his arrival, it became clear to Louis that Basil was not about to acknowledge his right to that title.[40]

Two years later, referring (in this same letter) to the episode of the fleet, Louis indignantly rejected one apparent complaint (or Byzantine excuse): that Nicetas and his ships had arrived at Bari to find only the straggler remnants of a fighting force, with its men carousing and in no condition to be effective. Louis insisted, in the letter, that the fleet arrived so late in the year that his army had disbanded for the winter.[41] Possibly the fleet did arrive late; but surely there was more to the affair than that. Something had obviously gone very wrong. As a result, Bari had not been taken.

Shortly thereafter, in the early winter of that same year of 869, Anastasius Bibliothecarius went to Constantinople as Rome's chief delegate to yet another ecumenical council. He was also to explore the possibility of resuscitating the marriage agreement.[42] But the mission was not a success. It is now generally agreed that Anastasius Bibliothecarius was himself the author of at least the weightier part of Louis' letter of 871, the portion that

grandiloquently proclaimed vast Carolingian (and papal) rights and powers. Those claims, which have been analyzed by generations of scholars,
need not be reviewed here. But if anything like the views expressed in the
letter were put forward by Anastasius at Constantinople—and put forward
in his usual contentious manner—it is no wonder that his mission only
exacerbated matters.

Possibly some form of negotiation between Louis and Basil did nonetheless continue in the course of 870 but, if so, nothing came of it. Meanwhile, the Bari Muslims remained a menace; indeed, no sooner had the
Byzantine fleet sailed away than a raiding party ravaged the Gargano
peninsula, including the great Lombard shrine in honor of St. Michael.[43]
Other Arab bands, too, were causing great distress. Therefore, at some
point in 870, Louis organized another attack, striking not at Bari but deeper
into Apulia and into Calabria. The reports indicate that, as in 867, Louis'
forces did score some solid victories, freeing at least a few towns and
defeating any Arabs encountered.[44]

And so, undoubtedly heartened by these new successes, Louis now
attacked Bari itself, with a mixed force of Franks and Lombards and with
the assistance of a "Sclavini" (actually Croatian) fleet, but without Byzantine help. This time, miraculously, the assault was successful. In February
871, Bari fell, and Sawdan was led prisoner to Benevento.[45]

This should have been—and for a brief time appeared to be—the high
point of Louis' long and frustrating reign, the triumphant culmination of
his efforts to stabilize southern Italy. But in a few short months everything
dissolved into comic opera. In the first place, as reported in both south
Italian and Byzantine sources, Sawdan quickly became a tremendous success at Benevento, totally diverting the limelight from Louis. If the sources
can be believed, even though confined he had a constant stream of visitors.
We are told that the Beneventan Lombards were eager to consult him about
"the treatment and care of cattle and other matters" and that even Louis
himself "would summon him to his table and would eat with him."[46]
Moreover, in time—again, if we can believe the sources—Sawdan came to
be consulted about more serious matters than livestock. He became a
lightning rod, attracting Lombard complaints about the Franks and Frankish complaints about the Lombards. Then, as we shall see, he put to use
what he had learned from each side.

Louis and Engelberga had now been in residence at Benevento, off and
on, for nearly five years. It was apparently during the period immediately
after the capture of Bari (between February and August of 871) that Louis

and Anastasius Bibliothecarius composed the lengthy letter to Basil.[47] If so, Anastasius must have come to Benevento, for although the Lombards had urged Louis to come south solely to free them from Arab raids, and Bari had fallen, Louis showed no signs of departing.

Contemporary sources do not give a clear picture of Louis, beyond the usual rhetoric associated with all rulers. Yet it does not seem fair to dismiss him as "a weak and unstable monarch."[48] During most of his adult life, Louis had to cope with rivalries among his contentious Carolingian relatives, yet he seems to have been honorable in his dealings with all of them, including his two brothers (Lothar II and Charles of Provence) and his uncles Louis the German and Charles the Bald. For the most part, he also remained on excellent terms with a succession of popes. And, finally, he took very seriously what he viewed as his obligations to southern Italy, exhibiting endless patience with the difficult situation there. Now, however, Louis' wife, Engelberga, his trusted partner ever since their marriage in 851, contributed to his undoing. Engelberga's capabilities were amply demonstrated both during and after Louis' life, and Louis' absolute devotion to her, and hers to him, are unquestioned. Time and again she served as his envoy, once representing him at an important Carolingian gathering. Popes Hadrian II and John VIII also seem particularly to have valued her. But she was not without faults.

Engelberga's parentage is debated, but her demeanor throughout her life certainly suggests that she was high-born.[49] She was, in fact, all too often, overbearing. The *Annales Bertiniani* tell us that on one occasion, at an important meeting in the north of Italy, she alienated all the "primores Italiae . . . propter suam insolentiam."[50] And in the summer of 871, Engelberga's arrogant behavior at Benevento seems to have ignited a smoldering fuse. According to the *Chronicon Salernitanum*, Engelberga was not only openly contemptuous of the provincialism of the wives of Benevento's Lombard elite but also once publicly observed that their husbands plainly were not even capable of defending themselves.[51]

Adelchis and his fellow Beneventans now proceeded to demonstrate that they were quite capable of taking forceful action. One day in August, Louis, together with Engelberga and their daughter Ermengard, suddenly found themselves surrounded and then put under guard in close confinement. As a shocked Erchempert wrote at Monte Cassino, the Beneventans had imprisoned "that most holy man, the saviour of their province."[52]

Presumably some of Louis' men were killed in the course of this action, for word flew across Europe that Louis himself was dead at the hands of the Beneventans.[53] In fact, however, after a month the bishop of Benevento negotiated the imperial family's release. But a condition was imposed: Louis had to take an oath never again to return to Benevento.[54]

The author of the *Chronicon Salernitanum*, writing in the latter part of the next century, assigned much of the blame for the seizure of Louis to Sawdan; the *Chronicon* states that Adelchis sought Sawdan's counsel before taking the action.[55] Constantine Porphyrogenitus, too, assigned the major blame to Sawdan. The latter purportedly inflamed the Beneventans by warning that Louis planned to send many of them north, in chains; and indeed another (and contemporary) source reported that Louis intended to send at least Adelchis into permanent exile.[56] The evidence thus suggests that Sawdan had access to information from both sides, and that he passed it on in the manner most likely to be helpful to his own cause. It is noteworthy, moreover, that the Beneventans released Sawdan after Louis' death in 875.[57] Inevitably, of course, some have suspected Byzantine involvement as well (although Jules Gay dismissed that Frankish rumor). But at least there does appear to have been widespread Campanian complicity; the contemporary Neapolitan chronicler John the Deacon said that both Sergius II of Naples and Guaifer of Salerno were involved.[58]

In any case, so ended—with a whimper, one might say—the most concerted effort ever made by a Carolingian ruler to assert control over southern Italy. Perhaps, in fact, Byzantium did play a role in this; Basil could hardly have been displeased by the prospect of an ignominious end to Louis' imperial pretensions. Mainly, however, Louis had been thwarted by the southern Lombards themselves. Somewhat surprisingly, he did return south once more, but never again to Benevento. His final mission in the south came about, as we shall see in the next chapter, in reluctant response to a desperate plea from Salerno. And he and Engelberga then spent a considerable time at Capua before he died in 875. But the Benevento fiasco essentially marked the end of any hope that southern Italy could be absorbed within the *imperium* of Italy. The Carolingian rulers who held title to Italy after Louis' death showed no interest in southern Italy. They were far too busy contending for power within the Carolingian mainstream to govern even northern Italy properly, let alone look south. "Post cuius [Louis'] obitum magna tribulatio in Italia advenit," said Andreas of Bergamo, and he was right.[59]

Southern Italy from this point on was essentially left to the Lombards, the resurgent Byzantines—and the Arabs. It is time now to take a much closer look at the latter.

The Arabs

It is necessary to begin by establishing who and what they were, these "Arabs" who commenced appearing in southern Italy in the ninth century. In the first instance, it is a distortion to refer to all Mediterranean Muslims as "Arabs." For the period under study, there is some justification for using "Arab" as a generic term, in that at least the ruling elites of the Islamic world were still largely ethnic Arabs. But the conquered populations under Muslim rule, ethnically very diverse, were by now well along in the process of assimilation, and that certainly was true in the Mediterranean regions. Southern Italy experienced some of the effects of that partial assimilation. Southern Italy also provides a good vantage point for observing the growing fragmentation of Islam, and its effects.

Egypt, a traditional gateway to the East in Roman days, had been one of the earliest Muslim conquests, and began the ninth century still firmly under the control of Abbasid Baghdad. But Egypt moved toward political autonomy in the third quarter of the century after the first of the Tulunid dynasty (869–905) seized power there. Meanwhile, at the western extremity of the Mediterranean, Ommayid Spain was completely detached politically from Baghdad and in religious matters set its own course. And Muslim North Africa, as one might expect from its geographical position, fell somewhere in between. At the start of the ninth century, Hārūn al-Rashīd had appointed one Ibn al-Aghlab as emir or governor of North Africa, and granted him virtual independence; thus began the Aghlabid dynasty, which was to control North Africa (or "Ifrīqya") for more than a hundred years. Although there was no marked ideological separation from Baghdad, in essence these Aghlabids functioned autonomously, amassing wealth through the exploitation of trans-Saharan trade and also, in 827, embarking on the conquest of Sicily.

After 827, with their increasing domination of Sicily, the Aghlabids of North Africa, geographically the Muslims nearest to Italy, obviously became even nearer neighbors. Meanwhile, within North Africa, they rapidly converted the indigenous Berber tribes and soon began incorporating Berbers within their armies. Inevitably, the latter then came to share the ambitions of their overlords, and the results of this would be evident in southern Italy. Al-Balādhurī described the Muslim conqueror of Bari, with some disdain, as a former servant or freed slave from the North African capital of Kairouan; apparently he was a Berber. Some of the "Arabs" hired as mercenaries by the south Italian Lombards in the 840s also seem to have been Berbers, who had been with the Aghlabid forces conquering Sicily but had perhaps found themselves cut off from the major rewards generated by that conquest.[60] Even earlier, too, southern Italy had experienced the indirect effects of mainstream Muslim bias. As noted in the previous chapter, those dissident "Mauri" raiding the Tyrrhenian coast in the early ninth century seemingly were Spanish renegades living precariously in Egypt, where they appear to have been suspect not only because they were Ommayid but because they too were of Berber ancestry.

The fact that many of these Muslim raiders and mercenaries came from the fringes of Islamic society helps explain why Arab sources are largely silent concerning ninth-century "Arab" activities on the Italian mainland. These Italian developments were disregarded because those involved were not deemed worthy of notice. Furthermore, with the exception of the sack of Rome, none of the incursions tracked thus far in this study seem to have been in any sense "official." They were in no way comparable to the Aghlabid operations in Sicily, which were launched and directed from North Africa, with full governmental involvement.

The Arabs in Southern Italy: Perception and Reality

To those at the receiving end of Arab violence, the raiders' status could hardly have mattered. Nonetheless, south Italian chroniclers often attempted to distinguish among the Muslims now appearing in southern Italy, presumably because the differences frequently had practical significance. Thus we are told that Radelchis hired "Agarenos Libicos" and that Sikenolf retaliated by hiring "Hismaelitas Hispanos."[61] ("Agareni," meaning sons of Hagar, although sometimes used in south Italian sources as a generic term for all Muslims and thus an alternative to "Sarraceni," usually designated Muslims from North Africa or Sicily. The addition here of "Libicos" [Libyan] suggests Berbers. "Ishmaelite" was another common generic term for Muslim; as modified in this particular reference, it becomes a synonym for "Mauri," the term ordinarily employed in south Italian sources for Spanish Muslims.) Apparently there was at least coolness between the "Mauri" and the "Agareni" in southern Italy, just as there was sometimes open warfare between their respective home governments. In 813, the ruler of North Africa had had to explain to Pope Leo III that he could not speak for the Spanish Muslims because "non sunt sub dicione regni nostri."[62] South Italians needed no such explanations. They may not

have understood the full implications of ethnic and theological differentia-
tion among the Muslims, but they were beginning to know a good deal
about the Islamic world.

Over and above these distinctions, however, what was the general
attitude in southern Italy toward Muslims? Most nineteenth-century historians assumed that ninth-century south Italians would have instinctively
recoiled from non-Christians. Most twentieth-century historians have at
least assumed some strong sense of "we" and "them." It is certainly true that
ninth-century south Italian monastic chronicles, like contemporary papal
documents, consistently referred to the Muslim invaders as pagan mon-
sters. Nevertheless, among the secular leaders of ninth-century southern
Italy the attitude toward Muslims seems to have been pragmatic. Muslims
were the enemy—as and when they were viewed as the enemy—not because of their beliefs but because of what they did.

This is not to suggest that secular southern Italy in the ninth century
was a paradise of principled religious toleration. But ninth-century southern Italy was accustomed to religious diversity. With Christianity itself by
no means uniform or standardized, there could have been little sense of a
single Christian community. Within the secular world, the bonds linking
one individual to another were formed not by religion but by ethnic or
kindred relationships. Furthermore, over the centuries southern Italy had
been built up of layer upon layer of diverse peoples: first Samnites and
Etruscans and Greeks, then Romans, and later at least some Byzantine
Greeks and, of course, Lombards. As each new ethnic wave arrived, it had
washed over but surely never completely obliterated the population already
there. Only the current dominant group was in a position to leave records—to communicate with us, so to speak. Yet countless "others" and
descendants of "others" must still have been on the scene in the ninth
century, some of them doubtless given to rather exotic practices.[63] Moreover, in addition to Christians of various rites there were communities of
Jews in southern Italy, and undoubtedly also, here and there, various
foreigners of all sorts whose religious customs were divergent. There are
only a few mentions of "foreigners" in the contemporary charters and
chronicles, but chronicles and charters reflected the activities and concerns
of the dominant group. One would expect foreigners to figure in them only
to the extent that their activities interconnected. Nonmention of foreigners
should not be interpreted as proof that there were few in southern Italy.

Altogether, then, the arrival of Muslim "others" may not have seemed
as extraordinary as we might think. Their religion was ill-understood, but

that was surely irrelevant in secular contacts. Certainly the rulers of southern Italy evinced no interest in theology. In any case, Islamic beliefs and
practices would likely have seemed only slightly stranger than some approaches to Christianity encountered by south Italians.[64]

It also bears remembering, in this connection, that south Italians had
never been, indeed could never be, totally isolated from the rest of the
Mediterranean. At least to some degree, they always had extrapeninsular
contacts. For some long time, trade may have been less vigorous than it had
once been, but it certainly never ceased entirely. There is at least some
evidence that, as early as the eighth century, south Italians were already
trading with Muslim areas, particularly for olive oil.[65] And in the 720s, St.
Willibald had found at Naples a ship in from Egypt.[66] Moreover, although
those "Greek" slavers who were cruising the Tyrrhenian coast in the 770s
may not have been south Italians, the *Pactum Sicardi* certainly indicated that
Naples, by the 830s, was selling slaves overseas.[67] Presumably those sales
were to the Arab world; the ease with which Naples hired southern Italy's
first Arab mercenaries (in 835) seems confirmation that Naples was then
actively in touch with the Muslims of North Africa and Sicily. Furthermore,
the familiarity Muslim raiders demonstrated with other south Italian ports
suggests that Naples was not alone. "Arabs" were not known merely as
raiders.

Trading relationships could have explained, and indeed surely did
explain, the unwillingness of a Naples to wage indiscriminate war on any
and all Muslims. But trade need only have meant intermittent contact. Fully
to understand the intensity of feeling expressed in the monastic chronicles
concerning the Arab situation in southern Italy, the sense of being surrounded, we must take note of something else as well. A clue lies in the
Divisio, the document separating Salerno from Benevento in 849. One
clause of the *Divisio* ordained that no "Sarraceni" could thenceforth remain
in either principality—*except* for those already converted to Christianity in
the time of Sico or Sicard and not since relapsed.[68] By 849, then, there were
Arabs (including some ostensibly converted to Christianity) living in an
ordinary way in southern Italy. Indeed, since Sico had died in 832, some
must have come in even before Naples hired Arab mercenaries in 835.

Other indications that this was the case appear in a source so rich it has
never been fully plumbed: the multivolume *Codex Diplomaticus Cavensis*,
containing private charters executed in the ninth, tenth, and eleventh
centuries, mostly within the principality of Salerno.[69] These charters predominantly record land transactions, and many of the earlier ones, in

particular, involve interactions between laymen selling or leasing very small properties. In four, and possibly even six, of the ninth-century charters there is at least a hint that individual Arabs were then living in the Salerno region. First, in 819, a plot of land is described as adjoining *terra sarracini*.[70] Then in 842, and again in 844, "Saracino" is one of the witnesses to two otherwise unremarkable transactions involving small amounts of land. "Saracino" might merely be a nickname, but such informality is not otherwise encountered in Salernitan Lombard charters; and it is notable that he is not identified as "son of so-and-so," as many (in some charters, most) Lombard witnesses are.[71] Later, in 858 and in 868, we encounter two more "fatherless" witnesses with striking names ("Samso" and "Cakco") that may have represented awkward renderings of Arabic.[72] And finally, in 872, some property is described as near the *locum spianu maiure* [sic], surely "the place of the Spanish Moor."[73]

Obviously, this charter evidence is problematic. Cumulatively, however, it is at least interesting; and there is other, similar evidence. For example, Nicola Cilento noted that in the 860s the court doctor at Capua had an Arab name.[74] Altogether, ecclesiastical authorities in ninth-century southern Italy may well have been justified in fearing not only raids but increasing encroachment; they sensed a gradual but very real drift within the Islamic orbit.

It is unlikely that any of the Muslims coming into southern Italy in this period brought with them Islamic high culture. Nonetheless, everything about them was plainly of consuming interest to the south Italians. Not only did the tenth-century *Chronicon Salernitanum*, looking back, tell tale after tale about the Arab invaders. Ninth-century sources also document this fascination. Sawdan was a legend in his own time, and to a lesser degree so too were several leaders of smaller raiding bands. The local chroniclers particularly stressed the devilish ingenuity of these Muslims, their shrewdness and boldness, qualities always much admired by the south Italian Lombards. Even the distant author of the *Annales Bertiniani*, not normally given to anecdotes, repeated one story. Supposedly, some raiders on the Adriatic side of the peninsula had abducted a bishop and were holding him for ransom when he suddenly died; unfazed, they delivered him back propped up in full regalia, and collected the ransom before the ransomers discovered they had redeemed a dead body.[75] In the south Italian chronicles, there were also occasional reports of grand gestures on the part of these "nefandissimi." Once, we are told, when the monastery of San Vincenzo had been devastated by an earthquake, the leader of a Muslim band called off a raid, saying in effect that God had already sufficiently punished the monks.[76] The truth of these tales hardly matters; many of the same stories had doubtless been told before, about other invaders. What is notable, however, is the degree to which the southern Lombard chroniclers seem sometimes almost mesmerized by these Arabs.

Of course there was also, always, the harsh reality of the appalling devastation wreaked by the Muslim invaders. It was not merely the damage done to monasteries like Monte Cassino and San Vincenzo (although the monastic chronicles naturally emphasized that). The most ominous word in the sources is "depopularunt." Aside from the two major monasteries, the south Italian countryside could hardly have yielded much in the way of riches; one might therefore wonder at the continuous Muslim sweeps through rural areas, and we can only conclude that the loot was primarily human. We have the evidence of Bernard the Monk, who had seen at Taranto eleven ships packed with "twelve thousand Beneventan Christians" and other assorted captives, all apparently destined for Tripoli and other Muslim ports. Later, he and his companions sailed on one such slave ship, which was carrying its cargo to Alexandria.[77] Although the numbers may have been exaggerated in Bernard's tale, countless hapless individuals must indeed have been seized. We read that in the 840s Muslim raiders "omnes civitates Apulie depopularunt" and that some of the inhabitants of a captured town were put to the sword but the rest were sold into captivity.[78] In the early 850s, Erchempert reported, the raiders began steadily to "depopulate" the principalities of Salerno and Benevento.[79] And despite Louis' recapture of Bari, the situation was to become even worse in the 870s, as we shall see in the next chapter. The source of the Arab threat changed then, and became more official. But the raiders' aims would remain the same: the taking of any accessible treasure but also, continuously, the collection of innumerable potential slaves. Erchempert, again, reported that in the 870s, first the territories of Naples and Benevento and Capua, and then the whole of Calabria, were scoured.[80] One might note here the contrast with Viking raids; for the Vikings, treasure seemed always the prime objective. But the Vikings were raiding "up," into a richer and more splendid society than their own, one with much to offer. The Mediterranean Muslims were clearly raiding "down" in ninth-century southern Italy.

Typically, it appears, the ninth-century raiders established their inland bases along rivers, which obviously facilitated the transportation of human booty; many regions along river courses must have been stripped bare of all but the elderly. Undoubtedly many of the captives were from the indigenous servile population. Yet at least some were from minor Lombard families who owned and worked small parcels of land. We find this documented in the Salernitan land charters.[81]

Even the south Italian landscape suffered. In 841, the ancient city of Capua was sacked and burned during a raid by Benevento's Muslim mercenaries; fifteen years later the Capuans, "tired of living like goats in caves," built themselves a new city two or three kilometers away (the Capua we know today).[82] Thereafter, however, stray Muslim bands took to using the vast Roman amphitheater of "old" Capua as a base. Later, similarly, the deserted Greek temples at Paestum were used.[83] This ominous predilection for stoutly built classical structures led the Neapolitans eventually to raze the castle of Lucullus on the Bay of Naples (where once the last Roman emperor in the West had ended his days) in order to forestall Arab use of that stronghold.[84] We can surmise that similar actions were taken in other parts of southern Italy, thus speeding along what we might call the de-Romanization of the landscape. And at the same time defensive fortification increased. Nicola Cilento dated to the latter ninth century and the start of the tenth an accelerating tendency in southern Italy to ring towns with ever stouter walls and also to start building the fortified "Saracen towers" still evident here and there today.[85] The phenomenon we now call *incastellamento* obviously had complex roots, and will be further discussed in later chapters. It is well to note here, however, that in southern Italy its beginnings seem unquestionably Arab-related.

European contemporaries, hearing frightening tales of the Arabs in southern Italy, would hardly have been surprised to hear of fortification. Moreover, the efforts of Louis II to free southern Italy from the Arabs surely appeared rational and commendable: the Christian West saved from villainous attackers. Given the appalling devastation and suffering inflicted by the Muslims, the situation would have seemed unambiguous to outsiders.

Yet the closer one gets to the actual scene, the more muddled and perplexing the picture becomes. Time and again we find the south Italian rulers, even as they fortified their major towns, unwilling to wage all-out warfare against the invaders. As we shall see in the next chapter, this south Italian ambivalence was not only to affect the papacy but also contributed to the resurgence of Byzantine power in southern Italy. Nonetheless, as we shall also see in due course, there were sound reasons for this ambivalence. Despite Arab depredations, Campania, at least, had much to gain from an Arab connection.

4. Firming the Elements

NO DECADE BETTER DEMONSTRATED ambivalence toward the Arabs than the 870s. Events illustrating this began with a seemingly minor incident in Salerno, probably in the spring of 871—just after Louis had taken Bari.

According to the *Chronicon Salernitanum*, Prince Guaifer was striding through the city of Salerno, heading back to his palace from the local baths, when as he passed through the forum an Arab hailed him, saying he much admired Guaifer's handsome head covering. Guaifer, apparently in one of his rare good moods, tossed the cap or bonnet to the Arab. The tale is intriguing because it suggests that Arab visitors were commonplace. In addition, however, the incident was to prove significant. For not long afterward (the *Chronicon* reports) the Arab, back home in North Africa, encountered an Amalfitan merchant and gave him an urgent message for Guaifer. In return for Guaifer's generosity, the Arab wanted him warned that preparations were under way for a massive Aghlabid attack on Guaifer's capital.[1]

Whether or not this colorful tale was true, Salerno does seem to have had advance warning of an impending attack, and all of Campania knew this to mean a crisis for the region. There were frantic efforts to prepare for what was coming. The defenses of the city of Salerno were strengthened and military reinforcements poured in from the other Lombard principalities and even farther afield. In addition, emissaries set off north, one by one, to find Louis and beg his help. The emissaries apparently included Guaifer's son and heir, Guaimar, two of Campania's leading ecclesiastics (Bishops Landolf of Capua and Athanasius II of Naples), and even papal representatives.[2] Everyone doubtless realized it would not be easy to lure Louis south again after the treatment accorded him by the Beneventans only a month or two earlier.

Understandably, Louis at first resisted all entreaties. (He even imprisoned briefly the young Guaimar.) Meanwhile, the Aghlabid forces— thirty thousand "Saraceni," according to Erchempert—landed in Calabria and made their way north, capturing "many towns" along the way. When they finally reached the city of Salerno, its defenses proved strong enough

to keep them out, but it was impossible to protect the surrounding countryside. While the main force held the city under close siege, others of the
Aghlabid invaders settled like locusts throughout the area, keeping food
supplies from reaching the city and capturing or killing virtually everyone
they encountered.[3]

The siege seems to have begun in the late fall of 871.[4] Time and again,
hunger nearly drove the inhabitants to surrender; at the very worst point,
after many months, the Salernitans survived only because Amalfi managed
to smuggle some supplies into the city. (We are told that Amalfi took this
action only after much debate, for Amalfi "pacem cum Agarenis a primitus
habebat.")[5] Of course, even with this Amalfitan aid, the Salernitans could
not have held out indefinitely; in the end, after over a year of siege, it was
Louis who saved them. Presumably worn down by the desperate pleas, he
dispatched a Frankish force supplemented by various Lombard contin-
gents. Word of this approaching army caused the invaders to abandon the
siege and depart.[6]

The siege of Salerno represented the first try on the part of the Aghlabid rulers of North Africa to take a major Campanian city. It would also
prove to be the last, but no one could know that. Overall, the situation must
have appeared grim, especially since this massive attack on Salerno occurred
just as the Aghlabids were tightening their grip on Sicily; only six years
later, Syracuse, the last great prize, would fall to them. True, at the time of
the Salerno attack Louis had just taken Bari. But Bari was merely an
adventitious outpost, not linked to any major Muslim offensive. And its
recapture had only limited significance as long as Taranto and other key
Apulian ports and towns remained in Arab hands. The fall of Syracuse in
878 was to be far more momentous. Syracuse was the administrative capital
of Byzantine Sicily and unquestionably its most important city. Its loss,
capping decades of Muslim advance across Sicily, meant that the Muslim
world now really did extend to peninsular Italy's doorstep.[7] One can
imagine how doubly ominous the fall of Syracuse would have seemed, had
Salerno also fallen, six years earlier.

For that matter, saving the city of Salerno may have seemed to contemporaries only a qualified victory. The main Aghlabid force sailed back
home, but for decades afterward either remnants of that force or newly
arrived Aghlabid bands were much in evidence throughout Campania and
neighboring parts of southern Italy. And over the next thirty or forty years
virtually all major developments in Campania would be related in one way
or another to this Arab presence.

Meanwhile, for southern Italy as a whole, the first major development was the reappearance of Byzantium on the scene. In 873, just after Salerno had been rescued by Louis' army, a Byzantine naval force attacked some Arabs then holding Otranto, in the heel, and reclaimed that port for Byzantium. Two years later, in 875, Louis died, leaving a Carolingian vacuum in southern Italy. Constantinople hastened to take advantage of this. In 876, a Byzantine force drove from Bari the Lombard gastald installed there in 871 after Louis' victory. Together with Otranto, this now gave Byzantium two key bases on the Apulian coast. For the time being, however, Taranto (crucial for any Byzantine drive westward) continued in Arab hands, and its Arabs remained a menace both in the interior and at sea.[8]

Byzantine officials now attempted to enlist the support of Benevento, Salerno, and Capua in fighting Muslims in southern Italy. After all, their region, too, was affected. Yet all three Lombard leaders refused, despite Salerno's recent travails. In fact, Naples, Gaeta, and Amalfi (together with Salerno) were all described by Erchempert as now formally "at peace with the Saracens."[9] Plainly, Byzantium would have to mount on its own any military attempts to clear southern Italy of Arabs.

Pope John VIII: A Dream Denied

Yet in this period Constantinople did for a time have one indomitable ally: Pope John VIII (872–82), who devoted much of his papacy to attempts to halt the slide of southern Italy into the Islamic orbit. John VIII was the last in that series of strong popes who had dominated Rome for more than a century. (His murder in 882 plunged the papacy into "the darkest decades of its history.")[10] When John became pope, he surely knew the grievous problems he faced. In his youth, he must have witnessed the Aghlabid sack of Rome; when he took office, the emirate of Bari had just been extinguished, but Salerno was under siege. Now, Arab raiders sweeping up from southern Italy were destroying the economy of the papal patrimony. Rural areas in the vicinity of Rome were becoming a desert, the inhabitants dead, captured, or too frightened to work their fields. At one point, Pope John even lacked fodder for his own horses and had to cancel a journey.[11]

No one could have labored more valiantly or creatively than John in trying to deal with this state of affairs. For one thing, he seems to have been the first clearly to recognize the chief factor motivating at least some elements within Campania. Almost immediately upon becoming pope, he wrote to Amalfi, offering both monetary reward and trading concessions at

Rome in return for Amalfitan naval help against the Arabs.[12] No record
exists of the response, but judging from Amalfi's later behavior, the Amalfitans doubtless accepted both the money and the special concessions at
Rome but provided only token naval assistance. Three years later, in 875, we
hear that "Saracen ships" (or Saracens coming by sea) were causing Rome
great distress.[13] And so in 876 Pope John toured Campania in person in an
effort to organize an anti-Muslim coalition. Salerno and Capua seem to
have agreed almost immediately, presumably not wishing an open breach
with this forceful new pope, and in June of the next year, 877, delegations
from Salerno, Capua, Naples, Gaeta, and Amalfi all journeyed to Traietto
for a group meeting with John. The meeting seemed a success, and later
that year a formal pact was apparently signed.[14]

One of the steps agreed on was papal payment of 10,000 silver *mancusi*
to Pulcarius of Amalfi; in return, Amalfitan ships were to patrol the Tyrrhenian coast from the Traietto area up to Civitavecchia.[15] Although costly,
that seemed promising, and the next year Pope John was also pleased by a
change in ruler at Naples; Bishop Athanasius II ousted a pro-Arab duke
and assumed total control of the duchy himself. Pope John quickly wrote to
congratulate both Athanasius and the people of Naples—and the letter
indicates that he had committed 1,400 *mancusi* to aid the coup.[16] In the
following year, 878, John chose to sail from Naples, on a trip to France in
search of Carolingian military and financial support for his anti-Arab campaign.

Unfortunately for this mission, however, on Louis' death in 875 John
had backed Charles the Bald's claim to the imperial title, and then only two
years later (the year before John's trip to France) the newly crowned
Charles the Bald had died. The pope therefore arrived in France with no
dependable ally among the contentious Carolingians, and in the event no
one proved willing to provide him with any help.[17] He had to return to
Italy fundless and with no promise of future aid. In order to secure Rome's
safety during his absence John had sent a bribe of 25,000 silver *mancusi* to
the Arab bands threatening papal territory. Now he could not even count
on a replenishing of the papal treasury.

Moreover, John's letters show that even before the trip to France he
had reason to be concerned about Campanian developments in relation to
the Traietto pact. In the winter of 877–78, he had written to Salerno and
also to the bishop of Capua, complaining that the Amalfitans were refusing
to patrol the Tyrrhenian coast on the pretext that they had been promised
12,000 *mancusi*, not 10,000.[18] After his return from France, he obviously
encountered new evidence that Campania was reverting to its old ways. In

September 879, we find John asking Pulcarius of Amalfi to return the 10,000 *mancusi* if he was not going to fulfill his part of the bargain.[19] But Amalfi's ruler was obviously not the sole problem. Later that month, in letters not only to Pulcarius but also to Bishop Peter of Amalfi, and to Athanasius II, bishop-duke of Naples, and to both bishop and ruler at Gaeta, Pope John declared that unless they all broke their "pactum cum Saracenis" by December 1, he would anathematize all of them.[20] Athanasius had not proved to be a loyal anti-Muslim after all, and at Amalfi and Gaeta, too, the bishops were seemingly as uncooperative as the secular rulers. The warning letters plainly had no effect. In October 880, Pope John dispatched to the "universo populo Amalfitano" an all-embracing sentence of excommunication, and a few months later the entire duchy of Naples was also excommunicated.[21]

John later made one final try with Amalfi. Not long after the sentence of excommunication, he wrote offering to lift the sentence and also to pay Amalfi 10,000 *mancusi* annually (with an additional 1,000 *mancusi* at the start "pro benedictione") if only Amalfi would give up the "society" of the Saracens and its evil alliances with them. But if Amalfi persisted in its wickedness, he would see to it that its merchants would "everywhere" be prohibited from doing business.[22] This last might have seemed a telling threat, but the Amalfitans undoubtedly knew it was unenforceable. In any event, like all previous efforts with Amalfi, this one too was a failure. John also made one last try with Naples, with equal lack of success. In 882, shortly before he was murdered, he wrote to Athanasius offering to expunge the sentence of excommunication if only Naples would repent, break with the Saracens, and send the Saracen "maiores" as prisoners to Rome.[23] Again there was no response.

It is notable that by 882 John had only exhortation to offer. The papal treasury was presumably drained and with nothing to show for it. That, combined with the obvious lack of Carolingian support for John, must have badly weakened him in the eyes of all Italy, and undoubtedly contributed to increasing factional strife at Rome, and ultimately to his murder.

And there was one further factor. In his desperate attempt to cleanse southern Italy of its Arabs, John VIII had made gestures toward Byzantium that surely outraged many powerful individuals in Rome and would have appalled his immediate predecessors. Presumably there was no objection when he asked Constantinople for naval help; there must have been general rejoicing when, in 879, a Byzantine fleet had arrived to patrol the Tyrrhenian coast. Papal territory would now at least be protected from attack by sea.[24] Moreover, at that point John was careful not to carry this new relationship too far; when the Byzantine *strategos* at Bari journeyed to Nola for a formal meeting with John (and persuaded the rulers of Benevento, Salerno, and Capua to join him), the pope failed to appear.[25] But a year later, in 880, having had to excommunicate the entire population of Naples and Amalfi, John apparently concluded that Byzantium represented his only hope of seeing the Arabs driven from Italy. He therefore took a further, extraordinary step. He participated in the total rehabilitation of Photius, now once again patriarch. Hadrian II's 869 sentence of anathema was revoked, along with several other papal decrees objectionable to Byzantium; claims to papal authority in Bulgaria ceased to be pressed; and John seems not even to have reacted publicly to assertions that the Byzantine patriarch was equal in standing to the Roman pontiff.[26]

Altogether, it does not seem excessive to suggest that the intransigence of the south Italian states led inexorably to the downfall of John VIII and thus to "the darkest days of the papacy." Obviously, there were other causes as well. The ecclesiastical and political strife in that period, from Rome north, was horrendous, and John's actions on many fronts had won him enemies. Nonetheless, reading his increasingly obsessed and anguished letters to and about southern Italy, one senses that he came in the end to stake everything on a decisive resolution of the Arab problem. When he appeared to have lost even that gamble, he was doomed.

As a grim coda to these failed efforts, ecclesiastical southern Italy suffered its worst blow at the hands of Muslim raiders around the very time John was assassinated. Although there were now Byzantine forces in southern Italy, they were by no means numerous enough to police the entire region. The great monasteries of Monte Cassino and San Vincenzo al Volturno were totally unprotected. In 881, the year before the pope's murder, San Vincenzo was essentially destroyed in a particularly fierce raid, with almost all of its monks killed.[27] Two years later, in the fall of 883, it was Monte Cassino's turn; the abbot was struck down before the high altar, and most of the buildings were burned to the ground. The surviving monks fled to Teano, within Capuan territory.[28] The Monte Cassino community was to remain there until 914. They then moved on to the new city of Capua, for another twenty years, and did not return to their hallowed mountaintop until 934.

Campania and Its Arabs

The Arab bands that destroyed San Vincenzo al Volturno and Monte Cassino had come from Aghlabid Sicily, and were recent arrivals on the scene. Very likely, in fact, it was the appearance of these Arabs in Campania that had led to Pope John's first threat of anathema for Naples and Amalfi in the fall of 879. For we do know that by 880 one Aghlabid band had already settled at the foot of Mount Vesuvius and that it had been permitted to do so by Naples' bishop-duke, Athanasius II.[29] Soon another band was ensconced at Cetara on the Gulf of Salerno, midway between the city of Salerno and Amalfi.[30] These Aghlabids not only attacked San Vincenzo al Volturno and Monte Cassino. From an advance base at Sepino (in a rugged area north of Benevento), they also ravaged the principality of Benevento as well as papal territory in the area around Rome. Some even went all the way north to Spoleto.[31]

References in contemporary chronicles and in the letters of Pope John VIII suggest that there were now quasi-formal pacts between the Aghlabids and Naples, Amalfi, and Salerno. No doubt the latter—seeing Sicily absorbed within the Islamic sphere, noting little evidence that the Carolingians now would or could provide a counterforce, and uneasy about Byzantium's return to southern Italy—felt it expedient to strengthen their relationship with these Muslims. Their motives were doubtless in part defensive but also, surely, economic. The more wide-ranging benefits of trade with the Arab world would not be fully apparent until the tenth century, but fruitful intercourse had already begun. Furthermore, it is possible that there were economic advantages to be gained by harboring Aghlabid bands; just possibly, Naples and Salerno (and perhaps Amalfi too) received some share of the spoils from raids.

Not surprisingly, however, both Salerno and Naples soon discovered that these raiders could not be controlled. The Cetara Arabs proved devastating to Salerno, as Salernitan charters from the year 882 reveal. A woman wishing to sell property could not produce either of her sons (to validate her action in accordance with Lombard law) because one son had been captured by these "Saraceni" and the other lived at Nocera, along the road to Naples, and could not get past the "generationes barbares saracenorum" to reach Salerno.[32] Another woman stated that she was forced to sell her property because "a Saracenis sumus circumdati et a periculis famis nos perire cogitamus."[33] The only people who seem to have benefited from the situation were two presbyters at Nocera, who in this same year of 882 busily bought up land at distress-sale prices and leased land at exceptionally advantageous rates.[34]

Naples too, after allowing an Aghlabid band to settle at the foot of Mount Vesuvius, soon had cause to regret it. Therefore, in 883 or 884, Naples and Salerno joined forces and drove all of the raiders out of their immediate region. Apparently, most of those expelled initially moved further south, to Agropoli, below Paestum (at the southern edge of the Gulf of Salerno). Soon, however, some came north again, this time to join in establishing that major encampment along the Garigliano River near Gaeta which was to prove so worrisome in the early tenth century.[35]

It appears that these raiders moved to the Gaeta area at the explicit invitation of Gaeta's rulers, who were feeling threatened by Lombard Capua. In other words, only extreme provocation had led Naples and Amalfi to take action against the Aghlabid bands, and their action certainly did not signify any general aversion to the presence of Arabs in Campania. Moreover, the raiders themselves had not taken offense; they continued to be more than willing to serve as mercenaries or surrogates in the local power struggles, which once again were keeping Campania in bloody ferment. It was the 840s all over again, but worse, for the lines now were less clearly drawn; the Campanian rulers were changing alliances and enemies almost daily, and their Muslim recruits proved happy to do the same. The author of the *Chronicon Salernitanum*, looking back from the latter tenth century, described it thus: "When they [the Garigliano Arabs] were at peace with the Salernitans, they grievously afflicted the Neapolitans and the Capuans, and when they made peace with the Neapolitans, they attacked the cities of Salerno or Benevento . . . they would invade the smaller towns [*castella*] and then openly sell their Christian inhabitants."[36]

There were several underlying reasons for local turmoil in Campania in the 880s and 890s. First, from 878 on there were recurrent power struggles over the Beneventan throne, with none of the temporary victors proving very effective rulers. Second, at Capua, which had broken away from Salerno at midcentury, there was a bitter contest for control in the 880s, mainly between two rival brothers, each of whom had supporters among the other Campanian leaders. Third, Naples under the expansionist Athanasius II became very aggressive, continuously attacking its neighbors. All of this turmoil proved a boon to the opportunistic Arabs.

Byzantium *Redux*

No doubt Constantinople was well informed about the situation in Campania as well as the situation elsewhere in the Italian peninsula. Shortly after Monte Cassino's destruction in late 883, Basil the Macedonian dispatched Nicephorus Phocas to southern Italy with the largest Byzantine army seen there in centuries. For the next two years, that brilliant general moved through the region, staying clear of Campania and the Lombard core areas but otherwise restoring order and defeating any Arab bands he encountered. Four years earlier, a smaller Byzantine strike force had finally reclaimed Taranto from the Arabs. By the time Nicephorus Phocas was recalled to Constantinople in 886, he had further solidified Byzantine control throughout most of Apulia, had retaken for Byzantium virtually all of Calabria, and had even settled Byzantine garrisons (and sometimes Greek bishops as well) in major towns in the deep south such as Cosenza, which in the *Divisio* document of 849 had specifically been listed as part of the principality of Salerno.

Preoccupied with their local battling, Salerno and Benevento at first seemed not to react to these moves. And, as Gay noted, Nicephorus Phocas took pains not to alienate the local populations in the areas reclaimed; the army was forbidden to loot or take slaves.[37] So, quietly and methodically, Byzantium carved away from the southern Lombards more than half of the vast land area they had once claimed. The whole of the lowest portion of the peninsula and almost all of the Adriatic coastal area now came under Byzantine domination. For decades, Arab occupation of the key towns and continous Arab raiding had presumably made these regions nonproductive for Benevento and Salerno. Nonetheless, for the Lombards to lose even nominal possession of so much territory was a significant development.

Almost all of the Campanian rulers thus moved quickly now to arrive at some accommodation with Byzantium. In early 887, Guaimar of Salerno (who had succeeded his father and was at the moment the most secure and powerful of the Lombard rulers) journeyed to Constantinople. A year or two earlier, either Salerno or (more likely) Benevento had already begun to issue *denarii* inscribed "Basil-Leo-Alexander." And Naples' *denarii* started bearing the legend "Basil Imperator," the first sign of deference to Byzantium on Neapolitan coinage in a century.[38] Now Guaimar returned from Constantinople a *patricius*.[39]

Commenting on Guaimar's trip to Constantinople, Jules Gay observed that Guaimar now became "le plus fidèle vassal de l'empire byzantin."[40] But "vassal" was an inappropriate term. True, throughout the balance of Guaimar's rule, all Salernitan charters identified him as *imperialis patricius*.[41] However, as Vasiliev noted, "Naples, Beneventum [and] the principality of Salerno . . . frequently changed their attitude toward the Byzantine Empire in correspondence with the course of the Byzantine campaign against the Arabs."[42] In practice, in other words, Campanian deference to Byzantium waxed and waned in direct relation to current perceptions of Byzantium's strength, as demonstrated through victories over the Arabs. In the late ninth century, after the victories of Nicephorus Phocas, some sort of connection seemed, at the least, politic. Furthermore, a Byzantine title constituted a splendid embellishment. Yet nothing in Guaimar's subsequent behavior suggests that he attached any deeper significance to his title.[43] And in fact, as it turned out, Byzantium over the next century was never consistently strong enough militarily in southern Italy to secure genuine and permanent submission.

Meanwhile, in the late 880s, a Byzantine connection was also valuable because of what Byzantium could do for its friends. When Guaimar went to Constantinople in 887, Salerno badly needed help against Naples; the latter, together with some locally recruited Arabs, was harassing Salernitan territory. As the chronicler Erchempert put it, "[Salerno] nimium affligeretur ab Athanasio episcopo cum Saracenis." The Byzantine response was gratifying. Salerno received money, a shipment of wheat, and a detachment of Byzantine soldiers.[44]

Athanasius II, observing this, obviously decided it was time to remind Constantinople of Naples' ancient links to the Byzantine Empire and to ask for his own Byzantine troops. In due course a small Byzantine force arrived—which, according to Erchempert, Naples then used not to fight Arabs (the stated aim) but instead to harry Capua.[45] Altogether, the Byzantine soldiers must have found service in Campania rather puzzling. At one point, the Neapolitans deployed their Byzantine unit side by side with Saracen mercenaries to attack a mixed force of Capuans, Beneventans, and other Saracen mercenaries.[46]

In retrospect, it is clear that the late 880s and the decade of the 890s constituted a period of adjustment, not unlike the period a hundred years earlier when southern Italy had had to adjust to Charlemagne's absorption of northern Italy. Then the external factors had been, on the one hand, the disappearance of Byzantium from southern Italy, and, on the other, a resurgent and forceful papacy vigorously supported by the Carolingians. Now the situation was different but equally challenging. The intermittent Carolingian interference of the past century was over, leaving little trace beyond a sharpening of intra-Lombard rivalries. The papacy, for the first time in a hundred years, had ceased to be a significant force. But Islam, now approaching the peak of its power in the Mediterranean, had (with its conquest of Sicily) moved closer. And within southern Italy, Byzantium was back.

It is not necessary to track all the details of the settling-in process at the end of the ninth century. Yet a brief survey is desirable, if only to illustrate the disorderly situation from which the very different world of the tenth century emerged. René Poupardin, a contemporary of Jules Gay, once observed that "de 774 à l'an 1000, la plupart des [southern Lombard] princes sonts morts de mort violente ou ont été expulsés pour être remplacés par des usurpateurs."[47] Even in relation to the ninth century, this was a gross exaggeration. And it was patently untrue of three-quarters of the tenth century, when the Lombard principalities (and indeed all of Campania) enjoyed exceptional stability. Nonetheless, violence and ugly infighting unquestionably characterized the last years of the ninth century.

Byzantium made its own contribution to the turmoil of that period. In 887, the same year in which Guaimar of Salerno went to Constantinople, a new Byzantine *strategos* suddenly came from Bari into Campania with a small strike force. Ostensibly, he had come to attack the Garigliano Arabs, but disregarding the example set by Nicephorus Phocas, he also attempted to take several minor Lombard towns within the Beneventan heartland. Not surprisingly, this infuriated the Beneventans, and their ruler, Aio, responded by marching on Bari and seizing it. But this expedition left the core areas of Benevento temporarily unprotected, so Athanasius II of Naples invaded, whereupon Aio rushed back from Bari and ravaged the Terra di Lavoro, Naples' fertile inland plain.[48]

Aio may have felt encouraged to attack Bari because word had come that Basil the Macedonian was dead; perhaps his heir would not prove equally forceful or equally interested in southern Italy. However, the new emperor, Leo VI (Leo the Wise), had no intention of losing the territory his father had just reclaimed. Within a year, the Byzantines had retaken Bari from the Beneventans, and when the Sicilian Aghlabids began to threaten Calabria again, they were fought off, both on land and in a series of naval battles.[49]

After these Calabrian confrontations in 888–89, factionalism among the Sicilian Muslims prevented any further attacks for more than a decade. Leo's representatives in southern Italy could concentrate on consolidating their hold, and in fact they even expanded Byzantine territory temporarily at the expense of the southern Lombards. In 891, when Aio of Benevento died and was succeeded by a weak heir, the Byzantine *strategos* swept up from Bari again and took the city of Benevento itself, ousting Aio's successor. He then proceeded to make Benevento his new administrative capital for Byzantine southern Italy, in place of Bari.[50] A year or so later, a new *strategos*, still operating from Benevento, apparently even tried to take Salerno, doubtless sensing that Guaimar's loyalty to Constantinople was not dependable.[51] That attempt failed, but otherwise Byzantine power in southern Italy seemed to be increasing rapidly.

In 892, Leo VI set a seal, so to speak, on the military accomplishments of the preceding decade by establishing formal mechanisms for the governance of Byzantine southern Italy. All of the reclaimed and freshly conquered territory was incorporated into a new theme, pointedly named Longobardia.[52]

The New Political Configuration

At the time Leo established this south Italian theme, the Byzantines still held Benevento and doubtless hoped that even more Lombard territory would soon be theirs. Three years later, however, in 895, they were driven from Benevento. Bari reverted to being the operational capital for the theme of Longobardia. The political configuration of southern Italy was about to be set in a form that would last almost to the end of the tenth century.

Byzantium would thenceforth control more or less all of southern Italy below a hypothetical line across the peninsula from the Gulf of Manfredonia on the Apulian coast to the Gulf of Policastro on the Tyrrhenian side. The rest of southern Italy, despite Byzantium's wishful thinking, would remain essentially autonomous.. (In the mountainous interior that formed the Byzantine-Lombard border zone, sovereignty was ill-defined and would be frequently contested.)

Before the situation stabilized, however, there was one last round of violence and disorder. It tells us a good deal about the character of the late ninth century.

The individual who drove the Byzantines from Benevento in 895 was yet another Guy of Spoleto, grandson of that Guy of Spoleto who had played so prominent a role in south Italian affairs in the late 840s, and son of the Guy of Spoleto who was briefly the western emperor (891–94).[53] Although Charlemagne, after 787, had awarded the Lombard duchy of Spoleto to a Frank, the new Frankish dukes of Spoleto had soon begun to intermarry with the ruling families of Lombard southern Italy—an astute move, given the traditional importance of Spoleto to the Lombards. Thus the Guy of Spoleto who "liberated" Benevento was, like his grandfather, a brother-in-law of Salerno's ruler; Idta, wife of Guaimar I of Salerno, was Guy's sister.

Even more to the point, Guy's mother, the dowager empress Ageltruda, was a Beneventan, sister to Aio, the late ruler. Guy could therefore claim familial justification for involving himself in Beneventan affairs.

For two years after his expulsion of the Byzantines, Guy himself ruled the Beneventan principality. Then in 897 he was called back north, so he offered Benevento to his brother-in-law Guaimar. Unfortunately, however, most Beneventans were appalled by the prospect of subordination to a Salernitan, particularly one like Guaimar who was known to be violent and ruthless. On his way to Benevento, Guaimar was therefore waylaid, and blinded. Guy rushed back south but could only accompany the wounded Guaimar home to Salerno. Guy's mother, Ageltruda, then urged that Benevento be awarded to her youngest brother, another Radelchis; and the latter did rule from 897 through 899. But he was hopelessly inept, dismissed in the chronicles as "Radelchis the Foolish."[54] And so, in January 900, Atenolf of Capua seized the Beneventan throne. Atenolf was related to one of Benevento's leading families and for years had been assiduously cultivating Beneventan dissidents.[55] He was immediately acclaimed, we are told, in a great ceremony at Benevento's Sancta Sophia attended by all the "populus necnon et proceres."[56]

Atenolf's coup might have seemed merely one more round in the endless intra-Lombard struggles, but it proved to be a decisive development. It spelled the end of the old Beneventan dynasty. From then on, for most of the tenth century, Capua and Benevento were ruled by Atenolf and his heirs as more or less a single entity.

Meanwhile, at Salerno in that same year of 900, the fierce (and now maimed) Guaimar I was succeeded by his more moderate son, Guaimar II. The latter would then govern Salerno for a remarkable forty-six years, and his son (Gisolf I) for another thirty. Thus throughout the first three-quarters of the tenth century all of the Lombard regions were to have notably stable governance. And Salerno, with ever stronger links to Amalfi, would enjoy a surge of prosperity. Consideration of this development must be left for later chapters. Here, however, we need one last look at southern Italy as the ninth century ended, with particular attention to the autonomous regions.

The Autonomous States

The extent of Byzantine dominance at the end of the ninth century (and on through the tenth) has already been noted; Byzantium held most of modern Apulia, Basilicata, and Calabria. Calabria, now Byzantium's western frontier, could perhaps be a staging ground for retaking Sicily. Basilicata, in the rugged center of the peninsula, linked Calabria to Apulia. And that most of Apulia was now in Byzantine hands was even more significant; for one thing, it gave Byzantium excellent ports on Italy's Adriatic coast and on the Gulf of Taranto. Moreover, much of Apulia's hinterland was (at least theoretically) extremely productive, so there was once again hope for a solid income from southern Italy. Throughout Byzantine southern Italy, in fact, while the population would remain mostly non-Greek, taxes could presumably be gathered.

Conversely, of course, for the Lombard rulers the territory from which they could expect revenue was now much reduced. Nonetheless, in the tenth century the Lombard princes of Salerno and Capua-Benevento were clearly prospering. The Salernitans, it appears, were compensating for their loss of territory through intense cultivation of their remaining lands. (We explore this in Chapter 6.) For tenth-century Capua and Benevento, we have little direct documentation. But records survive from the monastery of San Vincenzo al Volturno, just to the northeast of Benevento, and these also show increased cultivation. It therefore seems safe to assume an agricultural surge in Benevento and Capua as well.

This tenth-century agricultural development was surely not owing to deliberate policy on the part of the Lombard rulers (although they deserved credit for creating a climate of stability). A southern Lombard ruler's role, in both the ninth and tenth centuries, remained for the most part what it had been in Arichis's day: supreme arbiter in judicial disputes (and powerful locally in matters pertaining to the church), preeminent military leader, and, often particularly crucial, prime representative of his people in all external dealings. In ninth-century southern Italy, this last had frequently seemed the most significant role. It is instructive to note the skill with which it had been played by Capua's leaders.

When Atenolf of Capua seized power at Benevento in the year 900, it represented the triumph of crude ambition and political entrepreneurship over tradition. Benevento had been the heartland of the southern Lombards, the first area they had settled. Moreover, the city of Benevento, with Sancta Sophia and the other monumental buildings erected by Arichis, evoked memories of that great leader and his successful defiance of Charlemagne. Paul the Deacon had walked its streets; southern Lombard poets and chroniclers had praised its splendors. Even after the 849 *Divisio*, and despite a series of largely unimpressive rulers, Beneventans plainly felt superior to other southern Lombards. Capua, in contrast, was initially merely one of many southern Lombard gastaldates; it had been awarded to Salerno as part of the *Divisio*. Yet in the classical era, as ninth-century Lombards remembered, the city of Capua had been "second only to Rome."[57] Perhaps for that reason the Lombards treated the gastaldate of Capua as somewhat special; in any case, its gastald held the additional title of count.[58] And in the 840s, his ambitions already obvious, Count-Gastald Landolf had proceeded to build himself, on a hill along the river near his city of Capua, a heavily fortified *castrum*, which one contemporary caustically called "Rebelopolis."[59]

Benevento's Arab mercenaries had burned the old city of Capua in 841, but by 856 a new and more defensible city of Capua had risen three or four kilometers away.[60] And by about 860, Landolf's successors had become sufficiently powerful to slough off their link to Salerno. From that point on, through the balance of the ninth century, Capua (together with a cluster of minor gastaldates that accepted its dominance) essentially acted independently.

The secret of Capua's success unquestionably lay in the skill, vigor, and ruthlessness with which Landolf and his heirs acted. And Landolf had ample heirs: four sons, three of whom in turn each had at least three sons. All, seemingly, were equally tough and ambitious. Most became either count or bishop of Capua; one, a second Landolf, youngest son of the dynasty's founder, was from 863 to 879 (emulating Naples) both count and bishop. Virtually all, especially this second Landolf, were adept at making and breaking alliances within and without Campania as Capua's interests (or their own) dictated. They also arranged advantageous marriages for their relatives with Campania's ruling families, including those of Naples and Amalfi. And they kept Benevento, Salerno, and Naples off balance by sometimes sheltering dissidents and at other times providing military help to one or another of those key rulers. (According to the chronicler Erchempert, a near contemporary and himself a Capuan, the first Landolf on his deathbed had advised his four sons never to let Benevento and Salerno be at peace with each other lest they then unite against Capua.)[61]

Count-Bishop Landolf and his immediate successor were also notably skillful in dealing with powerful outsiders such as Louis II and Engelberga, and Pope John VIII. Strong connections with Monte Cassino helped here. In the second half of the ninth century, there seems to have been only one brief period when the abbot of Monte Cassino was not related or at least warm friend to the Capuan dynasty. That was at the time Louis II came south to launch his final attack on Bari; the abbot then of Monte Cassino had apparently warned that Landolf was not to be trusted, and this had led Louis to seize Capua and temporarily put in place a Spoletan overseer.[62] Soon, however, Landolf had won over Louis, and after Louis' ill-treatment at Benevento in 871, he and Engelberga made Capua their south Italian base and seem to have spent much of their time there.[63] After Louis' death in 875, Count-Bishop Landolf briefly resisted Pope John's anti-Muslim campaign, but the threat of excommunication quickly brought him to a mutually helpful relationship with John, and Landolf soon began to serve as the pope's intermediary with the other Campanian rulers. By the time Landolf died in 879, Capua had become the pope's only reliable Campanian ally— and was amply rewarded.[64]

For a while in the mid-880s, a family dispute over the succession caused serious problems within Capua, and the wily Athanasius II of Naples took advantage of this to seize some Capuan territory. In 887, however, Atenolf, the most able of Count-Bishop Landolf's nephews, became count himself, and the steady march toward regional dominance resumed. By now, as a result of Monte Cassino's destruction, Capuan territory had become the site of Monte Cassino in exile, and was to remain so for half a century. Over time, this had significant cultural implications for Capua, but more immediately it surely also had political value, given Monte Cassino's image.

Altogether, Landolf's dynasty had done very well in the course of the ninth century. At the end of the century, Capua met with only one minor rebuff. In 897, Atenolf proposed to Guaimar I of Salerno that Atenolf's son marry Guaimar's daughter; but Guaimar's wife, Idta, immensely proud of her Spoletan (and hence now imperial) connections, loftily rejected the match as unsuitable.[65] Undaunted, Atenolf married his son to the daughter of Athanasius II of Naples. And three years later he must have mightily enjoyed Idta's discomfiture when he himself became ruler at Benevento and thereby acquired the grand title of "Langobardorum gentis princeps."

The geographical position of Capua and Benevento had promoted contacts with popes and emperors; a pope or western emperor would inevitably come first to that area of southern Italy. (In the tenth century, much would be different, but not the geography. Thus the Ottonians were to come first into Capuan-Beneventan territory. And in part because of Benevento's proximity to Byzantine Apulia, Capua-Benevento, far more often than Salerno, would find itself in confrontation with Byzantium.) In the ninth century, before the destruction of Monte Cassino, its geographical closeness had often proved useful for both Capua and Benevento, facilitating contacts with Monte Cassino's important visitors. Yet geography could only provide opportunity. Capua in the ninth century had made the most of it. But Benevento, even with the additional advantage of its traditional status, had foundered.

Salerno's geographical position was very different. Arichis had rightly judged the city of Salerno sufficiently isolated (protected as it mostly was by mountains to the north and northeast) to be safe from any Carolingian threat. And most of the principality's territory lay south or southeast of the city, seemingly even more secure from interference. Throughout most of the ninth century, Salerno's rulers could therefore leave it to Benevento and Capua to deal with popes and western emperors. Salerno had been free to concentrate on other matters. Of course the return of Byzantium to southern Italy, late in the century, had initially seemed ominous. There could now be encroachments from the south or southeast, and as we have seen, Nicephorus Phocas had moved swiftly to take some of the more remote areas claimed by Salerno. Guaimar I had therefore gone to Constantinople in 887 and, for the balance of his reign, displayed his Byzantine title. Yet in practice Guaimar treated his title as no more than a cosmetic touch. Even while sporting the title, he sent troops against Byzantine forces on occasion.[66] And the Byzantines did nothing to punish him. In effect, the Salernitans were still free to pursue their own interests, still essentially protected by their geographical setting.

In addition to the Lombard principalities, there were, of course, three other autonomous entities in southern Italy: the erstwhile Byzantine city-states of Gaeta, Naples, and Amalfi. Each had played a distinctive role in ninth-century developments, and to round out the picture we need to examine those roles. However, since Amalfi will be the focus of the next chapter, here only Gaeta and the duchy of Naples will be considered.

Gaeta lies along the Tyrrhenian coast just to the north of present-day Campania; the modern city, perched at the end of a rugged hook of land overlooking a superb natural harbor, still evokes its medieval past. In the tenth century, for a variety of reasons (including the altered character of the papacy) Gaeta was to be comparatively little involved in Campanian developments. But in the ninth century it was very much involved. With the papacy then much concerned with southern Italy, Gaeta was important because of its location, close to the coastal route south from Rome. That same geographical position also put Gaeta near the center of action in the crisis-period of the Arab attack on Rome in 846. Furthermore, until about

839, Gaeta seemingly functioned as a quasi-dependency of Naples.[67] Indeed, in the late eighth and early ninth centuries, popes—and Byzantine governors of Sicily—had plainly viewed Gaeta, especially in relation to naval help against the Arabs, as more or less interchangeable with Naples and Amalfi.[68]

As the ninth century wore on, Gaeta, like Naples and Amalfi, had come to seem ambivalent toward the Muslim world. Its location on the very edge of papal territory gave Gaeta reason to worry about papal dominance. In the ninth century, the Gaetans may also have been involved to some extent in overseas trading. These two factors doubtless predisposed Gaeta toward tolerance of the Arab presence in southern Italy. But more important, Lombard Capua, bordering Gaeta to the south, posed a continuous threat; it was fear of Capua that had led Gaeta, in the 880s, to invite that Aghlabid band to settle nearby along the Garigliano River.

Nevertheless, Gaeta also seemed in some ways to remain deeply Byzantine. The fustily elaborated phrasing of its charters and an addiction to rather antiquated titles suggest a society living in the past.[69] One senses that ninth-century Gaeta, small and ingrown, had difficulty adjusting to a world in which, with Sicily gone, its Byzantine connection could no longer be maintained. Through 934, Byzantine imperial dating continued to be used in Gaetan indictions.[70] Many witnesses to Gaetan charters continued to sign their names in Greek letters, and Gaetan notaries proudly noted their competence in both Greek and Latin.[71]

Much of this was also true of Naples.[72] Yet somehow the overall tone at Naples was very different. And if Gaeta is largely peripheral to our story, Naples is decidedly central.

It seems almost miraculous that Naples had survived as an independent entity. When the ninth century began, the Lombards for two hundred years had been nibbling away at Naples' territory. Successive popes and Byzantine governors in Sicily had been sympathetic but unable to help. Naples' only comfort came from occasional portents; in 787, when the death of Arichis had freed Naples of its greatest enemy, Vesuvius erupted.[73]

By the mid-eighth century, Naples' dukes had already begun to be chosen locally, without reference to Byzantium.[74] Once, in the early ninth century, the Byzantine governor of Sicily was asked to arbitrate a disputed claim to power, but in that same period Naples also demonstrated its independence by disregarding a Byzantine plea for naval help.[75] By then the duchy had long since ceased to honor the Byzantine emperor on its coinage.[76] With Byzantine power fading in the Tyrrhenian, and Byzantium thus unable to supply help against the escalating Lombard threat to Naples, it is no wonder that the traditional hierarchical relationship collapsed. In any case, Naples' move away from its Byzantine connection proved to have been the start of further fragmentation, more severing of relationships. In the late 830s, both Amalfi and Gaeta broke their links to Naples.[77]

In 840, Sergius I became duke at Naples, beginning a dynasty that was to dominate Naples for more than a century. By then, Naples had already been the first to bring Arab mercenaries into Campania, and Neapolitans present at the taking of Byzantine Messina had apparently sided with the Arab attackers. Throughout the balance of the ninth century, Naples enjoyed an exceptionally close relationship with the Muslim world, to the horror of successive popes and of Louis II. In his 871 letter to Basil the Macedonian, Louis said bitterly that Naples was "a second Palermo or 'Africa.'"[78] And contemporary sources do suggest that at Naples there were more Arabs around, more consistently, and more intimately involved in local affairs, than anywhere else in Campania. Only rarely, as when in 842 some Sicilian Aghlabids had landed on the island of Ponza, and when in the 880s the Aghlabid band on Mount Vesuvius's flanks proved too troublesome, did Naples take action against them.[79]

The most dramatic illustration of the strength and persistence of this relationship had come in the 870s. The grandson of Sergius I, Duke Sergius II, virtually turned Naples over to some Sicilian Aghlabids when he attained power in 870. His two uncles, Bishop Athanasius I and Caesar (the old hero of the naval battle of Ostia), opposed his actions, whereupon Caesar was thrown into prison and Bishop Athanasius was besieged on the tiny offshore island where he had taken refuge. Louis II, hearing of this, persuaded Amalfi to send ships that rescued Athanasius.[80] Sergius, however, remained in power, and the unfortunate Caesar died in his prison.[81] Pope Hadrian II dispatched Anastasius Bibliothecarius to Naples, and Louis II sent the abbot of Monte Cassino, but to no effect.[82]

Later in the 870s, in the early stages of Pope John VIII's anti-Muslim campaign, Sergius temporarily abandoned his pro-Arab stance; he was party to the Traietto agreements. But he soon relapsed. Thus, as we have seen, Pope John backed a coup to bring to power Sergius's youngest brother, Bishop Athanasius II. There was every reason to believe that this second Athanasius would expel all Muslims; he was known to be a man of great culture, and he was certainly expected to be loyal to the church. Also, he had unquestionably acted firmly toward Sergius; the latter, brother or no, had been blinded and sent to Rome to die. Yet within months Bishop (now also Duke) Athanasius II had Naples once again swarming with Aghlabids. It was the Naples of Athansius II that Pope John sorrowfully excommunicated.

In the later 880s, after the death of Pope John, Naples under Athanasius II was perhaps the most powerful force in Campania.[83] Sometimes allied with Capua (and freely using Arab mercenaries), the duchy dominated its immediate region. Athanasius seemed also to be restoring Naples' antique grandeur. Culture flourished. His saintly uncle Bishop Athanasius I had established schools of reading and singing and had lavished embellishments upon Naples' churches.[84] Athanasius II assiduously sought Greek manuscripts of every sort, and he established scriptoria not only to copy but in some cases to translate those works.[85] Indeed, we benefit today from his devotion to Byzantine-Greek culture; he secured and thereby preserved for posterity many important manuscripts. And early in the next century, following his example, the wife of another duke of Naples obtained many more manuscripts from Constantinople, including the first version of the Alexander stories to come to the West.[86]

Athanasius II involved Naples more deeply in Campanian politics than had any of his predecessors. The degree to which he was successful was demonstrated by the fact that Atenolf of Capua sought a marriage alliance with Naples after being refused a Salernitan bride for his son. Once viewed by the Lombards merely as a tempting target, Naples by the latter ninth century was plainly seen as a very desirable ally. Campania was certainly no longer divided into hostile and nonintersecting Lombard and Byzantine spheres.

Yet after Athanasius's death in 898, Naples would never again, at least in this period, seem quite so important. It was almost miraculous that the duchy had survived into the ninth century. But equally surprising is Naples' fading from prominence in the tenth century. This mystery, however, is best considered in connection with the rise of Amalfi, the subject of the next chapter.

5. Amalfi in Context

BY THE BEGINNING OF THE TENTH CENTURY southern Italy's autonomous states had achieved political equilibrium. From this point on, we can therefore devote less attention to political events; the chief issue becomes the use to which those states put their newfound stability. To investigate this, a good place to begin is Amalfi, for Amalfi's connections with the wider Mediterranean world were significant for developments throughout the region.

Signs of Change: 902 and 915

To put Amalfi's rise in perspective, we must look first at two tenth-century happenings far from the Amalfitan peninsula. Like so many south Italian events of the ninth and tenth centuries, both involved Arabs. The first, in the fall of 902, was the largest Muslim assault ever mounted against southern Italy. The second was the celebrated campaign of 915, which wiped out the Arab encampment on the Garigliano River. The two were interconnected; fear generated by the 902 assault led to the united resolve of 915. Both were thus relevant to Amalfi's story. For after 915, although Arabs remained a serious threat to the Byzantine portions of southern Italy, in much of Campania "Arab" became synonymous with opportunity.

The events of 902 and 915 both demarked change. The 902 attack was the dying explosion of the Aghlabid dynasty that had ruled Muslim North Africa since 800; after 902, that tension-filled province would fall to the Fatimids, significantly different in their goals and attitudes. The Garigliano campaign represented change of another sort: a new maturity on the part of Campanian rulers.

The 902 assault was personally led by Ibrāhīm II, emir of North Africa since 875. Fierce and ruthless, Ibrāhīm had reasserted North African control over the splintered Muslim factions of Sicily, and in the summer of 902 his North African-Sicilian army took Taormina, the last major pocket of Byzantine resistance in eastern Sicily.[1] In September, hardly pausing to draw breath, he led a huge force across the Straits of Messina into Calabria. This time, there was no doubt about the character of the Muslim assault; this was *jihad*.

In both Arab and Christian sources, Ibrāhīm is described as exceptionally violent and cruel.[2] Even when a town meekly surrendered, he was likely to slaughter all its inhabitants. In 902, his reputation preceded him into Calabria, and defenses crumbled as he and his army approached.[3] Fear seems to have gripped virtually the whole of southern Italy. It was now, for example, that Naples leveled the "castle of Lucullus," at the outer edge of the Bay of Naples, lest Ibrāhīm reach Campania and make use of it.[4] And to the Greek hermit-monks of the Calabrian mountains, Ibrāhīm seemed the Anti-Christ. Some years before, one of these holy ascetics, St. Elias the Younger, had fled to Calabria from his native Sicily. In the spring of 902, seized by a vision of Taormina's impending fall and sensing the danger that portended for Calabria, Elias fled again, this time to Amalfi. He had presumably heard of Amalfi's special relationship with Muslims and perhaps hoped this would provide protection. In any case, once there, he set to praying with special intensity, and his prayers were answered. The terrifying Ibrāhīm suddenly died in late October while besieging Cosenza.[5] His huge army faded away. Within North Africa, Aghlabid power fragmented and then collapsed; for some time thereafter, political and religious turmoil preoccupied both North Africa and Sicily.

But the magnitude of the threat had made a profound impression on Campania. For three-quarters of a century, Campanian rulers had not only tolerated but welcomed Arab bands. The last such had operated since the 880s from the Garigliano River region; initially invited there by Gaeta as a shield against Capuan aggression, this band had steadily grown more menacing. These were more or less the same Arabs who, earlier, had destroyed Monte Cassino and San Vincenzo al Volturno. For two decades now they had been raiding papal territory, even going beyond Rome as far as Farfa. And they had certainly caused grief within parts of Campania. Therefore, in 903, the year after Ibrāhīm's invasion, Capua, Naples, and Amalfi (in unusual alliance) launched an attack on the Garigliano Arab encampment.[6]

It was not surprising that Capua wanted these predators gone; they were a constant scourge in Capuan territory, which lay just south of their base. Naples' and Amalfi's interest is less clear, but Atenolf of Capua was allied by marriage with the ruling families of both Naples and Amalfi. Moreover, the Garigliano Arabs blocked the overland routes north, which must have affected Amalfitan trading ventures to Rome and beyond.[7] For that matter, access to Rome would surely have been important to all of Campania.

The Garigliano Arabs repelled this 903 attack with the help of the Gaetans, who still valued these Arabs. Yet Capua was not about to abandon the effort. The sources are problematic here, but possibly there were additional Capuan attempts over the next five or six years. By about 910, however, Atenolf seemingly decided that Byzantium represented his only recourse. He therefore sent his son Landolf to Constantinople, and the latter returned a *patricius* and apparently with a promise of military help.[8] The death of Emperor Leo the Wise in 912 and the chaotic year-long reign of the dissolute Alexander temporarily interrupted planning. But in 914 there was a second Capuan embassy to Constantinople, and things began to move.[9] A Byzantine *strategos* arrived in Campania, the first high-level representative to come there from Constantinople on a friendly mission in a century and a half. Trying all possible persuasive tactics, he now awarded the title of *patricius* to the rulers of both Naples and Gaeta.[10] (Both, with their past Byzantine links, no doubt thought this honor long overdue; after all, the Lombard rulers of Salerno and Capua-Benevento had already received that gratifying indication of importance.) The mere appearance of the *strategos* in Campania emphasized the seriousness of the projected campaign. Plainly, this was an endeavor it was best to join. Even Salerno, heretofore apparently not committed, promised support.

Only Gaeta, it would appear, still needed additional persuasion. And this was now supplied by the new pope, John X, in a manner most revealing of the current papal situation. Liutprand's report of John X and the Garigliano campaign is highly colored and demonstrably full of inaccuracies; it also immediately follows his description of John reaching the papal throne by way of Theodora's bed—with its implication that, as pope, John functioned as Theodora's puppet.[11] Here, as so often with Liutprand, the narrative requires deconstruction; surely we can view Theodora as the misogynist Liutprand's symbol or sign for Rome's most powerful family. Lands owned by the Roman nobility must have been greatly affected by the Arab raids; such families thus had good reason to want the Garigliano encampment destroyed. And, for this, it was vital to ensure that Gaeta not provide refuge to the Garigliano Arabs. We therefore find John X formally reconfirming to Gaeta total sovereignty over a huge stretch of erstwhile papal territory first proffered by John VIII thirty years earlier for Gaetan help against the Arabs. And Theophylact, husband of Theodora, appears in the confirmation document as preeminent among the papal representatives.[12]

About two hundred square miles was involved: an oblong of territory edging the Tyrrhenian coast from Terracina down to the mouth of the Garigliano. (Gaeta had heretofore held little more than its hook of land.) Much of this territory was mountainous and would likely have had little value. Yet some ancient towns and productive lands were included, and more aggressive popes, like Hadrian I, had been very concerned to retain this area.[13] Now, not only did the pope grant Gaeta total sovereignty, with all rights and revenues, but the document even provided for Byzantine and Capuan guarantees that the grant would be respected.[14] John X was making a major papal sacrifice to buy tranquillity for Rome and its environs. This was, of course, not an unworthy objective. It would benefit everyone in and around Rome. But benefits would particularly accrue to those Roman landowners who seem to have been the prime movers.

Gaeta's cooperation—essentially a promise of nonintervention—was thus finally assured. (As a final touch, the papal document promised compensation if any Gaetan property suffered damage during the campaign.) In the spring of 915, a combined force of Capuans, Beneventans, and Salernitans, together with Byzantines and "others" from Byzantine Apulia and Calabria, took up a position south of the Arab encampment. Papal or Roman forces, along with troops led by Alberic of Spoleto, encircled the encampment on the north.[15] And a Byzantine fleet guarded the mouth of the Garigliano so that the Arabs could not escape by water. By late August, after three months of siege and sporadic fighting, the Garigliano Arabs had been wiped out.

Pope John later noted proudly that he himself had twice gone into battle.[16] Indeed, it has been customary to refer to the entire campaign as a papal accomplishment. Certainly the papal grant did secure the crucial cooperation of Gaeta. Yet, as Pietro Fedele noted a century ago, Leo Marsicanus, undoubtedly drawing on contemporary sources, gave the major credit to the Capuans, together with the Byzantine support they had secured. In the spring of 915, John X had been pope for barely a year, and there is no indication that he had become involved in the planning early.[17] Capua seems unquestionably to have initiated the effort. Furthermore, no one could have achieved more than temporary military victory, and perhaps not even that, without genuine, broad support within Campania as a whole. (Louis II and Pope John VIII had learned this, to their sorrow.) Atenolf and his son Landolf had become determined to expel all Arabs from their area. They (and the Byzantines) then drew in Naples and Salerno as well—and apparently without equivocation on the latters' part. Most of Campania had plainly wearied, at last, of Arab raiders in their midst.[18]

There is no mention of Amalfitans in connection with the 915 campaign, even though Amalfi had joined Capua in the 903 attempt. We can only surmise that the 915 campaign acquired a crusadelike tone that made the Amalfitans uncomfortable, given their connections with the Arab world. Or perhaps they were simply too busy with their commercial ventures. The population of Amalfi and its territory could not have been very large in this period, and summer was the sailing season. In any case, Amalfi by now often seemed detached from happenings in Campania.

Yet, whether or not the Amalfitans realized it, this 915 victory, clearing Campania of the Arab bands that had preoccupied everyone for so long, would have major, positive consequences for Amalfi and its entire region. The character of the relationship between this part of southern Italy and the Arab sphere would now change from a defiant, limited commerce to something much broader and more constructive. One sign of this—and perhaps the most interesting—will be considered in the next chapter. Here, however, we must now turn to Amalfi.

The Rise of Amalfi

The full story of Amalfi and its trade before the Crusades was for a long time deliberately misrepresented or not squarely faced. Matteo Camera, a nineteenth-century native son whose works on Amalfi stood for nearly a century as the definitive treatments, allowed his local patriotism and devotion to the church to blind him to the facts of Amalfi's Arab contacts.[19] It is no wonder. Some who glimpsed the truth found it shocking. Beazley, for example, praised Venice as differing from Amalfi in that Venice was not "stained by [any] disgraceful alliance with the Moslems to the damage of Christian lands."[20]

Both Wilhelm Heyd and Adolf Schaube did recognize the importance of Amalfi's Arab trade and described the situation objectively.[21] Yet Camera's portrayal, emphasizing Amalfi's Byzantine connections and crediting them for Amalfi's rise, continued influential. This view also dominated the next significant work on Amalfi, that of Adolf Hofmeister in 1920; Hofmeister insisted that Amalfi functioned in every way as a Byzantine dependency, and he showed considerable ingenuity in explaining away all evidence to the contrary.[22] In the 1930s, Italian scholars began producing perceptive articles on Amalfitan history, but their focus was primarily local and institutional. The Arab connection received little attention. The tide truly turned only in 1967, when Armand Citarella published a major article concentrating exclusively on Amalfi's trade with the Islamic world.[23]

Since 1967, some new evidence has come to light. We have also reached a better understanding of the structures of Amalfi's sea ventures, including the physical and technological components. It is therefore time for a new look at Amalfi.

The hard evidence for Amalfi's overseas commerce, through the tenth century, can be quickly reviewed. Most of the ninth-century evidence has already been noted, including the fact that in the Roman period there was no Amalfi, indeed no town at all along the south coast of the Amalfitan peninsula. The *Chronicon Salernitanum* said that Amalfi had been founded by people fleeing the city of Rome as their world collapsed around them; they had hoped to reach Constantinople but suffered shipwreck and other vicissitudes and, after years of wandering, settled on the Amalfitan coast.[24] Whatever the truth of that legend, in 596 we find the first indication of a town; Gregory the Great deplores the bishop of Amalfi's propensity to stray beyond his *castrum*, neglecting his duties.[25] We are not told why the bishop was straying, but his predilection seemed a portent.

We then find no further mention for two hundred years. But by the late eighth century Amalfi must have seemed worth having, for Pope Hadrian I wrote Charlemagne that Arichis, from his new base at Salerno, had attempted to seize the town.[26] Since Amalfi was still then linked to the duchy of Naples, a Neapolitan force rushed to Amalfi's defense and drove off the Lombards. Yet shortly afterward the Amalfitans participated in the Salernitan plot to assassinate four Frankish envoys.[27] In combination, these episodes seemed another portent: in this case, of Amalfi's always complex relationship with Salerno.

In the early ninth century, for the first time, there were concrete references to Amalfitan seafaring. In 812, at the request of the Byzantine governor of Sicily, Amalfitan and Gaetan ships had pursued "Mauri" raiders harrassing the Tyrrhenian coast.[28] Since the chase went all the way to Lampedusa (an island between Sicily and North Africa), we can conclude that Amalfitans were already used to long voyages. And it is plain that by the 830s, Amalfi was increasingly active in trade and at sea. The first evidence of this was Amalfi's mention in the *Pactum Sicardi* (836).[29] Although only the title of the section survives, that title ("concerning the

Amalfitans, wherever they may travel") is powerfully suggestive. Next, a Byzantine source reported that when the Arabs, moving across Sicily, threatened the island of Lipari, Amalfitans sailed there to rescue St. Bartholomew's remains.[30] A third mention involved yet another rescue; in 839, when members of a Salernitan faction needed to free their would-be leader, imprisoned at Taranto, they turned to Amalfi because Amalfitans in the guise of merchants could sail there unsuspected.[31]

The previous year, 838, the Lombard ruler Sicard, emulating his predecessor Arichis, had attempted to enfold Amalfi within Lombard southern Italy. Local sources suggest that at least some Amalfitans were not opposed to this; Sicard certainly took the town with little difficulty, and he then moved many of its inhabitants to his city of Salerno. Sicard had already demonstrated interest in economic matters by reforming the Lombards' coinage; now he apparently hoped to profit through Amalfitan trading activities. His assassination, shortly afterward, ended that dream; most of the Amalfitans drifted back home. Nonetheless, for Amalfi this episode marked a turning point. Thereafter, little by little, quasi-Byzantine Amalfi and Lombard Salerno appeared to draw closer together. Moreover, we find no further evidence of Amalfitan subordination to Naples. After 839, Amalfi clearly functioned as an independent entity, choosing its own rulers, shaping its own destiny.[32]

So far, there had been no hint of any special relationship between Amalfi and the Arabs. Amalfitans made long voyages, to Lampedusa, to Lipari, to Taranto. But the Lampedusa and Lipari ventures were in opposition to the Arabs, and at the time of the Taranto expedition Taranto was not yet in Muslim hands. Moreover, in 842 it was not Amalfitan but Neapolitan merchants who had reportedly welcomed the Aghlabid conquerors at Messina. It was Naples, too, that brought the first Arab mercenaries into Campania and that later seemed to Louis II a "second Palermo."

Yet in the 880s Pope John VIII found the Amalfitans so committed to an Arab connection that neither huge monetary payments nor excommunication could move them. Their enthusiasm was apparently not dampened by the Aghlabid attempt to take Salerno in the 870s, or by the presence of Muslim raiding bands in the decades leading up to the Garigliano campaign. At most, the Amalfitans had sometimes joined forces with Salerno or Capua or Naples to drive raiders from their immediate vicinity. Amalfitan trade with the Islamic world must therefore have begun much earlier than the surviving sources indicate. The tale linking Amalfitan merchants with warning of the 871 Arab attack on Salerno provides the first documentation. (The *Chronicon Salernitanum*'s author may have roman-ticized the details of that episode, but Salerno clearly did have advance warning, and very likely by way of Amalfitans.) Surely, however, the Amalfitans must have started a lucrative Arab trade well before 871, or Pope John VIII would not have found them so obdurate.

In the tenth century, in any event, varied evidence shows Amalfitans circulating all over the Muslim Mediterranean. Early in that century, the Byzantine patriarch Nicholas the Mystic thanked them for redeeming Christian slaves from the Arabs.[33] In 942, in a mention only recently noticed, an Arab source refers to Amalfitan merchants in Spain, in the caliphate of Cordova.[34] In 978, we hear of an Amalfitan merchant voyaging to the newly founded city of Cairo; and in 996, during a tense period, large numbers of Amalfitans were apparently massacred there.[35] Moreover, as proof of extensive trade with the Fatimids in particular, in the early tenth century both Amalfi and Salerno began using, in local transactions, gold *tari* (quarter-dinars), which either had been obtained in Sicily or North Africa, or were locally minted in imitation of that coinage.[36] The use of *tari* will be discussed again in the next chapter. Here, however, it needs to be noted as a telling reflection of commercial orientation.

In addition to the unequivocal proof of Amalfitan-Muslim trade, there is other, indirect but suggestive evidence. The Arab term *Rūm* (Roman) was once thought to mean only Byzantine Greeks. More recently, however, those working with Arab sources have concluded that *Rūm* could designate any foreign Christians, and certainly any who could speak Greek. Some-times, in fact, *Rūm* seemed specifically to mean "south Italian." It thus could very likely have referred to Amalfitans—which would give us consid-erable additional evidence of Amalfitan trade, since *Rūm* merchants were frequently mentioned at North African and Egyptian ports. It is now thought plausible, for example, to associate Amalfitans with a "market of the *Rūm*" mentioned at Fustat (the future site of Cairo) in 959.[37]

Certainly Amalfitans also traded with the Byzantine world in the tenth century. There is Liutprand's scornful remark that the purple fabric treated with such reverence at Constantinople could be seen even on the backs of prostitutes in Italy, thanks to Venetian and Amalfitan merchants.[38] In 992, when Constantinople favored Venice with customs fee reductions, it was with the proviso that the Venetian ships not carry goods or merchants from such places as Amalfi.[39] Altogether, a great many Amalfitans must have gone to Constantinople. At the time of Liutprand's second embassy, in 968, he reported that some Amalfitans were even recruited to lead a hastily gathered Byzantine strike force; and in the late tenth century an Amalfitan monastery was founded on Mount Athos.[40]

Unquestionably, Amalfi valued its Byzantine connection, and that connection became even more important in the eleventh century. Meanwhile, in the tenth century, most Amalfitan rulers welcomed Byzantine titles. Yet though Constantinople liked to consider Amalfi part of greater Byzantium, the Amalfitans seem to have viewed the relationship somewhat differently.[41]

Furthermore, as Citarella has suggested, it surely was the Arab connection that made the crucial difference in Amalfi's rise to commercial prominence. Not only was that connection highly productive in itself, but combined with the Byzantine relationship it gave Amalfi access everywhere in a period when cabotage (trading mixed loads along the coasts) prevailed. In the early or middle eleventh century, the Amalfitans would found a hostel in Muslim Palestine, which suggests there had been an Amalfitan presence in that significant border region for some time.[42] Of course trading ships based in the eastern Mediterranean also ventured back and forth between Byzantine and Muslim territory. We have the evidence of a recently excavated early eleventh-century wreck off the coast of Turkey, its cargo and the crew's personal possessions part Byzantine, part Islamic.[43] But Amalfi was the only major *western* port consistently associated with this two-pronged trade.

There is reason to believe that Amalfi benefited markedly from the change in dynasty in North Africa in the early tenth century. In 909, a Fatimid (Shiite) *imam* declared himself ruler of the North African territory formerly governed by the Aghlabids; roughly speaking, this was modern Tunisia and the coastal areas of modern Libya.[44] The Fatimids, despite their theological conservatism, proved in many ways more tolerant than the Aghlabids toward non-Muslims, whether Christian or Jew. Certainly they seem to have been more open to trade; significantly, the capital was now moved from inland Kairouan to a new city, Mahdia, on the coast. Moreover, in 969, Fatimid rule spread to Egypt as well, and later, if less securely, to Palestine and Syria. This unified, under a single ruler, all of the Muslim territories from present-day Tunisia to the Red Sea and on up the eastern shore of the Mediterranean. And it seems generally agreed that, at least until the latter eleventh century, most of this huge region was exceptionally prosperous.[45]

The Fatimid era largely coincided with Amalfi's rise to commercial prominence. Archibald Lewis, tracking naval power, once designated the century and a half from 827 to 960 as "the Islamic imperium," thus implying an end in the 960s when Byzantium reconquered Crete.[46] If one considers only naval power, that reconquest can indeed be viewed as a watershed. For maritime commerce, however, as Lewis would readily have acknowledged, the Muslim Mediterranean continued important well after that point. And although Amalfi's rise had begun in the ninth century, it reached its apogee in the tenth and eleventh centuries. The inference seems plain.

Open Doors: Trading with the Arab World

It is easy to understand why an enterprising city-state might have sought trade with the Arabs; we need only contrast the glitter of the Muslim Mediterranean with the Europe of that period. But some issues still need exploring, including the feasibility of this commerce.

In the early eighth century, according to al-Balādhurī, a governor of Egypt insisted that papyrus or cloth sold to "the Greeks" bear inscriptions in praise of Allah, even if this interfered with trade. Al-Balādhurī also told of Syrian merchants forced to adopt Islam if they wished to circulate at will "in the countries that have become ours."[47] Over time, however, such strictures seem to have largely disappeared. In periods of disruption, foreign merchants and non-Muslims were certainly at risk; one example was the apparent massacre of Amalfitans at Cairo at the end of the tenth century. Yet on that occasion the government hastened to punish the aggressors and restore all pillaged goods to their foreign owners.[48] In general, by the tenth century, and particularly in Fatimid territory, there seem to have been few barriers to international trade beyond customs duties or taxes, and these did not appear overly arduous.[49] Furthermore, there is marked emphasis on trade and its virtues in the writings of tenth-century Muslim geographers such as Ibn Hawqal. Speaking disparagingly of contemporary Sicily, which he found dirty and impoverished, Ibn Hawqal blamed its sorry condition on heavy taxation and execrable treatment of merchants.[50] Elsewhere he admired, above all, busy harbors and the steady flow of goods.

Ibn Hawqal described Amalfi as the most handsome and prosperous city in the whole of "Lombardy."[51] This may have been true. But his Italian information is thought to have been derived at second hand, so he may well have heard this from Amalfitan merchants—and Ibn Hawqal would always have been inclined to credit the reports of assiduous traders.

Envisioning Mediterranean commerce in the tenth century, we can picture an Arab orbit that circled out now to encompass part of the Italian peninsula. Yet it is important to remember that the "Arab" world was not monolithic. Throughout the Muslim Mediterranean, and certainly in Sicily, North Africa, and Egypt, there were substantial numbers of Christians and Jews. Some, over time, converted, with some converts rising to high office in Fatimid service but never entirely shedding their identity.[52] And many did not convert but continued to be practicing Christians or Jews. We know the Jewish communities of Fatimid Egypt through the magisterial studies of S. D. Goitein.[53] And we know of Egypt's Copts. In addition, however, there were other Christian communities scattered throughout the Arab Mediterranean; in the ninth and tenth centuries we read of Christian bishops or patriarchs in North Africa, Egypt, and Palestine.[54] The Amalfitans were thus not venturing into a totally alien environment when they sailed to these areas, and they would have found non-Muslims fitting quite comfortably into Muslim society. Goitein's work has taught us this about the Jewish communities.[55] Such relative integration appears to have been equally true of resident Christians. St. Elias the Younger, as a youth in Sicily, was captured by raiders and sold as a slave to a North African Christian family. Years later, when traveling through Byzantine territory, he was at one point imprisoned by a Byzantine *strategos* who suspected him of spying for the Arabs; presumably, in the variegated world of the pre-Crusades Mediterranean, Christians with connections to the Muslim sphere could not always be trusted.[56]

The Jews of Southern Italy

For the ninth and tenth centuries, the sources provide only one problematic indication of Amalfitan interrelationship with Jewish communities in southern Italy and the Muslim states. The *Chronicle of Ahimaaz* tells of a tenth-century Capuan Jew bearing a gift from the ruler of Amalfi to the Capuan's brother in North Africa.[57] This particular story may have been pure romance but we do know that south Italian Jewish communities were in communication with their counterparts in the Muslim areas. The history of southern Italy's Jews in this period has received considerable attention, for they figured in important pan-Mediterranean developments within Judaism and produced celebrated scholars and poets.[58] Unfortunately for our purposes, the surviving writings rarely mention economic matters and supply no information about trans-Mediterranean trade. Nevertheless, it seems reasonable to suppose that, in addition to religious and scholarly intercourse, there was some commercial interchange between the Jews of southern Italy and those in Palestine, Egypt and North Africa, and Spain. If so, Amalfi may perhaps have benefited.

Until the 920s, the principal south Italian Jewish communities had apparently all been in Apulia: at Otranto, Taranto, Oria, Bari (and at Venosa, nearby in upper Basilicata).[59] "From Bari the Law, from Otranto the Word of God," the old saying ran, and we might add "from Oria, Hebrew poetry." But there was a devastating Arab sack of Oria in 925, and in that same decade the Emperor Romanus Lecapenus began a fierce persecution of Jews in Byzantine territory. A general move into Lombard southern Italy thus seems to have begun.

Apparently there already was a small Jewish colony in Benevento, and in ninth-century Salernitan charters we encounter names (Jacob, "Josep," "Josueb," Rebecca) that seem to indicate the presence of Jews there as well.[60] (One of these, a ninth-century "Josep medicus," will be discussed in connection with Salerno's medical tradition.) In any case, in the tenth century one senses a surge in Campania's Jewish population. Even more references come in the eleventh century, but already in the tenth century we hear of two Jews (father and son) becoming at least minor officials at Capua; at Naples there is a reference to a synagogue and (in 1002) mention of a "vicus judeorum"; and two tenth-century Salerno charters cite lands or houses belonging to Jews.[61]

In a Salernitan charter of 1012, a property is described as "inter muros et muricino, ad ipsa judaica." That, together with the Naples reference to a "vicus judeorum," implies distinct Jewish quarters by the eleventh century.[62] But if Salerno's ninth-century Josephs and Jacobs were indeed Jews, it is noteworthy that those men served on occasion as witnesses to ordinary charters drafted "in the marketplace."[63] Altogether, evidence for the ninth and tenth centuries would seem to suggest considerable integration in daily life—comparable to the relative integration within Fatimid society and also reminiscent of the degree to which Campania had assimilated resident Arabs.

We know that individual south Italian Jews traveled to and from Muslim territory in this period, but we have no sure information about what ships they used. With more and more Jews settling in Campania— and by the twelfth century Benjamin of Tudela would find at Salerno the largest Jewish colony in all of south Italy—it is tempting to speculate that they sometimes sailed on Amalfitan ships.[64] That can only be speculation. Yet we should never assume any hard and fast separation, in commerce, between Jew and Christian and Muslim in this period. They all faced similar obstacles (and hazards) in a singularly rough and dangerous time, as is illustrated by the report of the fall of Syracuse in 878. The Muslim conquerors of Syracuse seemingly rounded up all foreigners in the city, and a Byzantine monk found himself incarcerated not only with fellow "Christiani" but also with "Aethiopes, Tharsenes, Hebraei [and] Longobardi."[65] Surely at least some of these were merchants, sharing a common fate.

Why Amalfi?

There is one puzzling question to address before considering the structures of Amalfi's overseas trade. Why was it not Naples, rather than Amalfi, that made a name for itself in international commerce? Naples, too, had Byzantine connections and in the ninth century Naples had enjoyed extraordinarily good relations with the Arab world. Naples certainly also had ships. The key role played by its fleet in the Battle of Ostia in 849 was only one example of ninth-century Neapolitan naval activity. Moreover, the seafaring tradition at Naples stretched back to the Roman period and had survived even the dark days of the late sixth century. (Gregory the Great once interceded for a young man at Naples who wanted a *licentia navigandi*. And on another occasion Gregory reprimanded a bishop of Naples for spending too much time idling down on the waterfront with his clerks and occupying himself inappropriately with the building of ships.)[66] Yet despite this maritime tradition, in the tenth century there is virtually no mention of Neapolitan shipping. Ibn Hawqal, comparing Naples to the more splendid Amalfi, said of Naples only that excellent linen cloth was produced there.[67]

Unfortunately, there is no sure answer to the question, Why not Naples? We can only surmise that the leading families viewed the rough and dangerous work of tenth-century trans-Mediterranean ventures as beneath them; collecting manuscripts was perhaps more to their taste. And the hierarchical social structure at Naples may have worked against the emergence of a mercantile class capable of mounting ventures on its own.[68] Perhaps, too, ninth-century Naples had been chiefly involved in the transshipment of slaves—and the slave trade apparently disappeared from Campania after that century.

In addition, however, Naples had a fertile hinterland. If we change the question to Why Amalfi?, the striking contrast in situation becomes apparent. A thousand years of clearances and terracing have now made the declivitous flanks of the Amalfitan peninsula highly productive. But in the ninth century it must have presented a far more forbidding picture; we read of its "vastas silvarum solitudines."[69] The Amalfitans had to take to the sea to meet even basic needs, and they must have longed for arable land. Possibly that had influenced the apparent Amalfitan acquiescence when Sicard sought to join Amalfi to Salerno in the 830s. In any event, there is ample evidence that in the tenth century the profits from Amalfitan seafaring went into land purchases. In charter after charter, we find Amalfitans acquiring property along the more fertile eastern edge of their peninsula, near Salerno, and sometimes land deep within Salernitan territory. Indeed, of the documented tenth-century Salernitan land purchases, two of the most impressive (in land area and price) were made by a group of Atranesi, Amalfitans from the little port adjoining the city of Amalfi.[70]

Obviously, this acquisition of land was important for practical reasons. Yet something else was also at work here. This was, after all, a period in which ownership of property had broad connotations, and in his splendid study of medieval Amalfitan society, Mario Del Treppo noted that the Amalfitans seem not to have wanted to think of themselves as merchants. Reading Amalfitan sources, Del Treppo observes, one would think Amalfi a "società senza mercanti," the only important division that between "maiores" and "plebs."[71] As he acknowledges, it may be wrong to make too much of this. It may only indicate that Amalfitans took for granted an involvement in trade. Yet Del Treppo also noted that Amalfitans came to seem obsessed by genealogy. Salernitan Lombards were often described in charters as "son of so-and-so"; given the limited number of Lombard proper names, this doubtless was vital information. Tenth-century Amalfitans, however, usually had distinctive compound names, which should have obviated the need for further identification. Yet in charters of the latter tenth century we frequently find Amalfitans reciting their genealogies back five generations (and in the eleventh century, sometimes seven). On occasion, clearly, this was done to reinforce a property claim. But it was done quite consistently and, as Del Treppo points out, these genealogies typically ran back to the late ninth or early tenth century, the period when Amalfitan wealth began to surge and thus the period when one's ancestors might first have amassed significant amounts of land—and therefore significant status.[72]

Matteo Camera described medieval Amalfi as splendidly republican: "tutti egualamente si recavano a gloria la libertà."[73] This may have been true around the time Amalfi broke free from Naples in the 830s; there was no indication then of sharp stratification within Amalfitan society. And Amalfitan sea ventures seemingly operated through the egalitarian *colonna* system. (This remained true long after maritime states like Genoa adopted more sophisticated approaches to the capitalization and organization of overseas commerce.) Functioning "a colonna," everyone theoretically shared alike in financing the voyage, operating the ship, and in the profits.[74] In practice, surely not everyone involved could always have gone to sea, and there must have been at least some paid labor; but undeniably the *colonna* approach had a democratic flavor. Nonetheless, over time, Amalfitan sea-faring apparently enabled some Amalfitans to outstrip their fellows and become major landowners.

In due course, moreover, some tenth-century Amalfitans would eagerly claim the title of count, a title earlier associated only with a few of Amalfi's rulers, and never, initially, hereditary. In the ninth century, after Amalfi became autonomous, its rulers had apparently been selected and titled somewhat randomly. Sometimes they were called "prefects" and appeared in pairs, serving for only a year or two; occasionally the term was *judex*. But sometimes (more or less haphazardly?) the title was *comes*. Next, it became increasingly common for one individual or family to exercise power for several years. A hierarchy thus developed and, not surprisingly, by the latter tenth century it was highly desirable to be able to identify a distinguished forebear—best of all, a *comes*. For by the late tenth century that title was treated as hereditary, and having a *comes* ancestor could set one apart.

Meanwhile, Amalfi's ruler had come to be styled *dux*. The frequent elections reported in the ninth century ceased at the end of that century; thereafter, for the next sixty years, Amalfi was ruled by a single family. Then in 958 a member of a rival family seized power and, proclaiming himself Duke Sergius I, he established a dynasty that ruled Amalfi until 1073 and the Norman era.[75]

In the course of a century and a half, Amalfi had thus evolved from an obscure quasi-republic into an opulent duchy. The attainment of status was obviously not the sole motivating force. Yet the Amalfitans, once subordinate to Naples, had the example of that ancient duchy with its emphasis on lineage and rank. We must at least consider Amalfitan behavior with that example in mind.

The Structures of Amalfitan Trade

One important question remains. How, in practical terms, had Amalfi managed to achieve opulence? Excellent international connections were all very well, but anyone visiting Amalfi today is struck by the inadequacy of the city as a port. Ibn Hawqal spoke of Amalfi as "fortunately situated," but he could only have meant the security provided by its isolated location.[76] For the city offers only a narrow strip of open (and ill-protected) shore beneath the towering Appenines spur that constitutes the Amalfitan peninsula. Moreover, we now know that the legend of elaborate stone harbor works (supposedly extending well out to sea in the early medieval period) had no basis in fact.[77] Possibly the harbor at Atrani, abutting the city of Amalfi to the east, was also used; initially it may even have been the primary harbor.[78] But though it is slightly more protected, sheltered behind the cliff that separates it from Amalfi, Atrani's harbor area is even smaller than Amalfi's, certainly equally inadequate.

Amalfi's ships must therefore have been comparatively small; perhaps the majority also sufficiently shallow hulled to be pulled up on shore in winter. Some may thus have resembled the eleventh-century Serçe Liman ship, that barge-like vessel recently excavated by the Institute of Nautical Archaeology off the coast of Turkey.[79] All, presumably, were lateen-rigged, chiefly powered by large triangular sails of the type that had by now replaced the Graeco-Roman square sail in the Mediterranean. But it seems a fair guess that at least some also carried a complement of oars; relatively small boats equipped both with sails and perhaps eight oars or sweeps—a compromise between the leaner but less seaworthy galley and the "round" sailing ship—were apparently still common in the Mediterranean as late as the sixteenth century. There are indications that the *sagena*, the ship type associated with Amalfi in ninth-century sources, was just such a vessel. The sweep-like oars would have been useful for getting in and out of port and also invaluable for supplying bursts of speed in pirate-infested waters.[80]

Ever since the Renaissance, there has been speculation that Amalfitan seafarers had some secret weapon that gave them a maritime advantage. It has been said that the Amalfitans invented the lateen sail, or the maritime compass.[81] Neither can be true. It now seems clear that the lateen sail evolved gradually over many centuries, beginning in the classical era. And the compass seems also to have been a gradual evolution. Moreover, the compass is not mentioned in the Mediterranean until the thirteenth century, and it is hardly credible that Amalfitans could have invented any such device three or four centuries earlier and kept it secret so long. For that matter, Amalfitans of the ninth and tenth centuries, traversing the Mediterranean only in the normal (summer) sailing season, doubtless found navigation no greater problem than had the Phoenicians or the Romans. Possibly, at most, Amalfitans had helped to popularize the lateen sail in the central and western Mediterranean. And in the thirteenth century perhaps some form of portable compass was produced and sold at Amalfi, thus giving rise to the later legend.[82]

In any case, neither compass nor lateen sail could have helped with the most difficult problem Amalfitans faced: their stretch of the Tyrrhenian Sea offers the weakest wind systems of the entire Mediterranean. This is true today, and it is thought that wind conditions in the Mediterranean have not changed appreciably over the last two thousand years. Thus when coming home or leaving port, Amalfitan seamen must have had either to use their oars or exercise extraordinary patience. Only as they neared or passed Sicily could they normally expect to encounter better winds; until then, they were likely to have moved literally at a snail's pace.[83]

Of course, most Mediterranean sea voyages took unconscionably long in this era, just as they had in the classical period. A. L. Udovitch, analyzing voyages of the eleventh, twelfth, and thirteenth centuries, found the "effective speed" to average considerably less than two knots. This was of course not a measurement of actual speed under way; sea trips were typically interrupted by stops at intermediate ports, and the records typically give only the time taken, overall, on a voyage.[84] Nonetheless, the preponderance of evidence indicates that all too often ships actually sailed more slowly than a man could walk. With Amalfi less propitiously situated in relation to wind than, for example, Genoa or Venice, it would appear that, far from having a secret weapon, Amalfitans had to overcome an additional handicap.

Amalfi's only obvious geographical advantage was that, among Campanian ports, it was closest to the Islamic world and to the main east-west sea routes described by John Pryor.[85] Amalfi was also well placed to serve as both marketing and purchasing agent for the principality of Salerno, which in the tenth century became ever more productive and prosperous. And it was well placed, too, for supplying not only the rest of Campania but also Rome, especially since, in this period, it had a virtual monopoly on trans-Mediterranean trade in so far as the west coast of Italy was concerned.

Ibn Hawqal's knowledge of Campania, and particularly Amalfi, has sometimes been cited as evidence that Arab merchant ships went there. In reality, however, not until the eleventh century do we hear (and then only once) of an Arab merchant vessel at Amalfi.[86] This is hardly surprising. Amalfi's harbor was not inviting and presumably there was little to draw Arab shipping, or at least not enough to divert Arab traders from ports nearer home.

Yet the Amalfitans themselves had access to a variety of marketable products. Within the principality of Salerno there came to be a concerted effort to produce cash crops, as we shall see in the next chapter; there was much planting of vines, and of trees such as chestnuts and hazelnuts. Some of this activity, when not directed toward a home market, may well have been aimed at sales within Italy; the Amalfitans certainly traded up and down the coast as well as farther afield. But if the Muslim Mediterranean was by now virtually denuded of trees, as some believe, then every sort of tree product would surely have been welcomed there: from chestnut trees, for example, not only the wood itself but also the nuts, and the bark for tanning.[87] And despite the strictures against alcohol, wine was salable in many parts of the Muslim world.

One can speculate endlessly about what the Amalfitans found, near home or elsewhere in Italy, to sell abroad. There was, for example, the excellent linen that Ibn Hawqal associated with Naples. Claude Cahen once suggested that the Amalfitans even built ships for the Fatimids, and Armand Citarella has sought commercial significance in tenth-century Amalfi's numerous mills.[88] But in fact we can only be sure that the Amalfitans were finding something worth transporting, for somehow they were managing to return home with goods for the Italian market and with gold *tari*.

It is easier to imagine merchandise the Amalfitans may have brought back. Among luxury goods, the possibilities were endless: finely wrought textiles, Islamic glass, Byzantine and Islamic ivories, rich liturgical vessels, and elaborate jewelery from Byzantium. There is ample evidence that such things were coming into Italy in considerable quantity, and no doubt this was often by way of Amalfitan ships. And of course there were always spices, and dye stuffs or coloring agents not available in Italy. Only one known import deserves particular mention; we have no evidence to connect it specifically with the Amalfitans, but it demonstrates the need for trade with the Arabs. In the latter ninth century, even as Pope John VIII was fulminating against such trade, his papal chancery was using Egyptian papyrus.[89]

Since no shipping contracts have survived from medieval Amalfi, there is no way to determine the relative frequency with which Amalfitan ships visited various parts of the Mediterranean. For example, it would be interesting to learn whether the Amalfitans shifted more emphasis to Egypt at the end of the tenth century, when the Red Sea became the prime route for goods coming from the East.[90] But we have no way of ascertaining this. Nor can we tell to what extent Amalfitans were developing credit instruments. We do not even know whether tenth-century Amalfi had resident agents around the Mediterranean. Two centuries later, Amalfitan trading colonies were scattered all over southern Italy, and beyond; but that was the twelfth century. The many Amalfitans apparently at Cairo in May 996, when the massacre occurred, could merely have been merchants who had wintered over.

In sum, for Amalfi in the ninth and tenth centuries, we can only form hypotheses based on scraps of evidence and chance mentions. These indicate that, at least by the latter ninth century, Amalfitans had begun trading with the Arab world but with no greater plan than securing money to buy land. In setting themselves on this course, they had to overcome formidable handicaps—including, at sea, omnipresent piracy. Yet Amalfi did have assets. First, despite its inadequate harbor, Amalfi did enjoy some geographic advantages: its secure setting well out on the Amalfitan peninsula and relative closeness to Arab territory. Second, in this period there were so many practical obstacles to maritime commerce that for a long time the Amalfitans had little competition along the west coast of Italy. (The Venetians seem to have stayed entirely in the eastern Mediterranean, and the Genoese and Pisans had not yet begun to range widely.) And—a most significant asset—thanks to their good relations with both Byzantium and the Arab sphere, Amalfitans were able to profit from the favorable commercial climate associated with Fatimid rule and from the prosperity and relative openness of Byzantium under the Macedonian dynasty.

The eleventh century would bring Amalfi increased wealth and renown. Earlier, however, its dogged pursuit of riches seems to have served another—and important—function. As we shall see in the next chapter, in the tenth century Amalfitan ventures apparently provided the catalyst for economic expansion throughout its portion of southern Italy.

6. Salerno's Southern Italy in the Tenth Century

TO CONSTANTINOPLE, southern Italy in the tenth century must still have seemed a gray world, merely one more troubled frontier zone. Yet in at least some segments of the region, the tenth century brought bright prospects. One excellent example is the Lombard principality of Salerno. Through most of the century, Capua and Benevento would be far better known beyond southern Italy. But this was to Salerno's advantage; Capua-Benevento in effect served as a buffer, shielding Salerno from the major power struggles. Confrontations with Byzantium, for instance, usually involved Beneventan territory. Salerno was for the most part left alone, to the principality's profit.

And, as it happens, we too profit from this. Relatively unmolested, tenth-century Salerno left considerable documentation and it thus provides an ideal vantage point for a consideration of southern Italy in this period.

The Sources for Salerno

There are two particularly rich sources for tenth-century Salerno: the *Chronicon Salernitanum* and a large number of charters published in the *Codex Diplomaticus Cavensis*. This plenitude of sources stands in marked contrast to the situation for the rest of tenth-century southern Italy. From the Byzantine regions, aside from saints' lives, only a few charters and two minimal annals from Bari have survived. And the situation is no better for Capua-Benevento or Naples. From tenth-century Naples we have only a handful of charters; and Capua-Benevento, despite its importance, has left only scattered charters and one perfunctory annals. Later, two major chronicles were compiled in the Beneventan region: the late eleventh-century Monte Cassino chronicle of Leo Marsicanus, and the twelfth-century *Chronicon Vulturnense*, documenting the monastery of San Vincenzo al Volturno. But these, for the tenth century, mostly recorded monastic land transactions and concerns, giving the broader scene scant coverage.

The author of the *Chronicon Salernitanum* was also a monk, but his is secular history in the tradition of Paul the Deacon, and his attention to southern Lombard politics suggests a life spent close to the sources of power. At one time, the *Chronicon Salernitanum* was denigrated as derivative because it drew heavily on earlier sources for its ninth-century coverage. It was also dismissed as too colorful to be reliable. Now, however, its extraordinary value seems recognized. In her 1956 edition, Ulla Westerbergh proved its ninth-century section to be an ingenious interweaving of new and old material. Paolo Delogu noted that the *Chronicon*'s obvious biases rendered it a priceless mirror of tenth-century Lombard values.[1] Hans Belting has spoken glowingly of it.[2] Even the general accuracy of its reporting, despite the embellishments, now seems accepted.

The *Chronicon Salernitanum* essentially begins with the late 700s, the period of Charlemagne and Arichis, but it is particularly useful for the tenth century. Unfortunately, it ends, abruptly, in 974, and thereafter the *Codex Diplomaticus Cavensis* becomes the sole local source. Yet this compendium is equally valuable, supplying, for the ninth and tenth centuries combined, more than five hundred varied notarial documents, most of them executed within the principality of Salerno.[3] In addition to land transactions, there are wills, marriage contracts, and many judgments. Since many of the charters record lay transactions (and tend to be nonformulaic), these acts provide a wealth of revealing detail.

The *Codex Diplomaticus Cavensis* does present one problem. The nineteenth-century editors simply put all of the charters in chronological order, but they obviously represent several disparate groupings. Presumably the monastery of Cava (Santissima Trinità di Cava dei Tirreni), founded by one of Salerno's last Lombard rulers and later much favored by the Normans, came to serve as a regional repository, and over time unrelated batches of charters were jumbled together. Thus these charters do not form a homogeneous sample, and their varied nature and haphazard survival make them unsuitable for overall quantification. Nonetheless, we can roughly track developments in, for example, leasing practices, and later in this chapter this (and other) charter evidence will be considered. First, however, we must review the general situation from 900 to approximately 970.

The Scene Through the 960s

At least within Campania, the first six decades of the tenth century were relatively quiet. The Lombard principalities more than held their own against Byzantium, and in Salerno it was then that economic advance began to be visible. The Salerno the Normans encountered commenced to take shape. In the latter 960s, however, toward the close of his reign, Otto I started looking south, below Rome, and this marked a turning point. It meant the end of nearly a century of detachment from the European scene, and the story after Otto the Great therefore belongs to the final chapters of this study.

From 900 to 970, Lombard southern Italy consisted of two political entities, Salerno and Capua-Benevento. Both now had stable governments, ruled by dynasties that had assumed power in the latter ninth century. In both cases, events of the year 900 had been significant. In that year, Atenolf of Capua had become ruler of Benevento as well, thus providing his dynasty with an impressive dual power base; through most of the tenth century, Capua and Benevento would be ruled virtually as a single unit. And at Salerno there had also been a noteworthy development in 900. Guaimar I had then been prince for twenty years, governing "vehementer," according to the *Chronicon Salernitanum*. He had dealt with friendly and unfriendly Arabs, with political disorder in Campania, and with Byzantium's reappearance in southern Italy. But after 897, when he had been intercepted and blinded en route to Benevento, his temperament—not surprisingly—changed for the worse.[4] Initially, he had been less prone to indiscriminate violence than his father, Guaifer (founder of the dynasty). Now, however, he had a leading Salernitan publicly beheaded for disloyalty, and next, in a sudden mad rage, he ordered his palace scribe castrated for coming to work with his clothing perfumed. The Salernitans, the *Chronicon* says, could take no more. "In unum congregati," they went to Guaimar's son and insisted that he oust his father. The young Guaimar, agreeing, had his father seized (but with surprising gentleness, "blandisque sermonibus") and shut away within the precincts of St. Maximus, the newly built dynastic foundation. Thus Guaimar II became Prince of Salerno, "and all the people rejoiced."[5]

This tale, which there is no reason to disbelieve, reveals the delicate balance of power then in Campania. "Electus est" had been a recurrent phrase in the ninth-century chronicles and no mere euphemism. Time and again in the ninth century we encounter a genuine need for consensus, and rejection of any heir or ruler thought inadequate. As Paolo Delogu has observed, this was reminiscent of the old Germanic approach to rule.[6] Yet in ninth-century Campania this approach had not been restricted to Lombards; a similar attitude was evident at Naples. And the ninth-century rulers of Amalfi were indeed "elected," and for only brief terms.

Obviously, this was not genuine democracy. In the Lombard principalities, to be deemed worthy of ruling one needed some connection with a preeminent family. But with that requirement met, the *maiores* appeared always ready to alter the succession in order to secure strong leadership. This was demonstrated in the ninth century at Capua, at Benevento, and at Salerno. Furthermore, the "populus" (lesser Lombards) was always said to be involved as well.

The year 900 marked a turning point, however. After 900, "elections" were perfunctory. The rulers began formally associating their sons with them, to lock in the succession, and fortunately the sons proved acceptable rulers. Throughout most of the tenth century, the Capuan-Beneventan dynasty would remain solidly entrenched. Similarly, continuity in rule largely prevailed then at Amalfi (and at Naples). And in Salerno, disruption would come in the 970s only through outsiders.

Several factors, over and above the rulers' competence, promoted this new stability. Although boundaries remained somewhat fluid, the basic geopolitical divisions were now firmly set. Furthermore, at least until the 960s everyone seemed careful to avoid potentially threatening external relationships. But most important, surely, was the increasing prosperity of this part of southern Italy in the tenth century, and the fact that all of the *maiores*—as best we can tell—shared in this more or less evenly. Within Salerno, for example, not only did the ruling family steadily accumulate land but other well-connected individuals also seemed to be enhancing their holdings.

Guaimar II ruled Salerno from 900 to 946, his principality including roughly half of present-day Campania and a portion of Basilicata. Like his predecessors, he named gastalds to hold the key *castra* ringing the outer limits of the principality.[7] The sources also show gastalds in Guaimar's capital, the city of Salerno, serving in various ways as the prince's surrogates. "Gastald" seemed now an all-purpose term for any highly placed official recruited from among the *maiores*.[8] And orderly government plainly owed much to them.

What we would consider the first major event during Guaimar II's reign was the Garigliano campaign of 915. Surprisingly, however, the *Chronicon Salernitanum* makes no mention of it; for most Salernitans, apparently, this distant campaign was of little interest. There is also no hint of the revived Salernitan relationship with Byzantium that followed the Garigliano triumph. After Guaimar II had become prince, Salernitan indictions had at first noted no Byzantine honors. Then in 908—at a time when Capua-Benevento and Naples were both threatening Salernitan territory—Guaimar II had begun to be identified as "son of that Guaimar who was *imperialis patricius*."[9] And after he aided in the Garigliano victory he had his own Byzantine title; from 917 to 923, in all but one Salernitan charter he is *"imperialis patricius."*[10]

Yet the *Chronicon Salernitanum* does not mention this honor. To its proud Lombard author, the significant events of Guaimar II's reign were the battles fought against the Byzantines. A more aggressive attitude toward Byzantium seems to have developed in the 920s. Early in that decade, Guaimar, a widower, took as his new wife a Capuan, one Gaitelgrime, granddaughter of Atenolf and daughter of Capua-Benevento's current co-ruler. In addition, Guaimar married a daughter to the other co-ruler's son. These unions seemed to symbolize a resurgence of pan-Lombard ambition. In Byzantine-held Apulia, with its heavily Lombard population, there were uprisings in 921, and the co-rulers of Capua-Benevento promptly invaded. They seized the *castrum* of Ascoli, and in the process the Byzantine *strategos* was killed.[11]

The decade of the 920s was grim altogether for Byzantine southern Italy. Hungarian raiders appeared in Apulia in 922.[12] In 926, Michael, "rex Sclavorum," briefly captured Siponto, at the edge of the Gargano peninsula.[13] Arabs, too, once again began raiding the Byzantine areas. In 925, a North African band sacked Oria (inland from Taranto), killing large numbers of people and carrying off the rest to be sold as slaves.[14] Two years later, it was Taranto's turn.[15] And in Calabria the situation appeared even more ominous. The Sicilian "Cambridge Chronicle" reports raids on Reggio and other Calabrian towns in 918, 923–24, 925–26, 928–29, and 929–30. The local populace, with the concurrence of Byzantine officials, at least twice offered the Arabs annual payments and hostages, but each time this stopped the raids only briefly.[16]

Then in 929 a combined southern Lombard force struck, defeating a Byzantine army along the little Basintello River, east of Acerenza. This time, according to the *Chronicon Salernitanum*, when the *strategos* found himself surrounded by Salernitan troops, he shouted a reminder to Guaimar that, in a happier time, he had been godfather to Guaimar's firstborn son. He was therefore spared.[17] Plainly, however, such amicable relationships would not recur. Guaimar II had ceased to use his Byzantine title after 923; it never reappeared in Salernitan indictions during his lifetime.[18]

As the next major Lombard move, the meager sources cite an assault on Matera ten years later. But there must have been activity in the interim, for Matera represented deep penetration of Byzantine Apulia.[19] Moreover, it now took forceful intervention by Hugh of Provence to halt the Lombard campaign. Hugh, then king of Italy and negotiating with Romanus Lecapenus to marry a daughter to the Byzantine heir apparent, apparently put pressure on Capua-Benevento, and offered inducements.[20]

By the time Hugh intervened, according to the *Chronicon Salernitanum*, Guaimar and the co-rulers of Capua-Benevento had come to dominate "omnes civitates Apulie simulque et Calabrie."[21] That surely was hyperbole. Nonetheless, by about 940 Byzantium was unquestionably on the defensive in southern Italy.

This is therefore the place to make again a point made earlier in this study. It is wrong to view the Lombard principalities (or even Naples and Amalfi) as "vassal states" of Byzantium—and thus to consider the Lombard principalities "in rebellion" against Byzantium in the second quarter of the tenth century. Such terms force the realities into a totally inappropriate mold. Byzantium had never fully accepted the loss of any part of Italy; inevitably, then, Constantinople still claimed the entire southern half, and Constantine Porphyrogenitus referred to all of the Campanian states as part of the empire. But we should not be seduced by his comforting fantasy.[22] Unquestionably, all Campanian rulers admired the visible aspects of Byzantine culture. Also, claiming a special relationship with Byzantium was often useful.[23] Even in the case of Naples, however, the relationship was now tenuous at best. And as for the Lombard principalities, we would do well to note the attitude expressed in the *Chronicon Salernitanum*, which consistently portrayed the southern Lombards as proud and independent opponents of an external aggressor. For a Lombard, significant history had essentially begun with the Lombard arrival in Italy in the late sixth century; that anniversary is stressed in the sources.[24] Thereafter, Lombards, not Byzantines, had mostly dominated southern Italy; tenth-century Lombards therefore could (and did) view Byzantium as an interloper.

Nonetheless, the local rulers all recognized a need to bend when strong winds blew. Faced with the alliance between Hugh and Romanus Lecapenus, Salerno in 943 welcomed a visiting Byzantine *protospatarius*.[25] And in this same period a few Capuan-Beneventan indictions included Byzantine regnal dating.[26] There were no other submissive gestures, but also, for the moment, no further anti-Byzantine campaigns.

Instead, there was now, briefly, confrontation within Campania. Compared with the Byzantine regions, Campania had suffered relatively little disruption for decades. There is a report of Arab sea raiders in 928 demanding tribute from both Naples and Salerno.[27] And in 937 a fierce Hungarian raid struck Beneventan and Capuan territory and even the area around Naples, ending perilously close to the city of Salerno.[28] Yet otherwise life had been relatively calm. Now, however, in 946, Guaimar II died, and the Capuans threatened Salerno.

After Atenolf's death in 912, Capua-Benevento had been jointly ruled by his sons Landolf and Atenolf II. And in the early 940s the succession passed to a grandson, Landolf II. (The latter designated as co-ruler his own young son, who would be known to history as Pandolf Ironhead, the most ambitious and aggressive Lombard ruler of the tenth century.) When Guaimar died, leaving only a sixteen-year-old heir, Landolf prepared to invade Salerno. He was joined by the Duke of Naples, who doubtless had his eye on some Salernitan territory. Both assumed the young Gisolf would be thought too immature to rule. Landolf could also pretend to some faint claim on Salerno, being doubly related, by marriage, to the Salernitan dynasty.[29]

Landolf, however, had failed to consider two facts. First, Guaimar II, during his forty-six years as prince, had clearly achieved remarkable status. The author of the *Chronicon Salernitanum* extolled him as a flawless ruler, "bellicosissimus" in battle and yet moderate in his approach to governing.[30] There must have been great sentimental preference for continuing the dynasty. Second, Amalfitan interests were involved. Although the next half-century would see Amalfitans even more deeply embedded in the Salernitan economy, during the reign of Guaimar II their involvement was already reflected in Salernitan charters. Amalfitans were frequently mentioned in connection with Salernitan rural property.[31] They also owned houses within the city of Salerno and they lent money to Salernitans. The bishop of Salerno granted a church and its lands to some Amalfitans. And an Amalfitan *comes* bought property at Nocera, a Salernitan market town on the road to Naples.[32]

Not surprisingly, then, Amalfi took a keen interest in what was happening. The young Gisolf, we are told, was strongly backed by the "populus" of Salerno but, in addition, Amalfi rushed in reinforcements. Gisolf was able to mass a force in the pass north of Salerno so quickly that the invading army took one look and turned around. Whereupon the Capuans, much impressed, abandoned their Neapolitan alliance in favor of a "fedus" with Gisolf, and the Capuans and Salernitans proceeded to ravage Naples' territory.[33]

Plainly, Gisolf's reign was off to a promising start, and indeed he was to rule Salerno ably for more than thirty years. Among other attributes, he had a flair for display, which notably enhanced his image and that of his principality. This was first demonstrated eight years after he assumed the throne; in 954, he had the body of St. Matthew the Evangelist brought triumphantly to Salerno. All south Italian sources reported this momentous event (and the cathedral Robert Guiscard later built for St. Matthew is still one of Salerno's glories).[34]

Meanwhile, however, Byzantine southern Italy had been facing new problems. In Apulia, the Hungarians had continued their raids, striking Otranto at the tip of the Italian heel in the late 940s.[35] Byzantine officials did their best to deal with such attacks and also tried to reclaim areas taken by the southern Lombards; on the latter mission, in 949 and 950, Byzantine forces were reported active in upper Apulia.[36] But the Arab threat was particularly worrisome. According to the *Annales Beneventani*, Arabs raided the Gargano peninsula in the early 950s.[37] Moreover, in Calabria, so readily accessible from Sicily, it was no longer merely a matter of raids. By 952, Sicilian Arabs were so securely established in parts of Calabria that, in a truce signed then, Constantinople was forced to accept the building of a mosque at Reggio.[38]

This struggle over Calabria continued until the latter 960s. It is amply documented, in many sources. Both Byzantine and Fatimid fleets were involved, in addition to land forces, and there were major sea battles in the Straits of Messina. The momentum swung back and forth; Byzantine armies retook Reggio (and tore down the mosque) but could never achieve a decisive victory. When in 964 Nicephorus II Phocas sent a massive force to invade eastern Sicily, both the army and the supporting fleet met with disaster. At last, in 967, Byzantium agreed to pay substantial annual tribute, and a pact finally ended this decade and a half of heightened conflict.[39]

Both sides were plainly ready for peace. To Constantinople, the Calabrian situation must have seemed painfully reminiscent of events leading up to the loss of Sicily in the previous century. Byzantium had therefore made a major effort, but at great cost. Meanwhile, al-Mu'izz, the Fatimid ruler of North Africa, had also understood the stakes; and on balance his forces had been more successful. By 967, however, al-Mu'izz was looking toward Egypt, temptingly vulnerable because its Ikhshidid rulers were highly unpopular. In 969, the Fatimids would in fact sweep into Egypt and take possession.

In retrospect, the Fatimid decision not to press on against Calabria appears fateful. Victory there would have strengthened the Arab position in the central Mediterranean, in effect compensating for Byzantium's retaking of Crete earlier in that decade. At the time, however, Calabria had plainly seemed insignificant in comparison with Egypt.

To the autonomous areas of southern Italy, the 967 Arab-Byzantine pact seemingly mattered little. In the mid-950s, when the situation in Calabria was particularly grim, a Byzantine delegation had come to Campania, demanding cooperation against the Arabs. Afterward, briefly, Gisolf is identified in charters as *imperialis patricius*. This title quickly disappeared, however; everyone reverted to their old ways as soon as the Byzantine back was turned. Amari speculated that some in Campania may even have reported Byzantium's military plans to the Arabs.[40]

In any event, Calabria was a long way from Campania, and in the 960s very different developments, to the north, were capturing local attention. In 961, there was a preamble of sorts. Landolf II, senior co-ruler of Capua-Benevento, died, and suddenly a papal army marched south; Pope John XII, no doubt invoking old Carolingian grants, seemed bent on seizing Capua. This attempt proved ill-advised; Gisolf of Salerno rushed to Capua's aid, and mere word of his approach, we are told, was enough to disperse the papal forces.[41] Actually, since the new ruler of Capua was the redoubtable Pandolf Ironhead, it seems unlikely that Gisolf deserved all the credit. Nonetheless, the upshot was a moment of glory for Gisolf, since Pope John now asked him to a meeting at Terracina. And when Gisolf arrived there, with a magnificent retinue, the pope and his companions were said to have exclaimed, in awe, "At last we see [the marvels] we have long heard of!" Altogether, the author of the *Chronicon Salernitanum* surpasses himself in this passage, concluding with the ringing statement that everyone—Greeks, Arabs, Franks and Saxons—now revered Gisolf, and his subjects rejoiced, and feared no one.[42]

Otto the Great in Southern Italy

It is no wonder that the *Chronicon*'s author made much of the Terracina meeting; in retrospect, it must have seemed the high point of Gisolf's reign. For within months (in February 962) Otto the Great came to Rome to be crowned emperor. Perhaps the full implication for southern Italy was not immediately apparent. It may not have been widely known that Otto, while in Rome, reconfirmed papal rights to large areas of the south.[43] And if the stay at Rome stimulated Otto's interest in southern Italy, that too may not yet have been clear. Yet in September 962 we find Gisolf and his wife,

Gemma, making an extraordinarily large gift of lands to Monte Cassino, now restored to its traditional site and aggressively seeking to expand its holdings.[44] Possibly Gisolf merely wished to reinforce his new image. But he may also have sensed now a need for powerful friends, and Monte Cassino had a tradition of strong links with all western emperors.[45]

If Gisolf did feel concern, he was prescient, for Lombard southern Italy, after decades of relative isolation, was about to become entangled in a major power struggle. One indication came within two years. Pope John XII, in trouble with Otto for associating with the rebellious Berengar and Adalbert, tried to turn to Constantinople. His legates, however, were intercepted—and in Capuan territory.[46] Pandolf Ironhead was plainly seeking Otto's favor. Highly ambitious, Pandolf surely hoped thus to become a player on a larger stage. He may also already have envisioned Otto helping to reclaim Beneventan territory from Byzantium.

Meanwhile, at Constantinople in 963, Nicephorus II Phocas had become emperor. At first, facing many other problems, he appeared disinclined to worry about southern Italy (except for the Arabs in Calabria). For some time, Otto, too, was focused elsewhere, on the papacy. He tried to replace the intransigent John XII with a nominee of his own (Leo VIII), but the Romans threw Leo out. Finally, however, in January 967, Otto's second nominee, John XIII, was securely installed in Rome. Now Otto could look south.

It is interesting to note the difference in behavior, to this point, between Pandolf Ironhead and Gisolf. Pandolf, having committed himself to Otto early on, never wavered, whereas Gisolf, at least initially, appeared to side with Otto's opposition. In February 964, the bishop of Salerno attended a council convened by John XII against Otto and his "anti-Pope" Leo.[47] But Pandolf sheltered John XIII, Otto's second nominee, when the latter was temporarily driven from Rome.[48]

By the time Otto returned to Rome in January 967 to reinstall John XIII, Pandolf's loyalty had been rewarded. In an act signed then by Otto, Pandolf is mentioned not only as ruler of Capua-Benevento but also as margrave of Camerino and duke of Spoleto. Otto, still opposed by north Italians allied with Berengar and Adalbert, presumably saw Pandolf as someone who could hold central Italy for him.[49]

The next month, doubtless both to honor Pandolf and to see for himself the south Italian situation, Otto made his first trip into that region. He visited Benevento, and perhaps also Capua.[50] And a year later, in January and February 968, Otto was back again, spending time in both

Benevento and Capua.[51] By now, marking Pandolf's new importance, Capua had been made an archbishopric, the first in southern Italy.[52]

At some point while at Capua, Otto sent a message to Salerno, requesting Gisolf's presence. Gisolf, we are told, was nervous about this invitation, but could hardly refuse to go since the message stressed that Adelaide was with Otto—and, as Gisolf's "sister," longed to see him.[53] This statement in the *Chronicon Salernitanum* is puzzling; there is no evidence of any relationship. Michelangelo Schipa, convinced that the *Chronicon* could not be totally wrong and noting that Leo Marsicanus described Adelaide as "ex proceribus Tuscie," hypothesized some central Italian connection by way of Gisolf's grandmother, Idta of Spoleto.[54] Yet according to Liutprand, Adelaide was the daughter of Rudolf II of Burgundy and Bertha of Swabia. Perhaps, then, we should consider a relationship deriving from some common godparent.[55] In any event, Gisolf did go to Capua, and there (according to the *Chronicon*) he was lovingly embraced by Adelaide and showered with gifts, including a magnificent horse with a golden saddle.[56] Afterward, no doubt with considerable relief, he went home to Salerno, not having had to declare submission.

In the late winter of 968, at the conclusion of his second visit to Pandolf's principalities, Otto led an army into Byzantine Apulia. Heading southeast from Benevento, the invaders apparently slashed and burned as they went, taking at least some Byzantine outposts. But Otto's prime objective was Bari, and by some time in March he was besieging that major port, Byzantium's administrative center for the theme of Longobardia.[57]

Unfortunately for Otto, early medieval Bari (protected on three sides by water) was virtually impregnable—as Louis II had found. Thus, with the army stalled there, the grand scheme of sending Liutprand to Constantinople was hatched. Embassies had been going back and forth for a year to no avail.[58] Now Otto and Liutprand would make an ingenious (if misguided) attempt to snatch victory from defeat.

Liutprand's embassy in that summer of 968 is too well known to warrant description here, but it is instructive to consider some aspects from a south Italian perspective. First, in the tirades to which Liutprand was subjected, one theme recurred again and again. Otto was repeatedly charged with having subverted "servos" rightfully belonging to the Byzantine Empire: the princes of Capua and Benevento. (Pandolf now had as co-ruler his brother Landolf III; technically, the latter was Prince of Benevento, and Pandolf was Prince of Capua.) Nothing seems to have angered Nicephorus Phocas more. At one point, he claimed that the princes wished to return to the Byzantine fold but were prevented by Otto; at other times he shouted that they would be severely punished.[59] The illusory nature of southern Lombard loyalty to Byzantium had in fact been exposed by Otto.

While Nicephorus Phocas gleefully noted that Bari had not fallen, Otto was castigated for the ravaging of Byzantine territory.[60] Indeed, the angry references to widespread depredations (and to the Lombard princes) make one wonder if there had not been action even before Otto's brief spring campaign. In the summer of 967, Nicephorus Phocas had abandoned an expedition against the "Assyrians" on word that Otto was then about to attack southern Italy.[61] Perhaps that supposed "servus" of the empire, Pandolf Ironhead—acting with Otto's approval—had already begun preliminary probes.[62]

In any case, one wonders what Pandolf thought of the plan to send Liutprand to Constantinople. Liutprand was to say that the siege of Bari had been called off as a gesture of goodwill on the part of Otto, who would now generously turn over Apulia in return for a marriage alliance.[63] Pandolf should have known this would strike any Byzantine as appalling effrontery, especially since Otto, so far, had hardly demonstrated impressive strength in the south. Perhaps Otto (or Pandolf) had actually done more damage than the meager sources indicate, but the claim that Bari had been "spared" was disingenuous at best.

Predictably, Nicephorus Phocas dismissed with contempt all of Liutprand's overtures, asserting that Byzantine forces would quickly restore order—and punish the traitorous Lombard princes.[64] (He had, after all, just wrung a peace agreement from the Fatimids, no mean achievement.) Otto, however, then resumed his campaign, and in the winter of 968–69 apparently met with some success even in distant Calabria. And in May he was back in Apulia, besieging Bovino, a former Beneventan *castrum* now held by the Byzantines. But then Otto's campaign foundered; he had to return north, leaving Pandolf to continue the siege—and Pandolf was captured outside Bovino and sent prisoner to Constantinople.[65] Byzantine forces promptly invaded Campania, took Avellino (on the Salerno-Capua border) and laid siege to the city of Capua. That siege failed, but the Byzantine army, joined now by Neapolitans, did severe damage to Capuan and Beneventan lands. And afterward the *strategos* rested for a few days in Gisolf's city of Salerno, where Gisolf made a great show of providing sumptuous entertainment.[66]

Yet Otto was not ready to admit defeat. When word of these developments reached the north, an army of "Germans, Saxons, and Spoletans" was rushed down, shortly followed by Otto himself. Avellino and several other towns were retaken, and Naples was punished.[67] Both sides appeared committed to a long and bloody struggle, with Campania sure to suffer.

Then suddenly, in December 969, Nicephorus Phocas was assassinated. John Zimiskes, his successor, immediately instituted major changes in policy. Pandolf was dispatched to Otto to revive the proposed marriage alliance, and in 972 Theophano became the bride of the future Otto II. Before the marriage, Otto did once again visit Pandolf's Capua, but he conducted no further operations in southern Italy.[68]

It is easy to understand why Nicephorus Phocas and Otto had battled over southern Italy. The Byzantines had always viewed southern Italy as rightfully theirs. For Otto, acquisition of southern Italy would certainly have meant enhanced prestige. And for both there were also revenue considerations, and not merely the taxes that could be levied; Nicephorus Phocas raged to Liutprand that the fathers and grandfathers of the princes of Capua had always paid tribute to the Byzantine emperor.[69]

But, for us, the most interesting aspect of this struggle is the contrast in behavior between Pandolf and Gisolf. Western historians may be tempted to see Pandolf as a forward-looking proto-European and Gisolf as lacking in spirit. But we must remember the geography. Benevento, in particular, was caught between the two empires; Pandolf had to choose. And since Benevento had suffered much at Byzantine hands, Otto must have seemed to Pandolf the obvious choice.[70]

Salerno, however, had—or was allowed—another option. Otto apparently never pressed Gisolf to declare himself. Perhaps this was because of Salerno's location; enforcing Salernitan obedience, had that proved necessary, would have meant diverting troops. Perhaps Gisolf's relationship to Adelaide (whatever it was) softened Otto's attitude. In any event, Salerno was able to maintain its somewhat ambiguous relationship with Byzantium, even entertaining the *strategos* who invaded Campania. And despite that, when Otto's forces reclaimed Campanian territory (and punished Naples), Salerno was spared. Somehow, Gisolf had managed to retain the option of neutrality.

Moving Toward *Opulentia*

Notably, in his tirades to Liutprand, Nicephorus Phocas never mentioned Salerno, and Otto never went there. But this did not mean that Salerno counted for little; Gisolf had simply lain low, avoiding attention. He undoubtedly shared the sentiments of the *Chronicon*'s author, who praised Nicephorus Phocas as a good and just man—presumably because he had largely left Salerno alone.[71]

The Cava charters suggest that Gisolf had much to protect. In the absence of adequate documentation for most of tenth-century Campania, we can never know to what degree (or whether) Salerno was exceptional. Many characteristics of Gisolf's principality do appear to have been mirrored elsewhere. Nonetheless, it seems reasonable to assume that Salerno was at least somewhat more prosperous, thanks to its Amalfitan ties.

The city of Salerno, capital of Gisolf's principality, was a Roman town fortified by Arichis in the late eighth century. Even before Arichis, it was called a *castrum*, but Arichis and his successors had apparently expanded its walls so that they encompassed not only the palace and several churches but also a sizable popular quarter and even fields and orchards.[72] On the heights above the city the Lombards built a *turris* or defensive castle, whose ruins, visible from the autostrada, are still impressive. This stronghold provided refuge in times of trouble and could also serve as a watch post for surveying the coastal waters and the land routes north and south.

In addition to the city of Salerno, there were other *castra* within the principality, some serving as bases for gastalds. Gastalds also functioned in and around the palace. In the settling of disputes, *judices* now played the primary role, but gastalds also bore significant responsibility for justice, and not only in the outlying areas.[73]

Gastalds and *judices* alike adhered scrupulously to Lombard law, or at least continuously cited it. Actually, this adherence was not as pure as the southern Lombards thought; inevitably, there was some infiltration of Roman custom. Yet Lombard law formed a crucial element in the ethnic pride of the southern Lombards. We find, for example, both *mundium* and *morgencap* strictly observed.[74] Altogether, the Salernitan records convey the impression of a society bonded and strengthened by well-understood, traditional structures.

Far less documentation is available for Capua-Benevento, but presumably traditional Lombard structures largely prevailed there as well. And, reinforcing custom, both formal contracts and notaries surely proliferated within Capua and Benevento in the tenth century, as they did within Salerno. An active notariate was not a new development. For the ninth century, in the rural areas of the principality of Salerno, the charters show notaries moving between market towns.[75] But notaries had not then achieved their ultimate status; they were merely scribes, recording private agreements and with no official standing. Only in the tenth century do we begin to find some enhancement of their role: more standardization within the charters and also fewer witnesses, which at least suggests greater confidence then in professionally drafted instruments.[76]

We can give only glancing attention here to the evolution of compliance mechanisms, one of the most interesting developments revealed by the Cava charters. In the ninth century, inadequate enforcement techniques, combined with an apparent lack of ready money, had plainly created problems. In contracts relating to the sale of land, sellers did promise to pay large penalties if unable to deliver clear title or undisturbed possession, but everyone seemingly knew such penalties to be uncollectible. Alternative compositions were thus often written into the contract. One nice example occurs in an 850 sale involving a vineyard and orchard; if the seller's relatives, disregarding the sale, come back onto the property and take fruit, the buyer can take equivalent produce from the seller's other lands.[77] What would now be considered criminal cases could also present problems. In 894, two gastalds found a man guilty of rape and assessed a fine of 90 *solidi*, payable half to the victim and half to the palace. But the culprit protested that he did not have 90 *solidi*, and so the gastalds, clearly at a loss, could only order him "seized by the hair of his head" and turned over to the victim's family.[78]

In the tenth century, we find more use of *guadia* (pledges) and *mediatores* (guarantors) in Salernitan contracts. In other words, an old Lombard mechanism for the general control of behavior now strengthened notarial transactions. (Sometimes, but by no means always, the guarantor was a family member; otherwise, family members seemed no longer responsible for their relatives' debts or conduct.) In addition, ecclesiastical institutions and prominent families were now routinely represented by *advocatores*. Something resembling the legal profession had arrived—to the disadvantage, usually, of lesser folk.[79]

Yet some traditional approaches lingered, in combination with lawyers and written records. This commingling of old and new is splendidly illustrated in four documents otherwise celebrated as the first to include vernacular phrases. All four were drafted in Capuan territory in the 960s, by Capuan notaries, and all four show ecclesiastical institutions contesting the ownership of land with laymen. (In one instance it is Monte Cassino; in another, a more obscure monastery, and in two cases a convent.) Witnesses abound, on both sides, and swear on the gospels and in one case on relics.

The *judex* interrogates the witnesses in private, to ensure no undue pressure, and the court adjourns to the disputed property so that the *judex* can see for himself the physical situation. But in the end the decisions all favored the ecclesiastical institutions and hinged on two vital elements: the victors had sworn (the vernacular oath) to having used or occupied the land for thirty years, and the plaintiffs could provide no written evidence to support their claims.[80]

In Salerno, at this time, one often encounters many of these same procedures but, overall, less attention to oaths and more reliance on written records; in Salernitan disputes, both sides frequently now produced many documents.[81] Yet the Capuan examples have one aspect in common with typical Salernitan cases; all the principals have Lombard names. In Salerno there was, of course, the Amalfitan presence; otherwise, however, all property seemed held or leased exclusively by ethnic Lombards.[82] One might have expected to encounter, at least among those contracting to work very small pieces of land, occasional representatives of a surviving non-Lombard population. But if any such did survive, in a position to hold or lease land, they left no trace in the charters.

Little from the tenth century remains visible today, and what there is is hardly impressive in scale. Nonetheless, within the city of Salerno the charters indicate much building and enhancing of both ecclesiastical structures and dwelling places.[83] It all suggests an economy moving forward, and we can now turn to the particulars of that economy.

Overall, charter evidence for the autonomous areas of southern Italy is uneven in distribution and often frustrating in its diverse terminology. Nonetheless, some patterns emerge. The first relates to coinage. In ninth-century Campania, there had been considerable variation. Naples had gone its own way, minting at least copper coins, and otherwise presumably using Byzantine *solidi* and whatever else came to hand.[84] As for the southern Lombards, Arichis in the late eighth century had issued his own gold *solidi* and *tremisses*, well designed and of respectable fineness. For some time, his successors had apparently held to an equally sound standard. But after Salerno separated from Benevento, the Salernitan coinage seemed to deteriorate. In the 860s, charters began specifying payment in the old *tremisses* of Arichis, surely by then not easy to come by but apparently regarded as the sole dependable coin.[85] Later, when Louis II was active in southern Italy, southern Lombard rulers commenced issuing silver *denarii*, including some honoring Louis and Engelberga. And when Capua was allied with Pope John VIII, its *denarii* bore his image.[86]

Early in the tenth century, however, as life in this region stabilized, the approach to currency stabilized too. Gold *tari* (the local term for Fatimid quarter-dinars) began to be specified for transactions throughout most of Campania.[87] It is not clear how soon (or how many) local rulers minted their own *tari*. The first indisputably local issue (usually thought Salernitan) was modeled on the coinage of al-Mu'izz, instigator of the Calabrian campaigns of the 950s and thus a contemporary of Gisolf. In any case, Sicilian and North African *tari* also circulated.[88]

Interestingly, despite opposition to Byzantine political control, Byzantine *solidi* continued to be cited in the penalty clauses of tenth-century charters.[89] But prices were virtually always now quoted in *tari*.[90] This not only indicates the importance of trade with the Islamic world; such new constancy in currency also suggests a society focused now on its economy.

More or less coincidental with the adoption of *tari*, we find in the principality of Salerno a gradual shift from outright sales of land to innovative leasing. The ninth-century charter evidence is comparatively thin, perhaps not a dependable sample. Nonetheless, for the entire ninth century there are no Salernitan leases, only sales of land. Even in the reign of Guaimar I (880–900), the closest we come to leases is two charters with money advanced "in muctuum" but "asque opera" (without interest), the recipient instead to work the lender's land for the period of the loan.[91] Then under Guaimar II (900–946) the charters show, in addition to eleven sales, nine leases. And under Gisolf (946–77), we find fifteen sales—and thirty-five leases.[92]

The majority of these leases (indeed all, until after midcentury) employed inducements to expand cultivation. Most were characterized by a new term, "pastenare" (or "ad pastenandum"). In the Roman era, the *pastinum*, a pronged hoe, had been associated with the deep cultivation thought vital for good vine growth. In tenth-century south Italian contracts, "pastenare" and "ad pastenandum" implied new plantings of any sort.[93] Lay landowners in the Salerno region, particularly during the first three-quarters of the century, favored a *pastenare* lease that ran for a relatively short period, usually ten years. The lessee was to bring the land into cultivation in the manner outlined in the lease (planting vines, typically, or specified varieties of trees) and no shares were normally due the landowner until the latter part of the lease period.

No shares at the start was not a novel concept; although not previously encountered in southern Italy, something of the sort had already appeared in the north.[94] Yet one version of the *pastenare* lease, *pastenare ad partionem*, was indeed new, at least in the breadth of its application. At the conclusion of these leases, the lessee acquired outright ownership of one-half (sometimes one-third) of the land, whether woodland, vineyard, or arable. In the north, such division agreements were apparently encountered only in connection with vineyards.

In the *Codex Diplomaticus Cavensis*, the first Salernitan charter to use the term *pustenare* comes in 936. The lay owner of a small property grants a six-year lease to two brothers, who are to plant willows and graft chestnut (or possibly fruit) trees; at the end of the period, the land is to be divided, half-and-half. Furthermore, if the original owner ever decides to sell his share, the brothers will have first option, with thirty-six days to raise the money.[95]

Two decades before this 936 charter, local ecclesiastical landowners had also begun feeling their way toward some means of attracting men to work land and improve it. In 913, the abbot of St. Maximus (that major foundation of the Salernitan dynasty) had leased out a vineyard for ten years. For the first three years, the lessee would keep all "de ipso frugio"; after that, the "fruits" were to be divided half-and-half. And if the lessee wished to leave at any time during the lease period, voiding the agreement, he was free to do so.[96] The wider implications of this last provision are obvious (and will be discussed in Chapter 7). In any case, however, by midcentury this first tentative approach had evolved into the type of *pastenare* contract particularly favored by St. Maximus. These later St. Maximus leases usually ran for long periods, sometimes indefinitely (or for the life of the lessee). But the exemption from shares now ran equally long, usually ten years. Moreover, beginning in 979, some St. Maximus leases even stated that, if the lessee left for some reason, he could nonetheless reclaim the leasehold if he returned within three or four years.[97]

It is noteworthy that (with one exception) it was only lay landowners whose *pastenare* leases led to an actual division of property. St. Maximus certainly offered generous terms but almost never surrendered land. But whatever the variations, all of these contracts indicate that large areas had gone uncultivated for a long time. Again and again, the land leased is described as "vacua." The continual Arab raids of the ninth century (and the intra-Lombard battling) must literally have diminished the population, and scared survivors off the land. In the 940s, we still read of a former vineyard now "in desolatione et debastatione [sic]" and of "multa [terra] inculta" because of past Arab actions.[98] Furthermore, fear had plainly continued to be an inhibiting factor. Actually, this portion of southern Italy would never again suffer from Arab raids, but contemporaries could hardly have known that.[99]

The entrepreneurial development reflected in the Salernitan charters was not restricted to Salernitans. As we might expect, Amalfitans, too, were interested in enhancing agricultural yield. They, too, employed *pastenare* leases, and we also find some among the (relatively few) tenth-century charters from Naples.[100] Some comparison with the rest of tenth-century southern Italy would therefore be helpful. And fortunately, though the Byzantine regions have left virtually no charters, documentation is available from one other area: that dominated by the great monasteries of Monte Cassino and San Vincenzo al Volturno. The evidence from San Vincenzo is particularly interesting.

When monks returned to Monte Cassino in the middle of the tenth century, they found the surrounding region "neglectus ac destitutus et quasi desolatus."[101] Earlier (apparently by 916), the San Vincenzo community had also returned from exile in Capua, to find a similar scene. The monastery of San Vincenzo held rights over an impressively large area, just to the east of Monte Cassino's home territory.[102] At first, noting a need for money to restore the monastic buildings, San Vincenzo's abbots offered leases strictly for cash: either lump sums or annual money rents. Moreover, then as later, they typically offered long leases, usually for twenty-nine years; and in these earlier ones they showed little concern about the use to be made of the land. By 939, however, we begin to find an emphasis on rural repopulation and expanded cultivation. In that year, a twenty-nine-year lease, to nineteen men, required them to bring their "familia et animalia" to live on and work their new holdings. Next, in 945, a similar long lease forgave shares during the first four years, stressing that the land was to be brought into productivity ("ad cultum perducere"). And in 950 another such lease (again to men coming with their families and animals) was generous in its share provisions and for the first time included the term *pastenare*.[103]

Nonetheless, there were marked differences from what was taking place in the Salerno region. San Vincenzo either leased out huge estates (including settlements, churches, and extensive water rights) or else leased several sizable plots simultaneously to groups of men. Perhaps inevitably, since such leases involved varied terrain, they typically included only generalized references to agricultural activity. Altogether, it was macromanagement; San Vincenzo's abbots aimed at rationalizing their territory. They were concerned less with immediate benefit, more with productivity over the long term and with stability. In the second half of the tenth century, we find in these leases a growing emphasis on core settlements—in other words, the socioeconomic version of *incastellamento*. (*Incastellamento*, that thorny issue, receives further attention in Chapter 7.)

The situation within the principality of Salerno was totally different. In the Salerno region, at the start of the tenth century, there clearly were many small, independently owned plots; perhaps for this reason we find there more agricultural innovation. But something else was at work too; Salernitan landowners, in the tenth century, seemed to be responding to market forces.

J. K. Hyde has observed that increased commerce can hardly explain the economic revival that began in Italy in this period because commerce "would have benefited in the first instance only the sea ports and a few key inland centres."[104] In fact, however, the availability of a market for products can have a profoundly stimulating ripple effect, as economists studying underdeveloped regions have long known.[105] The *pastenare* contracts of the Salerno area seem to provide a textbook example of this. While San Vincenzo's abbots certainly encouraged cultivation, Salerno's tenth-century landlords seemingly had a very specific goal: cash crops. Among the plantings stipulated, vines predominated, but second in frequency came chestnut and hazelnut trees.[106] These could have provided a range of salable products, as was noted in Chapter 5: not only high-quality hardwood and nuts but also (in the case of chestnut trees) bark for tanning. Chestnuts must have been particularly valued, for chestnut meal was a substitute for flour—not as desirable as wheat flour, but still used as an alternative even in nineteenth-century southern Italy.[107]

Perhaps much of this produce was aimed at local consumption. Yet we must believe that some was pointed toward more distant markets—perhaps elsewhere along the Italian coast, perhaps even farther away—and therefore that at least some of this activity was related to Amalfi's interest in having something to purvey. Certainly the Amalfitans themselves were extremely demanding landlords.[108] Moreover, they were steadily acquiring ever more property within the principality of Salerno and vigorously defending their holdings there. In Salerno in the decade of the 960s, for example, Amalfitans figured in five of seven land disputes.[109] Their own sustenance needs (even the status value of land) could hardly have accounted for this avid interest in agricultural development and in productivity of a very specific sort. It must have reflected, at least in part, a desire to stock their ventures.

Since we have few tenth-century charters from Naples (let alone far-ther afield), we cannot tell how widely the "Amalfitan effect" may have been felt. It may not even be totally fair to call it the "Amalfitan effect"; other influences were doubtless at work. Campania, after all, had a long history of commercial agriculture; if Apulia had been the grain basket of Roman Italy, the area of great latifundia, Campania had been its market garden. More-over, vineyards had figured in ninth-century Campanian sale charters, and local viticulture still employed such Roman techniques as training vines on very high stakes or arbors, which suggests at least some continuity.[110] Nevertheless, all available evidence indicates that agriculture had suffered grievously for half a millennium. Something now stimulated a leap for-ward. No doubt it was in part the new political stability and the freedom from raids, but surely it was also the marketing opportunities provided by the Amalfitans.

Pastenare contracts continued hereabouts even into the twelfth cen-tury.[111] But *pastenare in partionem* contracts (leading to a division of land) were particularly characteristic of the first surge in development. Thereaf-ter, interest in agricultural land remained strong, but the charters show changes in both leasing and landholding patterns. First, after midcentury we start to encounter lay leases of a more conventional sort, with shares from the beginning and no dividing of the property.[112] And by the latter part of the tenth century we note far fewer small landowners in the Saler-nitan charters. By then, *maiores* and ecclesiastical institutions seemed in-creasingly dominant; charters concerning their lands proliferate.

Of course, powerful men had always sought to increase their holdings. Locally, ninth-century charters had given ample evidence of this. And during the reign of Guaimar II (900–946) he, togther with a member of his family and an Amalfitan *comes*, accounted for four of the eleven recorded land acquisitions. Yet in the second half of the tenth century all indicators point to an increasing concentration of land wealth. We find, as never in the first half of the century, lands leased out by men who hold them *in bene-ficium*.[113] And in a representative year at the end of the century (994), all of those shown in Salerno's charters to be leasing out land were powerful men: a ruler's son, a count, an abbot. Otherwise in that year (aside from intrafamilial divisions of property) we find only a dispute between two abbots over water rights, two gifts of land (one a huge estate) to ecclesiasti-cal institutions, and two instances of abbots enhancing monastic holdings through land trades.[114] The old, simpler, more intimate relationships— owners of small properties leasing to men who would personally cultivate the holdings—virtually fade from view.

The chief benefits of the economic takeoff thus accrued to the *maiores*. In any case, however, the Salerno region now seemed to contemporaries impressively prosperous. Some of the principality's coins would bear the legend "Opulenta Salerno," and that appears to have been a fair description.[115] Of course, it was only relative opulence, measured against an early medieval standard. Nonetheless, there plainly was a marked contrast with darker, earlier days.

The tenth-century author of the *Chronicon Salernitanum* would doubtless have credited this prosperity to Guaimar II and Gisolf and to the stable government they had provided. That must indeed have been a major factor, and one we must not forget even as we consider market forces. Notably, though they were quick to defend their principality when threatened, neither Guaimar II nor Gisolf showed any interest in enlarging their territory. In this—in their disinterest in territorial aggrandizement and their apparent recognition of a better way toward economic advance—these rulers seem to have been ahead of their time.

7. The Late Tenth Century and South Italian Structures

IT IS TIME NOW TO MOVE FROM the particular (Amalfi and Salerno) to the general and to consider the south Italian scene as a whole as the tenth century drew to a close. This chapter will focus chiefly on the structures of the society, its institutions and patterns of behavior. Although evidence is far more profuse for some areas than others, it is possible to reach at least a few broad conclusions.

Growth or Development?

In the preceding chapter, the term "development" was on occasion used in relation to tenth-century Salerno and its economy. But as J. D. Gould has suggested, one should perhaps differentiate between "development" and "growth." "Growth," according to Gould, is the appropriate term for "a sustained increase in real *per capita* income"; "development" is best reserved for something broader and more auspicious: growth accompanied by sustained structural change.[1] Gould was, of course, not discussing early medieval Europe, for which we have no way of measuring per capita income. And by "structural change" Gould chiefly meant economic diversification of a sort one could hardly expect in the tenth century. Nonetheless, Gould's distinction is provocative and it can be highly useful; we need only apply it in a manner more befitting a medieval model. For our purposes, "growth" must be translated as simply a sustained (if not per capita) increase in wealth, and for "structural change" we must look to the general structure of the society.

In Campania, in the latter half of the tenth century, we see no evidence of structural change in the sense of new societal configurations likely to underpin and promote long-term advance. Within the principality of Salerno, the rich simply got richer, the powerful more powerful. Neither there, nor in Benevento and Capua, nor at Naples, do we see a significant middle class emerging. Indeed our Salerno sample suggests that, if anything, the "middling class" suffered in the course of the tenth century. With dynasties now firmly established, the *populus* no longer played its historic role (however minimal) in the choice of leader. Small, independent land-owners seem to have lost ground—literally. Furthermore, the church sup-plied no countervailing power; nowhere in Campania do we find bishops challenging the local rulers. Altogether, while the *maiores* were increasingly prosperous—"growth," of a sort—the society was not exhibiting greater diversification. Rather the reverse.

Such a pattern was of course hardly uncommon in tenth-century Europe. Yet Campania had characteristics that may have made "develop-ment" particularly unlikely. In other parts of Europe, we often find correla-tion between economic improvement and the emerging of towns. In many cases, these towns gradually took on a life of their own, eventually creating a new force within their regions. But Campania already had its towns. Unimpressive though some were in comparison with the Roman era, nonetheless these towns had continuously served as focal points. Further-more, the established order was urban-centered. Within each of the inde-pendent principalities and duchies, the ruler was based at, and governed from, the chief town or city: the Prince of Salerno from the city of Salerno, the Prince of Capua from the city of Capua, the Duke of Naples from Naples. Within the Lombard principalities, even in the lesser towns there typically was a gastald, exercising local control. In tenth-century Campania, in other words, the towns already functioned as core elements within firmly governed polities.

To be sure, there were areas in northern Europe (and for that matter in northern Italy) where one found precommunal stirrings even in towns dominated by an entrenched local aristocracy. Sometimes, indeed, the local aristocracy was itself responsible for these stirrings. Within the Lombard principalities, however, stability of rule in the tenth century, reinforced by Lombard law and tradition, held the social fabric firmly in place. And although governance in Naples relied less on formal codes, there, too, it appears, a firmly structured hierarchy of power and control prevailed.

In such stable environments, agriculture could flourish and its surplus could be marketed. But as the tenth century wore on, the whole in-creasingly resembled a court economy, with wealth going mainly into conspicuous consumption: more rich ornament, more luxury goods. We encounter goldsmiths in the Cava charters, and a shoemaker, but otherwise few representatives of a middling class except for notaries—and their chief task now was to record the acquiring of ever more land by the *maiores*.[2]

Possibly the very fact of Amalfi helped to explain the nonemergence of a significant commercial sector elsewhere in the region. Tenth-century Amalfitans, so avid for aristocratic titles, would not have liked to be viewed as middle-class surrogates. Yet their activities placed them in that role. Neither Salerno nor Naples could feel the lack of a significant merchant element so long as they had the services of the Amalfitans. And the Amalfitans were certainly entrepreneurial in behavior, not only abroad but also nearer home. For example, in Chapter 5 it was noted that (like other Amalfitans) individuals from the little Amalfitan port of Atrani leased and purchased Salernitan properties, including a particularly impressive purchase in 977. On that occasion, a consortium of Atranesi bought from the bishop of Paestum two large tracts of land in the Cilento area (below Paestum) for 1,010 and 1,050 pounds of silver respectively. The contracts describe some consortial members as absent from the formal transactions because "ad navigandum sunt," so these were apparently seafaring traders applying their profits to agricultural enterprise. Furthermore, judging from some of the contractual provisions, they were using their maritime experience with the *colonna* system; they plainly were comfortable with the complex structures of shared endeavors.[3]

The charters do not show Salernitans (or Neapolitans) combining in this organized manner, for profit. Neither do we find anything of the sort elsewhere in the autonomous areas beyond Campania; the leasing of San Vincenzo al Volturno property to groups of men (who were to bring their families and work the land) had a very different flavor.[4]

In relation to precommunal tendencies, Del Treppo noted "i germi di una organizzazione communale" within territory held by Monte Cassino, citing in particular an episode in 997.[5] But no one has identified any other example.

It is true that, in the Byzantine-held areas, the urban population seems to have become increasingly active. A reference in the late tenth century indicates that merchants from Bari frequented Constantinople.[6] That in itself is not surprising; Bari was always an active port. But in addition, at Bari and some of the other major towns of Apulia, there may have been movements one could call protocommunal. By the latter tenth century, Byzantine southern Italy was divided into two themes: Longobardia, centered at Bari, and Calabria.[7] We know almost nothing about the controls imposed within these themes because evidence is sparse for the Byzantine regions. But an urban population unhappy not only with Byzantine taxation but also with Byzantine restraints could account for the reported uprisings in Apulia in the early 980s and for the assassinations of Byzantine officials and other troubles shortly afterwards.[8] In Apulia, of course, ethnic Lombards predominated, so resistance to Byzantine rule might be expected. But there are indications of town-centered discontent even in the "Greek" areas; in Calabria, in this same general period, there was the rebellious behavior at Rossano.[9]

Perhaps, then, we cannot rule out some tendency toward genuine social evolution within Byzantine southern Italy. Yet in the final quarter of the tenth century, as we shall see, the Byzantine regions once again became subject to severe Arab raids. Thus, even in the absence of official restraints, forward movement there would likely have been hampered.

Altogether, one should perhaps think of southern Italy at the very end of the tenth century as poised for change but not quite ready to move to a new phase. Some growth presumably continued, building on foundations established earlier. Even at Amalfi, however, Bruno Figliuolo has discerned a temporary slowing of momentum, internally, at the century's end.[10]

The Ottonian Effect

A pause may well have been needed in order to assimilate all of the changes that had already taken place. For southern Italy had obviously altered greatly over the preceding two hundred years. In Campania, moreover, the ten years following the death of Otto the Great in 973 had been tumultuous.

The disarray was caused in part by the wider Italian involvements of Pandolf Ironhead; the boundary between southern and northern Italy had begun to crumble, and locally old relationships no longer held firm. Increased wealth must also have heightened temptations to disorder. In any case, from 973 to 983 there were rumblings and coups, particularly centered on Salerno but involving other Campanian states as well. The entire ten-year period resembled a rolling storm, with the last thunderous burst in 982 when Otto II suffered a devastating defeat in Calabria at the hands of the Arabs. In the aftermath, Otto II died, in 983, and his regent-successors evinced no interest in southern Italy. Campania was thus once again left alone, at least until the last years of the century. But key southern Lombards had been killed fighting alongside Otto II. For that and other reasons, Campania after 983 was substantially altered.

Otto II's campaign into southern Italy needs to be tracked, but it is important first to note the situation in Campania in the decade in which he came south. Trouble had begun with a coup in Salerno in 973, the direct result of one of the most admirable Lombard traits, devotion to family. Lombard law dealt extensively with family issues, but in addition the Cava charters are replete with examples of genuine family feeling at all levels of society.[11] Royal families were no exception. Gaitelgrime, the mother of Gisolf of Salerno, was a Capuan, granddaughter of Atenolf and cousin to Pandolf Ironhead. Unfortunately, she had a disreputable brother, yet another Landolf; exiled (for good cause) by Pandolf Ironhead, this Landolf had been forced to take refuge in Naples. From there, in the late 960s, he appealed to his sister Gaitelgrime, and her tearful pleas persuaded Gisolf to make a place for this reprobate and his four equally disreputable sons. Landolf was made gastald of Conza, and his sons were also granted Salernitan territories, complete with "omnia fiscalia."[12] (One of the sons, exceptionally cruel and extortionate, therefore became a threat to a Byzantine hermit-saint living just south of Salerno's borders.)[13]

The *Chronicon Salernitanum* paints a devastating picture of Landolf of Conza and his sons. Yet by 973 Landolf had persuaded both the Duke of Naples and the young Duke of Amalfi, Manso III, to support him in a coup. Gisolf and his wife, Gemma, were seized late one night in their palace and carried off to Amalfi, and Landolf of Conza assumed Salerno's throne. He was not to enjoy it long, however. The Amalfitans apparently came to regret their involvement, and those Salernitans who had backed Landolf fell to quarreling over the spoils. Support grew for Gisolf's restoration. The only problem was sufficient military force, and so Gisolf appealed to Pandolf Ironhead, offering formally to adopt and designate as heir one of Pandolf's sons, Pandolf the younger.

Gisolf and Gemma were childless so the direct line would in any case have ended with his death. Meanwhile, however, still only in his mid-forties, Gisolf doubtless expected ample time to void this arrangement if it proved unsatisfactory. With Pandolf's help (and the support of most Salernitans) the restoration was easily accomplished.[14] But Gisolf then suddenly died, in 977, only three years later. The young Pandolf succeeded, and seemingly contrary to the understandings, the widowed Gemma was almost immediately pushed aside. And Pandolf Ironhead became co-ruler with his son, making him master of Salerno in addition to Capua, Benevento, and Spoleto.[15]

This new Lombard empire was probably doomed from the start. A Pandolf Ironhead might hold together such extensive and varied territory, at least for a while. But the governance mechanisms of the southern Lombards had been perfected within mini-states, and when Pandolf Ironhead died in the spring of 981, the unraveling began. In early fall (probably in September) there was another coup in Salerno. The Amalfitans were once again involved, and this time with a more ambitious aim. For the next two years, Amalfi's Duke Manso III would rule both Amalfi and Salerno.[16]

Amalfi in this period was riding the crest. It was about now that the Amalfitan monastery on Mount Athos was established, an indication of its widespread international connections; and at home, later in this decade, the Amalfitans would inaugurate a splendid new cathedral befitting Amalfi's new status as an archbishopric.[17] Fused together, Amalfi and Salerno could constitute a formidable force in southern Italy.

For a short time, it appeared that Manso would retain his new prize. Otto II, just then venturing into southern Italy for the first time, was apparently in Apulia when he heard of Manso's coup. He immediately turned back and after ten days at Benevento headed for Salerno.[18] Mindful of the Ottonian debt to the Capuan dynasty, Otto presumably hoped to dislodge Manso and restore the younger Pandolf to power. He therefore pitched camp on the heights above the city of Salerno and began a siege. But the Salernitans held firm, and Otto was forced to compromise. Manso was allowed to retain Salerno's throne in return for surrendering a son to Otto as hostage for loyal behavior.[19] Later, after the debacle in Calabria, Otto stopped in Manso's Salerno on his way north, and he also supported Salerno's bishop in a struggle with a predatory Capuan.[20]

Manso had thus survived Otto's initial opposition. Moreover, little seemed changed in Salerno under his rule.[21] Amalfitans had increasingly figured in Salernitan land transactions, and this trend now accelerated; but nothing in the local charters indicates any real disruption.[22] Nevertheless, there must have been discontent, for in 983 there was another coup. This time a rather mysterious figure, a Spoletan *"comes palatii,"* was declared Prince of Salerno. And his descendants, adopting names associated with the former dynasty (Guaimar, Gisolf), continued in power until the fall of Salerno to Robert Guiscard one hundred years later.[23]

Stability therefore returned to the principality of Salerno well before the end of the tenth century. But Capua and Benevento were not so fortunate. Pandolf Ironhead's two eldest sons (one the younger Pandolf) fell in battle during Otto II's engagement with the Arabs in Calabria. Pandolf's forceful widow, co-ruling with a minor son, managed for a time to hold things together; but after her death that son was assassinated. Meanwhile, Capua and Benevento had broken apart; both now suffered bloody struggles between rival contenders for power, and in 990 severe earthquakes took a fearful toll in both Benevento and Capua.[24] These political and natural disasters undid what Pandolf had accomplished. They also assured that, in the early eleventh century, the first Norman adventurers would easily secure employment as mercenaries in Capuan territory, and eventually their own holdings there. All in all, one might say that Pandolf Ironhead's ambitions led in the end to disaster for his house.

As for the rest of southern Italy, while it was not so dramatically affected, it was certainly brought into sharper focus by Otto II's disasterous expedition. We must therefore go back now to 981–82, to look more closely at that ill-starred campaign.

Otto II had shown no interest in southern Italy during the first eight years of his reign. Ostensibly, his concern was only aroused by a series of devastating Arab attacks in Byzantine Apulia and Calabria.[25] From the mid-970s on, Fatimid raiders had once again become a frightening menace in those regions. In Apulia, the major towns of Gravina, Taranto, Otranto, and Oria were all hit, with much destruction, bloodshed, and the taking of captives for enslavement. In Calabria, raiders penetrated well to the north and inland, reaching as far as Cosenza. Moreover, many of these raids bore an official stamp; some were led in person by the brother of Sicily's emir. And they were reported not merely in Italian annals but also in Arab sources—evidence of the importance the Fatimids themselves attached to this new assault.[26]

Jules Gay thought the Arab menace merely Otto's pretext for an attempt to absorb southern Italy once and for all.[27] No doubt Otto did wish to make manifest those claims to south Italian sovereignty earlier asserted by his father. Yet with some justification he could view the Arab situation as a threat even to Rome. At the time, Byzantium was totally preoccupied nearer home by what was in effect civil war. The defense of Apulia and Calabria had been left almost entirely to local Byzantine officials, and they plainly lacked adequate military resources. Otto must have heard many alarming tales during the months he spent in Rome before heading south in September 981.

In any case, after the brief diversion to Salerno (the attempt to oust Manso), Otto and his army began to probe into Byzantine Apulia, going first to Matera, then to Taranto. At both places Otto camped on the outskirts, seemingly not attempting to enter. While waiting for reinforcements from Germany, Otto was apparently testing the Byzantine hold.[28] What did Theophano, who accompanied him, make of this? We cannot know, but her presence is interesting because her marriage to Otto had supposedly signified amity between the Ottonians and Byzantium. Possibly, when she and Otto married, there had been understandings concerning southern Italy which led her to feel this venture justified.

But certainly the local Byzantine authorities were worried about Otto's intentions, as we learn through one of southern Italy's hermit-saints. At that time, St. Sabas was, next to St. Nilus, the most revered of these holy men. And just before Otto headed south, Sabas was apparently persuaded by a Byzantine official to go to Rome and beg Otto not to intercede "on behalf of rebels" who were said to be seeking his help. We have no indication that Sabas actually reached Otto, but the message he bore is revealing.[29]

Whatever Otto's complex motives in going south, he did in the end engage a major Fatimid force, and with a massive and most impressive army—much of which was destroyed. Virtually every important German bishop and noble seems to have come south in the spring of 982 to join Otto. And when word came that the Sicilian emir had landed in Calabria, the combined German and Italian force had moved to confront the Arabs, in mid-July, near Stilo on the southern Calabrian coast. The story of Otto's escape from the ensuing carnage, with the aid of a horse loaned him by a Jew, is too well known to need telling here. The one positive outcome for the devastated Christian army was the death of the emir in the course of the battle. Despite their overwhelming victory, the Muslim forces therefore dispersed back to Sicily, ending for the moment any further threat.[30]

Yet only four years after Stilo, Arabs returned again to plague Apulia and Calabria. The beleaguered Byzantine garrisons again proved unable to defend even the major towns. In Calabria, Gerace (in the toe) and once again Cosenza, farther north, were attacked; in Apulia even the outskirts of Bari were ravaged, a local attempt to defend Taranto led only to many Christian deaths, and in 994 Arabs took and briefly occupied Matera.[31]

In the first half of the next century the Arab attacks, for various reasons, would gradually taper off. As the tenth century drew to a close, however, there would have been no reason to expect that. Ibn Khaldūn would later write that the Mediterranean was then so entirely controlled by Arabs fleets that "not a single Christian board floated on it."[32] This famous statement was a considerable exaggeration. Yet at the end of the century it must have seemed by no means clear that Byzantium could continue to hold its south Italian territories.

Campania, however, had long since ceased to be troubled by Arab raids. Amalfi continued its busy trade with the Fatimids, following them as Fatimid power spread. It was in 996 that Amalfitans were reported at the new Fatimid capital of Cairo.[33] Salerno, with its new Spoletan prince, presumably continued to benefit from this trade (although the Salernitans may also have been paying tribute to the Arabs, as they would be reported to do in the next century).[34] Only Capua and Benevento had problems, continuing their downward slide. But that was not attributable to Arabs; at the very end of the century, Capua and Benevento suffered at the hands of Otto III.

This was perhaps not surprising. The young Otto entertained grand visions of a renewed Roman empire that would encompass the southern Lombard principalities and perhaps the whole of southern Italy. Also, as the standard surveys tell us, he had been imbued by his mentor, Gerbert of Aurillac, with the new spirit of ecclesiastical reform. And finally, though prone to bursts of extreme cruelty, Otto III was on occasion gripped by intense spiritual fervor. All of this came together in his encounters with Capua and Benevento. His intervention in the selection of bishops there, and his involvement in controversies between Monte Cassino and the rulers of Benevento, need not concern us here. But in 999, angry for several reasons with the Capuans, he sent a force into Campania to seize the current Prince of Capua. (For good measure, the Duke of Naples was also seized and imprisoned for a time.) In the end, Otto was not successful in placing a ruler of his own choosing on the Capuan throne, even though many leading Capuans were sent captive to Germany or killed. Nonetheless, until his premature death three years later, he continued to harass Capua.[35]

By 1001 the young Otto had also become enraged with Benevento. In the spring of 999, he had gone on pilgrimage to the shrine of St. Michael on the Gargano peninsula, and en route he had stopped at Benevento and announced that, on his way back to Rome, he would collect the body of St. Bartholomew, for installation in a new church on the Isola Tiberina. The Beneventans were horrified; this relic was the great glory of their city, brought there by Sicard in the ninth century after Amalfitans had rescued it from the island of Lipari. Desperate, they decided on a ruse; when Otto came back he was given a body, but it was that of St. Paulinus of Nola. Within two years, Otto learned that he had been duped, and he promptly laid siege to the city of Benevento. "Otto rex cum magno exercitu obsedit Beneventum."[36] The sources do not tell us the outcome of that siege, but no doubt Benevento and Capua (and Naples, too) would have continued to suffer at Otto's hands had he not suddenly died a few months later. By then, however, because of Otto's actions and their own internal dissension, both Capua and Benevento were irremediably weakened.[37]

It is fair to say that in Campania at the start of the eleventh century only Amalfi and Salerno were prospering. Their location—and their determination to stay clear of northern politics—continued to protect them. But Capua and Benevento, less favorably situated, were now facing forces too powerful to resist: German emperors ever stronger and more determined and a papacy no longer supine. Looking back, it must have seemed hard to believe that Benevento had once succeeded in humiliating Louis II. Now the only element lacking, to tighten the vise, was a resurgent Byzantium; and the early eleventh century would bring that as well. It is no wonder that, at least in parts of Campania, the Normans were initially greeted with enthusiasm.

And what exactly did the Normans find, in Campania and elsewhere in southern Italy? We must now examine the structures of the southern Italy they encountered.

Religion

Southern Italy would seem an obvious setting for ecclesiastical conflict between Byzantium and the papacy. Generations of scholars have thus looked there for evidence of pre-Schism schism; and it is not hard to find. To cite only two examples, there was the eighth-century edict of Emperor Leo III, placing Calabria under the patriarch's jurisdiction; then, in the second half of the tenth century, Rome and Constantinople made conflicting appointments involving sees within (or on the fringes of) Byzantine territory. This latter development—each side creating metropolitan provinces or archbishoprics with putative authority over sees claimed by the other—has been much discussed.[38] And yet this jurisdictional dispute, however interesting to specialists, tells us very little about the actual religious culture. For that, we must begin with the perception and role of Rome.

Until the middle of the eighth century and the edict of Leo III, the whole of southern Italy, even "Greek" Calabria, had unquestionably been subject to papal authority. Furthermore, even in the tenth century, and despite the vicissitudes then of the papacy, Rome (or what Rome represented) remained a powerful symbol and magnet, even for those plainly

"Greek" in orientation. In the latter tenth century several of the Greek hermit-saints of southern Italy made pilgrimages there.[39] In practical terms, however, papal authority meant little in the south. This is perhaps not surprising in the tenth century, with the papacy in disorder. But it appears to have been true earlier as well, as the failed initiatives of popes from Hadrian I to John VIII demonstrated. Both at Naples and in the Lombard principalities, it seemed clear that bishops answered to the local rulers or to local imperatives. (Bishop and later Duke-Bishop Athanasius II of Naples had been openly contemptuous of papal directives; and when the bishop of Salerno went to a papal meeting at Rome in the period of Otto I, it was probably more to show Gisolf's support for anti-Otto forces than to indicate respect for papal prerogatives.) From the regions Byzantium held in the tenth century, we have little evidence. Surely, however, Latin-rite bishops there, too, would have chiefly responded to local needs and local pressures.

The religious culture of southern Italy was thus an open culture. For convenience, we may speak of "Latin-rite" and "Greek-rite." Actually, however, liturgical practices in this period must have been far from uniform. Theological points of difference, as between Rome and Constantinople, may have been of interest to a few individuals—at Monte Cassino, for example. Yet, even there, when Nilus of Rossano came to visit in the late tenth century only friendly curiosity and admiration were in evidence.[40] And translations from the Greek, whether saints' lives or theological treatises, seem to have been widely disseminated in the Latin areas.[41]

The most obvious proof of openness was the reverence universally accorded to southern Italy's Greek hermit-saints, of whom Nilus was merely the most celebrated example. Of course, reverence for these holy men extended well beyond the boundaries of southern Italy; Otto III visited St. Nilus (and tried to lure him to Rome); and St. Sabas had seemed the ideal emissary to Otto II.[42] But it is their reputation in the Lombard, Latin portions of the south that concerns us here. Most of these hermit-saints had been born and raised in the beleaguered Byzantine enclaves of Arab Sicily and had then fled into Byzantine Calabria. There they had established refuges in the mountains and led lives of total austerity, presiding over simple laureatic communities, their followers apparently building rude huts in the surrounding wilderness. As their reputations grew, even the Arabs were said to demonstrate respect for these ascetics.[43]

One might have thought the values exemplified by these hermit-saints totally alien to the world of the southern Lombards—and to the commercial world of Amalfi. (St. Nilus once had his monks rip up vines that were too productive.)[44] Nevertheless, there were increasing contacts. St. Elias the Younger had taken shelter at Amalfi during Ibrāhīm's invasion of Calabria. In the latter tenth century, several of these hermit-saints moved their hermitages or communities northward to areas bordering the principality of Salerno. And St. Sabas seems even to have lived for a time just outside the city of Salerno.[45]

The religious culture was thus variegated. On one hand, in the Lombard areas, there was admiration for the hermit-saints and a devotion to relics. On the other hand, local charters reflect an institutional Christianity chiefly notable for the material support it could provide. We find the elderly sometimes granting their property to an ecclesiastical foundation while retaining lifetime use; this stratagem presumably gained both spiritual rewards and protection for the property.[46] The *maiores*, by the end of the tenth century, were leasing ecclesiastical lands on very favorable terms. For the Lombard rulers, in the ninth century the principal monasteries had functioned as de facto banks, their treasuries enriched in good times but depleted when the rulers had financial needs. (There had been significant withdrawals to pay Arab mercenaries; and Sikenolf had taken back from Monte Cassino his father's crown in order to bribe Guy of Spoleto.) By the latter tenth century, the rulers were handling matters more discreetly, but the results were equally satisfactory; favored gastalds were made *dominii* of the wealthier foundations.[47] All of this was, of course, not peculiar to Lombard southern Italy, but it seemed in sharp contrast to the poverty and self-denial preached by the hermit-saints.

Yet the charters, with their focus on property issues, may to some degree be misleading. For it would be wrong to believe that bishops and abbots in Campania had no sense of higher duty. Their election to office did usually depend on some relationship to the ruler, often a family connection. (Once, some of Monte Cassino's monks attempted to elect as abbot a simple fellow monk, nephew to the preceding abbot; the "pars potior ac sanior" quickly intervened, however, and sent instead for a son of Benevento's current prince.)[48] Lacking independent power, local bishops could sometimes be subject to indignities, as when in the ninth century the bishop of Salerno had been forced to turn over his house to a visiting Arab. Unquestionably, too, bishops (and abbots of lesser foundations) were vulnerable to various pressures in relation to their landholdings. Nevertheless, in the tenth century we find fewer crude exploitations of ecclesiastical property, and certainly nothing in the sources suggests that venal bishops and abbots abounded in tenth-century Campania.[49] It is true that there was not yet a structured, territorial parish system.[50] And we hear almost nothing about major baptismal churches like the impressive fifth-century example still to be seen at Nocera Superiore, between Salerno and Naples. Instead, a bishop concerned about the cure of souls was now faced with a preponderance of proprietary churches.[51] Nonetheless, bishops did make efforts to ensure that *eigenkirchen* met spiritual needs; and when individuals were permitted to lease churches—as frequently happened—the charters stipulated that the liturgical furnishings (and any *codices*) be properly maintained and preserved and that priests be secured to perform the offices.[52]

Furthermore, although only in ninth-century Naples had local bishops demonstrated political power, one ecclesiastical institution did consistently exemplify both power and spiritual values: the monastery of Monte Cassino. Throughout Campania in the ninth and the tenth centuries, Monte Cassino's reputation remained extraordinarily high. San Vincenzo al Volturno, the only other major monastery, could never hope to rival Monte Cassino's traditions; and the many small foundations were almost exclusively proprietary. Monte Cassino, however, functioned with almost total independence, and it was trusted; when Guaifer founded St. Maximus at Salerno, he stipulated that in case of dispute over the choice of *rector*, the abbot of Monte Cassino should decide.[53]

The preeminence of Monte Cassino did not signify any uniform "rule" or "order." The monastic situation in Latin southern Italy was as varied and haphazard as the terminology of local charters. ("Ecclesia," for example, was used indiscriminately to describe a church or something more like a small abbey or even, on occasion, a family funerary chapel.) Nonetheless, Monte Cassino was special. Particularly in the tenth century, with the papacy in decline, it came to seem even more important, as a symbol of stability.

Most of the Monte Cassino abbots in this period were Capuan or Beneventan. But the one with the longest tenure, Abbot Aligernus (949–85), was a Neapolitan, which points to another fact of religious life in ninth- and tenth-century Campania. In religious practice, Beneventans, Neapolitans, Capuans, Amalfitans, and Salernitans exhibited far more similarity than difference. Naples, despite its Greek heritage, professed obedience to Rome, but within the duchy there were many Greek churches and small monastic foundations. And in the latter tenth century, not only did the Amalfitans found a community on Mount Athos but we also find there a Beneventan Lombard community.[54] It all constituted proof of the openness of religious culture.

L. R. Ménager and many others have noted the tolerance of the

Norman *Regno*, with mosques, Greek monasteries and Latin bishops all coexisting.[55] In tenth-century southern Italy, the scene appears more jumbled but equally coexistent—and less self-consciously so. If, in the tenth century, the Greek hermit-saints were a revelation to Latin south Italians, it was not because of their "Greekness"; Greek and Latin religious spheres overlapped everywhere, in Campania as well as in the Byzantine-dominated areas. As the tenth century drew to a close, despite the sharpening rivalries between Rome and Constantinople nothing like schism had penetrated daily life.

Legal Structures and Their Implications

Other aspects of south Italian society exhibited an eclectic openness as well. Stylistically, tenth-century Amalfitan charters differ noticeably from their Salernitan counterparts; the prose of the Amalfitan charters is far more convoluted and they tend to be lengthier. Given the different legal traditions (Roman versus Lombard) we might also expect substantive differences. In fact, however, significant variation occurred only in transactions involving females; in Salernitan transactions involving women, Lombard law was cited and its restrictive provisions heeded, while at Amalfi matters seemed ill-defined.[56] But until the very end of the tenth century this difference was not articulated by Salernitan notaries. Then suddenly, in two transactions recorded at Salerno but involving Amalfitan women, we are told in the first charter (997) that the proceedings have been conducted *iuxta legem et consuetudo romanorum*, and in the second (998) that the woman has "the consent of her husband in accordance with Roman law." These are interesting statements, and they demonstrate increased sensitivity to legal niceties on the part of notaries, but we should probably not take these pronouncements too seriously. Very likely they represented not some new, more clear-cut distinction in practice, but rather an attempt by Lombard notaries to impart legitimacy to the amorphous Amalfitan situation, with which they must have been uncomfortable.[57] Otherwise, in any case, we find little evidence that legal distinctions were observed. Amalfitans owning property in the principality of Salerno frequently had land disputes adjudicated by Salernitan Lombard *iudices*, even when both parties were Amalfitan (and with no mention of "Roman law").[58] Furthermore, in sales and leases involving Salernitan properties, Amalfitans (even among themselves) had been quick to adopt the Lombard practice of guarantees by means of *guadia* and *mediatores*.[59]

Vera von Falkenhausen has described a similar melding of legal approach in the Byzantine-held portions of southern Italy. *Morgencap*, the Lombard marriage settlement by which a wife acquired rights to one-fourth of her husband's property, apparently became commonplace, even when couples were not ethnic Lombards. Moreover, the *Edict of Rothari* was translated there into Greek, and in a manner indicating practical use.[60]

The chance survival of so many Salernitan charters makes it easier to trace legal developments there than anywhere else in southern Italy; some developments were therefore discussed in Chapter 6. Here, we might simply note the use of *boni homines* in both Salerno and Amalfi. Sometimes *boni homines* simply functioned as witnesses to an agreement.[61] But at other times they served as a crude approximation of a jury. In one instance, if a wife asserting her *morgencap* rights should cause a land-sale to collapse, the buyer was to receive compensation "tantu[m] per estimo de boni homines."[62] In another charter, if a man proved unable to repay a loan he was to surrender to his creditor all of the lands pledged as security, at a sale price to be set by *boni homines*.[63] Sometimes *boni homines* were convened to help resolve boundary disputes, and once (in an Amalfitan lease) they were stipulated as arbiters of adequate cultivation.[64]

A judicial system with a corps of *judices* backed by gastalds and supplemented when necessary by *boni homines* seems impressive. Moreover, difficult cases were referred to the prince; and contracts could be voided or altered only with the prince's permission.[65] Orderly government was obviously one of the strengths of the principality of Salerno; its procedures demonstrate that (as Chris Wickham has observed) Lombard Italy retained a clear concept of public authority.[66]

Yet the inherent power of Lombard rulers—and, by extension, the *maiores*—was immense. Legal strictures were doubtless most scrupulously observed when they did not interefere with the goals of the reigning prince and other powerful men. In Salerno, during the first three-quarters of the tenth century, Guaimar II and Gisolf had seemingly exercised power with some restraint. But their dynasty's wealth had continued to grow. Southern Lombard rulers controlled (and received revenues from) port and entry fees, marketing privileges, and licenses of all sorts.[67] The estates of those dying without heirs passed directly to the ruler, and rulers also confiscated estates for malfeasance.[68] In addition, there were gifts of land to the ruler and his family, and many of the "sales" of land to members of Salerno's ruling family were probably less than voluntary.[69]

The end result was an amassing of wealth not only by the rulers and their relatives but also by the inner circle of gastalds. This has already been noted in relation to Salerno, but it bears repeating here, for the situation was surely the same in all three Lombard principalities. In 984, in a lengthy document related to Gisolf and Gemma's adoption of the younger Pandolf, we glimpse the extent of land held by Salerno's ruling family and other powerful Salernitans.[70] We can be sure that the descendants of Arichis (the rulers of Capua and Benevento) were equally rich in land; both their wide-ranging holdings and the valuable rights they controlled are reflected in their grants to Monte Cassino.[71]

And there is something else to bear in mind in relation to wealth in the Lombard principalities. By the 990s, more and more Salernitan charters were involving land owned by proprietary foundations such as St. Max-imus. In 997, a typical year, nine of fifteen charters (leases, confirmations, gifts, judgments or settlements) relate to such lands.[72] We must recognize the implications of this. As Monte Cassino's holdings grew, so did its independence. But increased holdings for a proprietary foundation meant enhanced importance and profit for its proprietors. (Huguette Taviani-Carozzi has noted that the reformist attack on proprietary churches in the second half of the eleventh century would deal a severe economic and political blow to many of the old Lombard families in southern Italy.)[73] That at the end of the tenth century a high number of charters should concern proprietary foundations is yet more evidence that powerful men were then increasing their power.

Servitude and Demographics

In the latter tenth century, it is not easy to glimpse the ordinary population through the charters. From that period, fewer charters drawn in the smaller towns have survived. Nonetheless, it is possible to reach some conclusions about changes over time in relation to freedom and servitude.

In the ninth and tenth centuries, most south Italian sources were imprecise in terminology. For example, we find "aldii" in ninth-century pacts and in royal grants to Monte Cassino, but in the Salerno charters no *aldii*, no shadings among the unfree, only "servi et ancillae" and (occasion-ally) "famuli" or "manicipiis." In transactions involving large estates, in both the ninth and tenth centuries (and beyond Salerno as well as within that principality), *servi et ancillae* are often listed with the lands.[74] But we also find the term connected with small properties and lesser individuals; in such instances the *servi et ancillae* are often to be freed on their owner's death.[75] Clearly, these were very general terms, covering all manner and degree of servitude, both domestic and agricultural. But was there, anywhere in southern Italy, agricultural slavery on an almost Roman model, or were there merely servile tenant families, *condumae*?[76]

We cannot know; we can only be sure of a few broad facts. First, there is no evidence, anywhere, at any time, of labor service. (In Salerno, when in the tenth century leases first appear, at most the leaseholder is required to transport the landowner's share of produce to the latter's storage facilities.) But in the ninth century there did seem to have been servitude on a rather massive scale, in addition to an aggressive slave trade involving not only the Arabs. Both major ninth-century pacts (the *Pactum Sicardi* and the *Divisio*) had clauses relating to runaway *servi* and the taking of captives for enslavement. And in 866 the Beneventan ruler Adelchis revised Lombard law on marriages between free women and servile men; such couples and their offspring would no longer automatically become the property of the prince. Instead, they could now be retained by the owner of the servile man.[77] One therefore needed only to establish the servile status of some male to acquire an entire family, and we can guess who held the advantage in regard to proof.

Yet by the end of the tenth century there clearly had been change, both in Salerno and elsewhere. In one sense, within the principalities lesser individuals seemed to have lost ground, since the *populus* no longer played a distinctive electoral role in southern Lombard society. Indeed, many may have been reduced to tenancy, their small plots acquired by more powerful men. Also, there seemed now to be more foreigners among those leasing or holding small plots, which presumably meant, for lesser Lombards, a weakening of the significance of ethnicity.[78] Nonetheless, at the very lowest level of society some improvement seems evident. For example, beginning in the late tenth century, we find a willingness in Salerno to disregard all laws, new and old, that relegated free women marrying unfree men to servitude; such women were now sometimes permitted to retain their free status and to extend it to their children.[79] *Servi et ancillae* still appear in the charters (and there are some affecting examples of children consigned to an unfree life). But we hear no more of a wide-ranging slave trade, and (according to Vera von Falkenhausen) there also is surprisingly little evidence of servitude in the Byzantine-held regions.[80]

A decrease in servitude could hardly have come about seamlessly, and one development of the latter tenth century is perhaps revealing. Starting in

965, when someone in Salerno contracts to work a small plot he is often pointedly described as a free man, "liber homo."[81] Earlier in the century, individuals making similar agreements were undoubtedly also free men, even if not so described. Possibly, then, "liber homo" was no more than a variation on the freedom-to-leave provision found in many of Salerno's first *pastinare* contracts. Yet this new statement of status could also hint at social tensions. In Campania, the emphasis on viticulture had traditionally meant small plots owned and worked by free men. With more and more of these small plots absorbed by large landowners (as one senses, although it cannot be absolutely proven), there may have been related attempts to tie men to the land. If so, in a society now wedded to documentation, the only secure defense would have been clear recognition of status in any lease.

Nevertheless, overall in southern Italy, there must indeed now actually have been more free men—men who had managed to secure or assert freedom. Like the San Vincenzo records, the royal Lombard charters collected by Poupardin show, for the latter tenth century, highly attractive conditions offered to "free men" willing to work lands belonging to Benevento's Sancta Sophia.[82] One wonders how closely the recruits' status was examined.

If the situation in relation to servitude had in fact eased somewhat, this surely must have been attributable, at least in part, to a population level inadequate to meet agricultural demand. Demographically, the autonomous areas must still have been suffering the effects of the internal strife of the ninth century and the associated Arab depredations. And the comparative tranquillity of the tenth century had provided little opportunity to acquire replacements for the servile population.

Freeing men sometimes seemed a way to ensure one's supply of cultivators. Del Treppo saw this in the ninth century, when men donating land first freed the property's *servos*, apparently with the hope then of gaining their services for other properties.[83] Perhaps for a time men thus freed could indeed be retained. But sooner or later many must have claimed absolute freedom, and this may account for some of the insistent statements of status in the Salerno charters. In any event, judging by the leases, landowners were increasingly finding it necessary to make concessions. At the end of the century, even though *pastenare ad partionem* had, for the time being, faded from view, ordinary *pastenare* leases were sometimes even more generous than earlier in the century.[84]

The suggestion that tenth-century southern Italy faced a population problem is obviously at variance with findings for other parts of Europe, where a growth in population is assumed to have fueled economic advance. Nonetheless, I think we must recognize the south's special circumstances. There, economic ambitions seem to have outrun a population still in the process of recovery from the vicissitudes of the ninth century.

Incastellamento

An issue often related to population levels is *incastellamento*—a troublesome concept, not least because it too narrowly suggests "castle" to an English-speaker. In fact, those who use the term to denote changes in tenth-century Italy typically have in mind three phenomena, occurring singly or in combination: the formation of new settlements (*castella*) for more effective land development, the fortification of settlements (new or old) for defensive purposes, and the vesting of many *castella* with jurisdictional powers.[85] The records of San Vincenzo al Volturno, as Mario Del Treppo first noted, provide a classic picture of *incastellamento*, incorporating all three phenomena in varying degrees. In several tenth-century San Vincenzo leases, the establishment of *castella* (in the sense of nucleated settlements) is specifically mandated.[86] Some have viewed this as indicating an increase in population. Yet actually this need not prove anything about demographics. There is no indication that the men to whom these leases were granted—men who were to bring their families to colonize San Vincenzo's underdeveloped lands—represented surplus population. Some may simply have moved, from some distance away, attracted by San Vincenzo's generous terms. And Del Treppo speculated that some were merely the freed descendants of local *servi*.[87]

As for *incastellamento* otherwise, though all three phenomena are identifiable in the territory controlled by San Vincenzo (and perhaps also in Monte Cassino territory), elsewhere in southern Italy the fit is far less clear. References to *castella* occurred in south Italian sources in the ninth century as well as the tenth, and with no greater frequency in the latter. The word seems usually to have meant a small town or village, not necessarily fortified or walled. But it was used without much precision; in one late tenth-century Capuan charter we find Avellino (usually described as a *castrum*) called both a *castellum* and, grandly, a *civitas*.[88]

Also, in Campania, fortification was well under way in the ninth century; it merely continued in the tenth century. Moreover, Campania had never lacked for towns, large and small; at most, once the Arab menace had receded, doubtless some people returned to villages in vulnerable areas.[89] And in Byzantine territory, we find in tenth-century Apulia no appreciable change in settlement patterns. In Calabria, moreover, significant change had begun long before the tenth century; as early as the seventh century, it appears, the population of Calabria began moving away from the coast, for reasons not entirely clear. Thereafter, with the exception of Reggio, the Calabrian towns mentioned are almost always inland: Stilo, Rossano, Gerace, Bisignano.[90] These were indeed new towns, but new long before the tenth century.

Altogether, it is hard to make a case for *incastellamento* as everywhere the defining feature of tenth-century southern Italy. Late in the tenth century, when there was fragmentation of power and jurisdiction within Capua and Benevento, it was accompanied by increased fortification. Nevertheless, *incastellamento* in its fullest sense (and as a new phenomenon) seemed primarily concentrated in the areas dominated by the two great monasteries, Monte Cassino and San Vincenzo. Both had always clung tenaciously to independent status for their territories, under imperial protection. The practical effect was a military and governmental vacuum in those areas, making them ripe for *incastellamento*: new settlements (sometimes fortified) to provide local control and protection. In the rest of the lower peninsula, however, there had been no such vacuum.

The Evolution of Standards

If *incastellamento* did not sweep across all of southern Italy, something else—less dramatic yet nonetheless significant—does appear to have characterized the latter part of the tenth century. For lack of a better term, it may be called heightened definition. It is evident in the Salerno charters, with their greater precision in relation to law and men's status, and also in one minor but telling development. During most of the two centuries covered in this book, charters had identified properties chiefly in terms of their boundaries: "next to the wall belonging to Iaquintus" and so forth. In the case of small lots, measurements were often given as well, in *passi* or *pedes*, but one might well wonder how precise those terms were. And then, in 984, we encounter for the first time a measurement in *pedes* with the foot defined as "de latitudine quantum ista cartula in capite lata est."[91] In a charter two years later we meet for the first time a public standard, in this case for *passi*: "signatum est in columnia marmorea sancti mathei de archiepiscopatum salernitanum."[92] Not all charters immediately became so exact in their descriptions, but we do soon hear of another public standard, in a church at Nocera, and in other ways too the charters now began to demonstrate a concern for precision.[93]

Had there in fact been standards for some time, only now made explicit in charters? If so, that it was now felt necessary to spell things out is in itself interesting. And if these standards were new, did this represent a purely local evolution, or was this new precision the result of external influence in the latter tenth century?[94] There is no way to know. But this new attention to accuracy indicates how much the society had changed over two centuries.

8. Campania and Its Culture in the Tenth Century

IN THE PREVIOUS CHAPTER, the term "structures" was used to characterize the institutions and demographic characteristics of south Italian society in the tenth century. The focus of this chapter is culture, particularly in that portion of southern Italy not under Byzantine control. This means primarily Campania, and the emphasis is not only on intellectual or aesthetic trends but also on culture in its broader sense: how individuals lived and acted from day to day. It is, of course, impossible to draw a hard-and-fast line between "structures" and "culture." *Incastellamento*, for example, was not a totally impersonal force; individuals decided whether to create a new settlement or to fortify an old one. And individuals decreed standards of measurement. Nonetheless, the developments to be discussed in this chapter—including the quality of life, with which we begin—do seem different in character, to a greater degree representing conscious choice, personal predilections.

The Quality of Life

At the end of the tenth century, southern Italy, viewed from far above, would probably have looked very like the southern Italy of Charlemagne's day. Much more verdant than today, it would have had dense tree cover in many areas now bare and dry. Rivers that often now carry only a trickle of water must then have been free-flowing, for many charters mention water mills, not only at Amalfi but throughout Lombard territory.[1] Moreover, Arab raiders had typically positioned their bases along rivers, and often well upstream.[2]

Closer up, however, one would have noticed some change since the late eighth century: more vineyards, more areas under cultivation, and at least in Campania the towns and cities more prosperous in appearance. Many new churches had been built in Campania, and there was also another sort of construction. Starting in the tenth century, within the city of Salerno (the only well-documented urban center) small building lots were busily leased. Contracts in the second half of the century often stated that a wooden house could be erected on the lot, with the leaseholder to dismantle the house and carry away its timbers when the lease expired.[3] (Soon St. Maximus began applying the *pastenare ad partionem* concept to such contracts, with only "half the house" to be removed at the end of the lease and the other half left.)[4] And by the late 970s we begin to encounter houses of stone on city lots, sometimes complete with domestic "aqueducts." The city was plainly becoming more densely populated and also more genuinely solid and urban in appearance.[5]

Of course, the Lombard ruling families and the gastald class had never lived in crude wooden shacks, nor had they lacked for luxuries. In the ninth century, Prince Sicard's wife soaked her feet in a silver basin; in the latter tenth century, when Gisolf of Salerno and his wife, Gemma, were seized in the middle of the night and taken captive to Amalfi, we are told that it was a particular humiliation for Gemma to be rushed off half-clothed for she usually appeared only in royal purple encrusted with gold and gems.[6] And if the splendor of Gisolf and his retinue had stunned Pope John XII at Terracina, it was not surprising; in the Lombard principalities goldsmiths seemed particularly favored, often rewarded with gifts of land.[7]

Now, however, lesser individuals seemed to be living more comfortably, and it was not merely a matter of stone houses. For ninth-century Salerno, there is one mention of public baths; Prince Guaifer was supposedly strolling back from the baths to his palace when he encountered the Arab who admired his headgear. But in the latter tenth century we hear of another "balneo publico," at Nocera (that Salernitan market town); and in a charter drawn at Amalfi a man leasing some rural Amalfitan property is permitted to build a *balneum* where he and his men might "freely go to wash themselves." We also find an abbess permitted to construct a public bath in the city of Benevento, apparently to provide income for her community.[8] We might view these baths as a Roman echo. But certainly nothing social was implied in the Amalfitan charter, only refreshing cleanliness; and we have no way of knowing how elaborate the urban public baths were. In any case, however, it all indicates an improvement in daily life.

Yet this was still the tenth century. Grand though some of these developments doubtless seemed to contemporaries, we know that tenth-century buildings—of whatever sort, for whatever purpose—were pitifully small by later medieval standards. Moreover, the modest level of wealth is indicated in many wills. In 968, a seemingly prosperous citizen of Nocera left several pieces of land, but the other possessions listed came to little more than a cart and harness, a two-edged sword, a cotton tunic and leggings, and a share in a heifer.[9] This last item reinforces the impression one gets from other Salernitan charters: that domestic animals were relatively scarce and highly valued. In one lease, involving grain-growing land, the tenants must surrender the holding if their oxen die.[10]

It is hard to be sure of the cultural level of men like the Nocera landowner, but we do know a bit more about the elite. Naples' leaders prided themselves on their learning (in both Greek and Latin), and this continued to be true in the tenth century, when Neapolitan rulers were still avidly collecting manuscripts. Moreover, at least some members of the Lombard ruling families were, by contemporary standards, well educated.[11] Even so, it is hard not to smile indulgently when the *Chronicon Salernitanum* proudly proclaims that in the ninth century there were thirty-two philosophers at Benevento.[12] And when the *Chronicon*, in deploring the castrating of the hapless palace scribe in 900, notes that he was "liberalibus disciplinis instructum," we may wonder if this emphasis does not suggest he was something of an exception in late ninth-century Salerno.[13] Yet it is noteworthy that, in Salerno, a high proportion of lay witness signatures were autograph, even in the ninth century, and even in the case of charters drafted in outlying towns and involving small properties—even, indeed, in the case of some women witnesses in those outlying towns.[14] At least to that extent, literacy thus appears to have been relatively widespread; altogether, the general cultural level seems not unimpressive and presumably had risen somewhat in the tenth century.

The issue of language is also interesting, especially in one regard. There are many Greek-derived words in the region's Latin chronicles and charters, and obviously many citizens of Gaeta, Naples, and Amalfi knew and used Greek. Moreover, the Latin-speaking Lombards were in frequent contact with Greek-speaking Byzantines. We must therefore assume considerable bilingualism. Yet there remains one mystery: how south Italians, whether Greek or Latin-speaking, communicated with the Arabs of Sicily and North Africa. The chronicles, and the *Lives* of the Byzantine anchorite saints, frequently report conversations but give no hint of how these were conducted. Was there a pan-Mediterranean lingua franca, perhaps a Greek-related dialect? It seems possible but we cannot be sure.

"Beneventan" Culture

What we know about the higher forms of culture in the southern Italy of this period is for the most part dependent on what ecclesiastical institutions preserved. (Monte Cassino is the most obvious example.) We need to consider this culture, but it is important first to note one fact: southern Italy in the ninth and tenth centuries was to a considerable degree isolated from the north. In Louis II's day, the Carolingian world had grazed the south, and the young son of the Salernitan ruler Sikenolf had been sent north to Louis' court, to learn "astucia mundi."[15] Thereafter, however, until the latter part of the tenth century, there were few northern contacts. And although Byzantine culture was in theory familiar, it often was encountered only in crude or diluted form. Imported "Byzantine" objects were as likely to come from some minor Byzantine province as from Constantinople.[16] The Greek hermit-saints had mostly come from Sicily. And the governors of the Byzantine themes, military men and under continuous pressure, were unlikely to have been transmitting high culture.

In the autonomous regions, the isolation from the north was responsible for many unique cultural features. For one thing, it meant that the Latin religious culture was conservative. Old liturgical forms persisted there long after they had disappeared elswhere. For example, in some of the south Italian Exultet rolls the Paschal hymn appears in an early, non-Vulgate form.[17] But perhaps the most notable evidence of conservatism was the distinctive script that E. A. Loew called "Beneventan" (although in fact it was employed throughout the Lombard south and at Naples as well). In evidence from the late eighth century on, it apparently derived from a pre-Carolingian Italian minuscule.[18]

The name Loew chose for this script warrants some attention, for it has come to be widely applied to all aspects of the culture and has sometimes caused confusion. Scholars initially had difficulty settling on a single term for the cultural manifestations of southern Italy's autonomous regions in the pre-Norman era. Some favored "Cassinese" because Monte Cassino played a crucial role in the dissemination and preservation of this culture. Yet the implications of "Cassinese" were and are too narrow. Important though Monte Cassino was, culturally, in the ninth and tenth centuries, it was by no means the sole source or center. Thus most scholars now follow Loew's example and use "Beneventan" because "Benevento" implies southern Lombard and the culture was preeminently associated with the southern Lombard world. For that matter, in these centuries Monte Cassino was itself largely dominated by Capuan and Beneventan Lombards.

This study is hardly the place to propose a new term; "Beneventan" is now firmly established. The term, however, must be understood to encompass not only Benevento and Monte Cassino but also Capua and Salerno and even Naples and its sphere. Both Beneventan script and the art forms characterized as Beneventan were encountered throughout the autonomous regions. Yet in the period with which we are concerned, with only rare exceptions these distinctive cultural manifestations did not extend into the Byzantine-dominated portions of southern Italy, not even into Latinate Apulia with its heavily Lombard population.[19] "Beneventan" is therefore valuable as a limiting term.

Historians of culture and specialists in manuscripts have found the Beneventan region rewarding because the script establishes the range of interests and the *corpus* of knowledge in a neatly defined sample-area. Especially since publication of Loew's magisterial survey of Beneventan manuscripts in 1914, studies have proliferated. And the range of Beneventan interests has proved to be impressive. To quote Loew, in the tenth century we find in Beneventan script "the classics, medicine, history, poetry, and canon law . . . Virgil, Livy, Josephus, the fables of Hyginus, Solinus; Dioscorides, Galen, and an extraordinary compendium of the medical knowledge of the period; Paulus' commentary on St. Benedict's rule, the works of St. Gregory, collections of canons, writings of the Fathers, etc." In addition, as Loew goes on to say, there were the works of contemporaries or near-contemporaries, from within Campania and from beyond southern Italy: Auxilius and Eugenius Vulgarius; the histories of Paul the Deacon, Erchempert, and the ninth-century Naples historiographers; and also from Naples the many translations of Greek authors.[20]

In other words, the Beneventan area was remarkably rich in literary-cultural resources in the tenth century, even if judged only by the manuscripts that have survived. And there must once have been many more. Many fragments of Beneventan script have been discovered incorporated into bindings or underlying palimpsests; and we know from references in the Salerno charters that even minor churches in the region often possessed *codices*.[21]

Some of the surviving Beneventan manuscripts include marvelously evocative colored line drawings: astrological figures, Old and New Testament personages, and narrative scenes. These are also a feature of the

Exultet rolls, one of southern Italy's unique treasures: long parchment scrolls designed for liturgical use on Easter Saturday. The earliest surviving Exultet roll is ascribed to the see of Benevento in the tenth century; thereafter, these rolls proliferate. And the lively drawings of the earlier rolls, as well as those in several other Beneventan manuscripts, provide graphic detail of the way contemporary men and women dressed, and ate, and equipped their horses, and cultivated their fields.[22]

The manner in which the Exultet rolls were used can remind us of the small size and restricted function of most of the period's churches. The drawings are interspersed with the text of the Paschal proclamation, but (in all but the first of the rolls) the drawings are upside down; presumably the scroll was draped over the pulpit, and as the deacon sang or chanted from the text he unfurled the scroll so that others could see the illustrations (right side up for them). The whole suggests an intimacy appropriate to the scale of the buildings—and to liturgical observances not designed for large, public congregations. In this period, it appears that laymen would have entered *ecclesia* comparatively rarely, perhaps chiefly in connection with baptismal and funerary rites.

Yet despite their modest size, many of the more important churches must have been quite splendidly decorated. Many incorporated antique columns, although they were otherwise architecturally crude.[23] In addition, some surely had lavishly painted walls and ceilings, as does one major surviving example at San Vincenzo al Volturno.[24] And charters indicate that many also had rich hangings and vestments and liturgical vessels.[25]

It was, of course, these portable treasures that in the ninth century had drawn Arab raiders to the monasteries of Monte Cassino and San Vincenzo. Ironically, it seems likely that, in the tenth century, many regional churches were embellished with artifacts brought from the Arab world. Documented references begin only in the early eleventh century and then primarily mention "Spanish" or "Moorish" textiles.[26] But the treasury of San Marco contains several tenth-century Fatimid objects (rock-crystal ewers and censers of ornate metalwork and the like), and surely Amalfi was even better positioned than Venice to bring in such items. Furthermore, in the case of some low-relief stone panels, found throughout Campania and dated roughly to the tenth century, the bizarre animals featured are thought to be derived from Sassanid-style textiles, probably (although not certainly) imported from Muslim territory.[27]

Yet questions of derivation and influence are not always easy to resolve. In the first place, although some imported objects were plainly Fatimid or

Byzantine, many do not so clearly proclaim their provenance. The Islamic and Byzantine spheres overlapped in the southeastern Mediterranean. In addition, most of the Arab-held Mediterranean littoral had earlier been subject to Byzantium, and in the tenth century many of the local craftsmen were still non-Arab, non-Muslim. (It has been noted, for example, that, until about 1000, Fustat pottery exhibited virtually no change in design or technique from Egypt's pre-Islamic days.)[28] Conversely, in the tenth century some elements of the Islamic aesthetic were adopted by Byzantine craftsmen.[29] Thus in the ninth and tenth centuries, goods such as Sassanid-style textiles could well have been produced in either sphere. Or they could have been produced in one sphere but transmitted to Campania by way of the other, for there was always traffic between the two, despite Byzantine restrictions.[30]

All in all, we can only be sure that no one in Campania was likely to have objected to putting Islamic wares to Christian liturgical use—for example, employing a Fatimid perfume censer in an ecclesiastical setting. Islamic textiles, sometimes adorned with cufic inscriptions signifying their Muslim origin, might even be used to wrap relics.[31]

Yet many objects must certainly have come in from the Byzantine sphere, and one might therefore expect at least some trace of authentic Byzantine style in tenth-century Beneventan art. There was, after all, ample local recognition of Byzantium's prestigious image; it was implicit in the fact that local Lombard charters continued to cite the Byzantine *solidus* in penalty clauses, despite political hostility. Nonetheless, clear and irrefutable evidence of Byzantine influence on the region's art is not found until the eleventh century, when Byzantine power in southern Italy reached its peak even as the Normans were about to drive out all Byzantine forces. Earlier, in the tenth century, locally produced art and artifacts mainly demonstrated the varied meld of traditions that characterized the society as a whole. Any Byzantine influence often seemed more old than new, deriving perhaps from the Graecified papal Rome of the eighth century. Moreover, even this somewhat problematic Byzantine influence is found coexisting with traditional Lombard elements, with echoes of classical Rome, with stylistic approaches associated with early Christianity, and with (in the stone panels) some Near Eastern flavoring. Altogether, as Janine Wettstein observed, "l'art Campanien déroute sans cesse l'historien par la diversité de ses sources . . . et une absence presque totale de constantes."[32]

This casual mix of diverse elements in no way resembled the deliberate conjoining of fully developed traditions associated with Roger II's twelfth-century court at Palermo. This was not a period of self-conscious high culture, and its art, whatever its antecedents, was by any standard crude. Yet one notes with interest that the diverse styles and approaches transcended local political boundaries. There was not a Lombard style in Capua and a Greek style in Naples, contrary to what one might expect. Ernesto Pontieri once referred to Amalfi and Salerno as deadly enemies ("capitali nemici"); in assuming that, he was reflecting the views of earlier generations of historians who pictured a total separation in Campania between Lombards and quasi-Byzantines.[33] But we now know that customs of all sorts spread indiscriminately across the region, that *tari* came to constitute a common currency, and that the ruling families frequently intermarried across ethnic lines and came to each other's defense. To this intermingling we must add the evidence of the Beneventan script and the art of this "Beneventan" area.[34]

Unfortunately, though we have a reasonably clear picture of the ecclesiastical culture, the secular world left fewer cultural traces. We know that in the tenth century the increasingly powerful Lombard rulers made impressive displays of wealth. But the products of those goldsmiths once watched admiringly by the young Radelchis have long since disappeared, along with Gemma's jewel-encrusted robes. Only one sort of treasure can be securely associated with secular society: ivory oliphants, the great tusks of African elephants crafted into horns and embellished with intricately carved, Fatimid-style decoration. Some eleventh-century examples may actually have been the work of south Italian craftsmen, but oliphants dated to the tenth century apparently were imported from North Africa or Sicily.[35] We are therefore free to imagine a Fatimid-derived oliphant decorating the princely chambers at Salerno, along with other splendid objects from both the Islamic and Byzantine worlds—the ultimate symbols of riches and prestige in this tenth-century Mediterranean society.

The Mediterranean Environment and Medicine at Salerno

A Salernitan ruler would undoubtedly have valued equally Byzantine and Islamic objects. Indeed, by the late tenth century, Byzantium and Islam had themselves reached a sort of equilibrium. On occasion, there continued to be fierce battling between these two great powers (and toward the very end of the century the balance appeared to be tilting toward Constantinople). Nonetheless, to a considerable degree there now was mutual acceptance. Romilly Jenkins has commented on evidence for this in the early tenth century, and later in the century we find the Byzantine *strategos* of Calabria selling wheat to Arab Sicily.[36] The *Lives* of the hermit-saints, like the monastic chronicles of Campania, may suggest implacable hostility between Christians and Muslims. But as the wheat sale indicates, in the real world there were continuous interchanges. Interactive commerce was by no means restricted to the occasional Amalfitan merchant. In effect, what the Arabs had not succeeded in achieving militarily, they had largely accomplished economically. Even southern Italy's hermit-saints seemed resigned to living in a world shared with Muslims. Several of these holy men moved fairly freely back and forth between Christian southern Italy and Muslim Sicily; and St. Nilus never seemed surprised to encounter Muslims as he journeyed through Calabria.

It was in this environment that Salerno became known as a medical center. There has long been debate about the origins of the medical school of Salerno. Everyone is agreed that it achieved its greatest eminence in the twelfth century, but when, exactly, can it be said to have begun?[37] To what did it owe its origins? How important was the Arab influence? (And was there, in fact, a Trotula?)[38] Local sources cannot give answers to all of these questions, but they can fill in the background and thereby perhaps sharpen the picture.

The fame of Salerno's doctors had already spread by the end of the tenth century. In 985, the bishop of Verdun journeyed there "causa salutis," even though, slightly later, Richer of Rheims would disparage Salernitan practitioners as woefully ignorant of theory.[39] There was surely then no medical school as such, but in contemporary Salernitan sources we do encounter two prominent *medici*. One, Lotharius, "clericus et medicus," served as witness to a major sale in 977; and the *Chronicon Salernitanum* tells of "Petrus, clericus precipuusque medicus," so highly valued by Gisolf that he was made bishop of Salerno.[40] Moreover, *medici* had figured in the Salernitan sources of the previous century. In 897, Guaimar I had granted some lands to Monte Cassino "per rogum Raiemfrid, medici et prepositi."[41] Earlier, in the mid-ninth century, "Josep medicus" (who was clearly not an ecclesiastic) had bought extensive properties, paying the largest land prices recorded at Salerno in that century.[42]

This "Josep" has already been mentioned in Chapter 5, for his name suggests that he was perhaps a Jew; that he later gave land to Salerno's dynastic abbey church, St. Maximus, may support this notion.[43] In any event, in a Salernitan charter of 1004 we find one Judah "ebreus" described as a son of Judah "medicus," so by the late tenth century Jewish doctors were unquestionably practicing at Salerno.[44] And this points to one of the most interesting aspects of the south Italian medical scene. In the late tenth century, in Calabria, St. Nilus of Rossano engaged in a debate with Donnolo, the most distinguished product of southern Italy's Jewish community and much celebrated for his skills as a physician.[45] Cilento believed that one Surano, court doctor at Capua in the ninth century, had in fact been an Arab; and in the tenth century a south Italian "prince" supposedly set off for Arab Palermo to consult the doctors there.[46] In the latter ninth century, we encounter at Benevento (and subsequently at Monte Cassino) a monastic official who is also a *medicus* and whose name, Criscius, may suggest Greek origins.[47] Finally, a number of medical manuscripts (including the *materia medica* of Dioscorides) are securely ascribed to ninth- and tenth-century southern Italy.[48] Plainly, in early medieval southern Italy, many medical traditions intersected.

At Salerno, the likely result was an eclectic approach to medicine. The disparaging remarks of Richer of Rheims suggest that Salerno's approach was also more empirical than theoretical, but the theoretical underpinnings may simply have differed from those familiar in the north. In any case, the bishop of Verdun was, unfortunately, not cured at Salerno. Yet something had induced him to make that long journey. Presumably northern Europe had begun to learn more about southern Italy as a result of the Ottonian ventures south. And perhaps word had spread that Salerno's doctors offered better than average prognostic skills.

Or possibly there was another reason. One may well wonder why the medical expertise of southern Italy should have coalesced at Salerno. As with overseas trading, Naples would certainly have seemed the more likely center. After all, for a thousand years people had flocked to the baths around the Bay of Naples for therapy as well as pleasure; this must have drawn physicians there as well. Of course Salerno's rulers could simply have come to be known as especially generous patrons of skilled practitioners. Yet there is another, more interesting possibility. Perhaps we should look to Salerno's close relationship with Amalfi. Albert Dietrich has observed that Arab medical theory made no significant advance over Galen and Hippocrates but that the Arab pharmacopoeia did become notably more extensive, presumably because of the spread of Islam eastward.[49] And John Riddle has noted in the early medieval Mediterranean an expanding *trade* in drugs, including new substances from the distant East.[50] Thanks to Amalfi, Salerno's doctors could particularly have benefited from this trade. Salerno may thus have been able to offer treatments unavailable elsewhere in the Christian West.

In any event, once we understand the environment in which Salerno's doctors functioned, it becomes easier to imagine their growing reputation. As in the case of "Beneventan" art, their approach to medicine undoubtedly represented the coming together of diverse traditions. Furthermore, given the stability and increasing prosperity of the principality of Salerno, it is not surprising that what they offered came in time to be institutionalized. Exactly when this happened—at what point there came to be a genuine "school"—we can never know. No doubt it evolved from a century or more of apprenticeships. But it should no longer seem surprising that all of this happened at Salerno.

Campania and Its Tenth-Century Ethos

The twelfth-century *Chronicon Vulturnense* looked back on the period "before the time of the Saracens" as southern Italy's Eden, when everyone could live on the land in peace, when there was no need for *castella*.[51] This statement has been challenged by those who view *incastellamento* as a tenth-century development, essentially unrelated to the Arabs—indeed occurring only after Arabs had stopped raiding San Vincenzo's region. In fact, of course, *incastellamento* in the sense of fortification did begin in direct response to the Arab threat. And even in the San Vincenzo region, in the tenth century, no one could be sure there would not be further Arab assaults; deeper in the south they were certainly continuing. Salernitan charters still reflected concern at the very end of the century.[52]

Nevertheless, the chronicle's statement does deserve challenge, for several reasons. First, southern Italy "before the time of the Saracens" was hardly an Eden. Instead, it was surely a grim world for all but the *maiores*, a world in which much of the population lived in servitude, and many others were ill-fed and miserable. Second, while the Arabs unquestionably caused much grief, at least for Campania the opening up to the Arab world had in the long run proved a positive step.

And, finally, the Arabs were hardly solely responsible for introducing violence to southern Italy. Most ninth-century Lombard rulers had been fierce and ruthless men. Both Sico and Sicard were unremittingly aggressive, and vengeful toward their enemies. Landolf, founder of the Capuan dynasty, preached violence to his sons. Guaifer, founder of the dynasty that was to rule Salerno until 977, once wantonly killed a poor peasant boy in a nearby field simply to demonstrate something to his son, the future Guaimar I.[53] Guaimar I was in turn captured and blinded by Beneventans, whereafter he behaved with such cruelty toward his own subjects that he was deposed. Also, at least one ninth-century ruler of Naples shared their proclivities; Athanasius II, that cultivated bishop of Naples, had become duke as well by wresting the throne from his brother and having him blinded and sent to Rome to die.[54]

The change in the tenth century thus seems remarkable. Even the coups at Salerno were apparently bloodless. When Gisolf was deposed in 973, he had only to spend a few months in minimal confinement at Amalfi before being restored to the throne; and later, after Manso of Amalfi seized the Salernitan throne but proved unable to retain it, he simply returned to being Duke of Amalfi, and his replacement in Salerno (Prince John) came in without violence. Only in Capua-Benevento, and there only at the very end of the century, do we once again find brother against brother in deadly power struggles.

Obviously, we cannot attribute the relative tranquillity of tenth-century Campania to lessons learned from the Arabs, who were hardly apostles of peace. But perhaps we can say that the opening to the Arab world provided a distraction, revealed means of aggrandizement even more interesting than ceaseless internecine warfare. Salerno turned to the enhancing of productivity and profits. The Capuans, it is true, still tried on occasion to enlarge their territory (mostly at Salerno's expense). And Amalfi, under Manso, had designs on Salerno. Increasingly, however, links were forged among the disparate ethnic and political entities of Campania. In the ninth century, whenever there were external threats or pressures, there had been short-term alliances, even between Naples and Capua or Naples and Salerno. But the tenth century brought something more like cohesion.

This cohesion was not institutionalized. Each Campanian state remained separate and distinct. But that separation was in fact desirable, a source of strength. The region's governmental mechanisms plainly worked best within relatively small political entities. The economy of each was free to develop naturally. At the same time, the entities could freely absorb elements from each other, as well as from Byzantium and the Islamic world.

The Beginning of the End

Unfortunately, a loose alliance of shared interests and tendencies could never withstand sustained attack by external powers. Furthermore, something plainly had been lost as ethnic differences blurred. In the tenth century the Lombards still adhered to Lombard law; they were still Lombards. But Pandolf Ironhead's fervent interest in becoming an Ottonian client would surely have horrified the earlier Lombard rulers of southern Italy. Pandolf had acted in part because of the threat posed by Byzantium; in addition, however, he clearly craved action on a larger stage.

Of course, all of the Campanian rulers had always been happy to accept Byzantine titles; the trappings of hierarchy had always had some appeal. And Monte Cassino and San Vincenzo al Volturno had continuously sought confirmation that they were imperial wards, under some emperor's protection. (When in the late ninth century no western emperor was ready to hand, San Vincenzo looked instead to Constantinople.)[55] But there were obvious practical reasons for this. Such special status could shelter the monasteries from fiscal impositions and territorial intrusions on the part of local rulers, just as a Byzantine connection could sometimes prove useful to a Lombard prince or a duke of Naples. In the latter tenth century, however, something more than pragmatism seemed to be coming into play. When Otto II came into southern Italy (on his way to the disaster at Stilo), the bishop of Salerno apparently journeyed all the way to Taranto to secure Otto's confirmation of the possessions of Salerno's episcopal church of St. Matthew.[56] We know of no particular threat to St. Matthew's holdings. The episode seemed simply to reflect new feelings about a properly ordered universe.

No doubt this attitude was welcomed by Otto II, just as he had welcomed Pandolf's overtures. And it is clear that Otto II's south Italian venture opened up southern Italy to Europe; from that point on, the south was never again to be so isolated from northern currents. In the new scheme of things, one stood apart at one's peril; at the close of the century, Capua and Benevento would learn that, forcefully, from Otto III.

In other words, the day of small independent entities was coming to an end. Byzantine emperors, too, were beginning now to want more than occasional signs of respect from Campanian rulers. Both eastern and western emperors had long claimed the whole of southern Italy; in the eleventh century Byzantium would mount its most determined drive in five hundred years to turn that claim into reality.

This last great Byzantine push has received ample attention elsewhere, particularly in Jules Gay's monumental work. Furthermore, it falls beyond the boundaries of this study, which has been deliberately designed to describe southern Italy *before* the tumultuous events of the eleventh century. Nonetheless, this eleventh-century Byzantine campaign influenced what the Normans inherited, and so in the epilogue I will describe at least some aspects of its impact and also the fate of Campania's principalities and duchies.

9. Epilogue: The Eleventh Century and After

BY THE LAST QUARTER of the eleventh century the Normans held virtually all of southern Italy. It had happened very quickly; and since Sicily was speedily taken too, and the Crusades provided additional distraction, it is no wonder that few, then or now, have looked back. Pre-Norman southern Italy seemed forgotten in the rush of events.

Yet that is where it had all begun. Fully to understand the variegated splendors of the Norman *Regno* and the comparative ease with which the Normans would exercise control over the mainland, a backward glance is essential. The southern Italy that has been the subject of this study did leave a mark on what was to come, and we need to assess this legacy.

First, however, we must take note of two developments that affected what was passed on. One relates to Byzantium's eleventh-century campaign. The second is the fate of the autonomous states whose history has been traced here through the tenth century.

The Byzantine Overlay

Byzantium's new effort to dominate southern Italy more or less coincided with the arrival of the first Normans, early in the eleventh century. The latter soon became key players—and ultimately the decisive factor. For the first few decades, however, when the Byzantine forces were led by the great Byzantine strategist Boioannes and the Normans simply marketed their services to the highest bidder (even if Byzantine), Byzantium's effort looked very likely to succeed. Jules Gay placed Byzantine power in southern Italy at its apogee in the last years of Basil II (1020–25) and he saw its decline commencing only in the 1040s, when combined Lombard-Norman armies began to win major battles.[1] Even then the decline was gradual; the end did not actually come until 1071, a generation later, when Bari fell to a Norman force led by Robert Guiscard.

For our purposes, it is particularly important to note the appalling violence of this eleventh-century struggle—and its total disruption of the "Beneventan" region. There, the Byzantine thrust was not the sole cause of disruption; German emperors, too, were now steadily making inroads in the south, installing their own abbots at Monte Cassino and harassing all of the Campanian states within reach. Forgetting cohesion, each Campanian ruler reacted differently, whether to interventions by popes and German emperors or to anti-Byzantine rebellions by the Lombards living in Apulia. Meanwhile, Norman mercenaries fanned out across southern Italy, now supporting Lombards against Byzantines, now Byzantines against Lombards, now Naples against Capua or vice versa. It was all reminiscent of the ninth century with its Arab mercenaries; but this was far more brutal and much more widely destructive.[2] Only Amalfi remained mostly detached.

And yet, despite the almost continuous violence of this period, it was now that Byzantium began truly to leave marks on the landscape and culture of southern Italy—a sign of how close Byzantium came to winning the contest. In the tenth century, there had been no flowering of Byzantine culture in southern Italy; as we have seen, Byzantium then had been mostly represented by garrisons, military governors, and the ascetic anchorite saints preaching disdain for things material.

In the eleventh century, however, Monte Cassino manuscripts began to reflect contemporary Byzantine style in their illustrations. And in the Byzantine-held regions the developments were striking. The painted Byzantine cave churches of Apulia probably date to the eleventh century, and also the most impressive Byzantine church still standing in southern Italy, at Stilo in Calabria.[3] In Calabria, too, entire new towns and cities were created.[4] Furthermore, Vera von Falkenhausen has noted a marked increase in Greek signatures to Apulian charters in the eleventh century.[5] This was especially noteworthy, for until then the population of Apulia had remained overwhelmingly Lombard. It seems clear that, in the eleventh century, Byzantium not only poured in more soldiers but also new settlers, and aimed not merely at subduing its portion of southern Italy but also rendering it more genuinely Byzantine. The end result was that, just as Byzantium was about to lose the whole of southern Italy, much of it did at last become "Byzantinesque"—thereby encouraging many scholars to assume, wrongly, a continuous Byzantine flavor over centuries.

The Fate of the Autonomous States

In the tumultuous eleventh century, each principality and duchy fared differently. But in at least one case the end of autonomy came quickly. The city of Benevento, rich in memories of Arichis and the great days of Lombard power in the south, had long been coveted by the papacy; Beneventan territory abutted on papal lands. And in 1051 the revitalized papacy achieved its objective. By then, the only alternative seemed to be subjugation to the Normans and so the Beneventans offered no resistance when Leo IX claimed them as papal subjects. From then on, the city of Benevento was a papal city, and the principality's territory was fragmented among various claimants. But Lombard Benevento did make one significant contribution to eleventh-century history: Desiderius, the great abbot of Monte Cassino who later became Pope Victor III, was a Beneventan. It seems altogether appropriate that he was a product of the Lombard principality with the most impressive traditions.

The principality of Capua, throughout the second quarter of the eleventh century, had as ruler yet another Pandolf, this one particularly prone to violence and duplicity. Over time, he alienated almost everyone on the south Italian scene, including all of his Campanian neighbors and most Normans. By the time he died in 1049, Capua was in disarray, and within ten years the principality was forced to surrender to a Norman, Richard of Aversa. Richard's uncle Rainulf had been the first Norman to secure a holding in Campania; Naples had given him Aversa (a minor town or *castrum* halfway between Naples and Capua) in return for military aid. Rainulf had also strengthened his position by marrying a sister of the Duke of Naples. With such strong local connections and the subsequent acquisition of Capua, these Aversa Normans were initially more powerful than the de Hauteville Norman faction. Eventually, however, they were compelled to swear homage to Robert Guiscard, the greatest and most celebrated de Hauteville brother. Later, after the Normans acquired Sicily, Capua remained a significant fiefdom (held, for example, by one of Roger II's sons), and "Capua" even became the generic term for much of Campania. Moreover, in the thirteenth century Frederick II seems to have been particularly attracted by the city's Roman past. But with autonomy gone, the Capua of Pandolf Ironhead and his forebears had in effect vanished.

Amalfi, out on its peninsula, managed to stay aloof from many of the vicious power struggles of the eleventh century. Its relationship with Salerno soured, however, and Amalfitan merchants were sometimes seized by the Salernitans and brutally treated. Finally, in 1131, the beleaguered duchy surrendered to Roger II. The Normans have usually been faulted for Amalfi's decline thereafter (although legend blamed the Pisan raid of 1135); and, plainly, Norman rule did affect Amalfi adversely. But there were also other factors: Amalfi's physical limitations as a port and the changing commercial climate of the central Middle Ages.

Naples, which had for so long resisted the Lombards, also managed for a considerable time to evade Norman domination. Sources for Naples are as meager for the eleventh century as for the tenth; for both those centuries, unfortunately, much of our information must be derived from retrospective mentions in Norman-era chronicles. Nonetheless, it seems clear that the duchy's independent survival, to 1139, was due partly to adroitness, partly to luck. Early on, Naples had hired Norman mercenaries, just as it had been the first to hire Arabs in the ninth century. And as the eleventh century progressed, Naples sought help wherever it could be found: from Byzantium, from the local Lombards, or from dissident Normans. On one occasion, Naples withstood a Norman siege only because the besiegers became distracted by other events. Finally, however, eight years after Amalfi had fallen to Roger II, Naples too was forced to surrender and the duchy was dissolved.

Given its late incorporation into the *Regno*, it is perhaps not surprising that the city of Naples did not then play a major role in Norman activities. Salerno, closer to Palermo and much interwoven with the Norman beginnings in southern Italy, seemed far more important. Only in the thirteenth century, under Frederick II, did the city begin to reacquire significance; and after Frederick's heirs were eliminated by Charles of Anjou, Naples became the Angevin capital. By then, it bore little resemblance to the Naples of Duke-Bishop Athanasius II. Yet in 1224 Frederick II had founded the University of Naples; the tradition of scholarship had plainly lived on and had had its reward.

For some time it appeared that Salerno would enjoy a happier fate than any of the other autonomous states. In the early eleventh century it was the most stable and prosperous of the Lombard principalities. Guaimar V, ruler during the crucial second quarter of the century, was forceful, intelligent, and immensely popular with his subjects. He also had a reputation for probity, and even when he took sides he seems to have retained the respect of popes and emperors and even the Normans. For more than two decades, Guaimar preserved Salerno's full independence despite increasing pressures from every direction. And in 1058, after Guaimar had been succeeded by his son (Gisolf II), Robert Guiscard discarded his Norman wife and married Sikelgaite, Gisolf's sister. Salerno's future thus seemed promising; but not quite twenty years later, in 1075, Robert Guiscard ousted his brother-in-law and assumed the throne of Salerno for himself.

Despite the loss of independence, even this at first appeared only to enhance Salerno's importance. There was a close relationship with Monte Cassino, reflected in similar (and ambitious) building programs.[6] It was in the city of Salerno that Gregory VII, fleeing from Rome, took refuge and died. Culture in general flourished, and as a medical center Salerno became ever more celebrated. Moreover, in the early twelfth century, before the Norman *Regno* was consolidated, the mainland Norman rulers treated the city of Salerno as their capital, and both Roger Borsa and Duke William of Apulia were buried there in the new cathedral built by Robert Guiscard. Later, when Roger II joined southern Italy to Sicily, the city remained, in effect, the mainland capital. Several key officials of the Norman court at Palermo were Salernitan, and one of the Normans' most important chroniclers, Romuald of Salerno, came from an old Lombard family.

But after the death in 1189 of Roger's grandson William II, Salerno's close connection with the Norman dynasty proved its undoing. The Salernitans opposed the claim of Emperor Henry VI to the *Regno*, and sided instead with Tancred. Since, as the daughter of Roger II, Henry's wife, Constance, provided Henry with his claim, the Salernitans seized her when in 1191 she paused at their city to break a journey. They then sent her, captive, to Tancred. In due course, papal maneuvering led to her release, but three years later, after Henry had defeated Tancred, he took terrible vengeance on Salerno and its citizens. Much of the principality's territory had long since been nibbled away by Norman feudatories; now the half-destroyed city fell into obscurity.

The South Italian Legacy

With the virtual destruction of the city of Salerno, the last of the old Lombard strongholds was gone, the last powerful symbol of Campania before the Normans. And with even the Norman *Regno* gone after the twelfth century, one might well think this the end of the old southern Italy.

Yet there still remains, today, one tangible reminder. It is perhaps not surprising that the modern *regioni* of southern Italy largely replicate the pre-Norman segmentations. (For example, the modern administrative regions of Apulia and Calabria are little different in outline from the Apulia and Calabria of the tenth century; and while "Basilicata" is a newer term, Campania has also endured.) But in addition, and most interesting, within these *regioni* once Lombard, many of today's administrative subdivisions closely correspond to the old Lombard gastaldates.[7] The origin of these subdivisions (many of which later became Norman fiefdoms) can serve to remind us of the tight local control exercised by Lombard rulers.

And this in turn points to a significant fact. Of the areas conquered by Normans in the eleventh century, not only Anglo-Saxon England but also Lombard southern Italy had exceptionally well-developed local structures. Norman feudalism, with all its special characteristics, was unquestionably imported whole and new into southern Italy. Lombard gastalds were certainly not vassals in the Norman sense, nor was the office heritable (although doubtless sons had on occasion succeeded gastald fathers). But the Lombard pattern of gastaldates as local administrative units must greatly have facilitated the imposition of feudalism.

It is true that during the Normans' first half-century in southern Italy the only foothold any Norman secured in Campania was Aversa. Initially, the Normans found it far easier to take territory in the Byzantine sections of southern Italy. Nonetheless, they were often employed as Lombard mercenaries, which gave them ample opportunity to observe the workings of government within the Lombard principalities. And eventually, of course, they acquired Salerno, the best governed of the principalities.

No doubt Normans were as scornful as nineteenth-century historians of Campania's fragmentation into independent mini-states; the advantages this offered would presumably have escaped them. Yet they could not help but notice the effective administrative and judicial systems in the Lombard regions and the high degree of public order.

It is not clear to what extent the Normans retained Lombard mechanisms after they had finally taken all of the principalities; this issue has never been fully explored. For the mainland, Evelyn Jamison hypothesized only some Byzantine influence on Norman administrative systems. Jamison, however, seemed unfamiliar with the southern Lombard scene, and some of the procedures she described seem more Lombard than Byzantine.[8] But at this point one can only say that *judices* continued to preside over local disputes and Lombard law was sometimes cited.

By the mid-twelfth century, of course, when Roger II was well along in centralizing government and the seat of government was Sicily, any Lombard legacy may have been so fully absorbed as to be unrecognizable. In the early days, however, the Normans would have been foolish not to retain, at least in the Lombard regions, procedures both effective and locally accepted. Moreover, one aspect of Lombard government must certainly have pleased the Normans: the strong tradition of regelian rights.

The southern Lombard rulers had customarily derived considerable income from fines, fees, permits, riparian jurisdiction, and marketing licenses. Those rights had been exercised for centuries; they were unquestioned, and it must have been easy to carry them forward into the Norman era.

Some structures, however, were definitely not carried forward. When we turn to the Norman treatment of religious institutions, we find a clear and deliberate break with the past. For the most part, the Lombard rulers had kept bishops firmly in their place; only occasionally did bishops intervene even as peacemakers. In ninth-century Capua and Benevento (as in non-Lombard Naples) the leading bishop was often the ruler's brother or close relative.[9] Moreover, many churches (and smaller monasteries) were proprietary in nature. On the other hand, there was no attempt to regularize religious practices, no theological interference, and there seem to have been few attempts to involve church leaders in secular objectives. The Normans changed all that. It is sometimes hard to distinguish between Norman policy and the mandates of the eleventh-century reform movement. But we do know that the Normans established many new foundations and brought in new (and carefully selected) abbots and bishops, and that the overall result, by Roger II's time, was a regularization of the ecclesiastical scene, with leading ecclesiastics also expected to perform a variety of services for the ruler. Additionally, though Greek churches and monastic foundations were permitted to continue (and indeed in the twelfth century some new ones were established with royal approval), the old blurring of lines between Latin Christianity and Greek was a thing of the past. A church integrated into the polity had to be conformist.

Yet if the Norman approach to religion represented a break with the past, the cultural scene revealed legacies. It is true that the Islamic flavor of Norman Palermo's architecture was entirely Sicilian; one cannot claim that for the mainland. The Arabs had left virtually no physical trace in mainland southern Italy, where they had merely come and gone on hit-and-run raids or camped for a time in makeshift bases. If they were responsible for any building in Bari during their tenure there, no doubt local craftsmen were employed; the buildings would thus not have been Islamic in design. The same was very likely true when they erected a mosque at Reggio in the tenth century.[10] Nonetheless, Campania had demonstrated openness toward all Mediterranean culture, including the Islamic. The autonomous areas had eclectic medical traditions and collected manuscripts reflecting wide-ranging, even esoteric interests. This seemed almost to anticipate Roger II. Furthermore, there had been centuries of trade with the Arab world, preparing the ground for additional intercourse.

Mainland southern Italy also had long had a taste for things Byzantine, and that taste had been notably reinforced in the eleventh century, when even in the autonomous areas Byzantine craftsmen had begun to be brought in.[11] In Sicily, in contrast, by the time the Normans arrived the Arabs had firmly held the entire island for a hundred years; what was left of the Greek population was weak and fragmented. The Byzantine tone of Norman Palermo must therefore have owed a good deal, if only indirectly, to the Norman experience on the mainland. For it was there that the Normans had first found "Byzantine" equated with the highest forms of art.

And beyond these specific cultural elements there was something else, a broader legacy. The Normans had learned in mainland southern Italy to live in an ethnically diverse environment and to become Mediterranean in outlook. By Roger II's time this was obviously second nature. But it was a lesson first absorbed in the world on which this study has focused.

It would be good to end on this note. In one respect, however, there was no enhancing transmission, and this had much to do with the shape and feel of the Norman *Regno* and with the ultimate fate of southern Italy as a whole. The Normans did not learn from southern Italy how to live progressively and creatively with cities. They had arrived too soon, before the south itself had fully learned this lesson.

In the tenth century there had apparently been no precommunal stirrings in any cities in Campania—only, perhaps, in the Byzantine regions. By the twelfth century, however, urban-centered revolts were occurring throughout southern Italy—only to be ruthlessly put down by the Norman rulers. When the city of Bari proved as restive under Norman rule as it had been in its Byzantine phase, Bari was leveled by William I, the implacable son of Roger II. The spirit of southern Italy's cities, obviously seen only as a threat, was deliberately extinguished.[12]

Cities like Bari in the old Byzantine regions, but also the major cities of Campania, plainly had the potential to develop in interesting ways. Indeed, it appears that tendencies not fully visible in the tenth century began to be evident not long afterward. At Naples, for example, around 1030 (if Capasso was correct in his dating) an exiled duke was permitted to return to power only after granting his subjects a charter promising no unjust imprisonments or confiscations, and further providing that decisions about war or peace would be made only after consultation and that there would be no interference with merchants coming to Naples.[13] It seems clear that Campania had retained memories of the consensus approach to rule that had prevailed before the tenth century. Moreover, there were other examples, beyond Campania. In the late eleventh century, Monte Cassino formally recognized the "ancient customs and liberties" of some communities within its jurisdiction.[14]

At least some south Italian cities might thus have evolved into something resembling northern-style communes, had they been left alone. And surely the same was true of the more vigorous cities in the Byzantine-held areas. But no such evolution was permitted. The turmoil of the eleventh century intervened and so the Normans simply inherited restless populations. They then co-opted those individuals who could be useful to them, and extinguished all vestiges of freedom.

In the last analysis, southern Italy in the ninth and tenth centuries must thus be viewed as a failed experiment. Its autonomous entities, advantageously situated in the midst of an increasingly flourishing Mediterranean world, had themselves flourished for a time, and made some contributions toward the future. But in the end they were unable to stand against the trend toward large, centralized states.

Notes

Introduction

1. Typical of these occasional visitors were the saintly Saxon Willibald in the early eighth century and the French monk Bernard in the latter ninth century; both, on their way to south Italian ports, called on local bishops and visited local shrines. Willibald, returning from Jerusalem, even spent several years at Monte Cassino. Their narratives indicate that, to Bernard in the latter ninth century, southern Italy seemed even more "foreign" than it had earlier to Willibald—partly, of course, because Arabs now held Bari and Taranto. (For Bernard and Willibald, see "Sources" listing in Bibliography.)

2. Evelyn Jamison's first article (1913) was on the Norman administration of Apulia and Capua; her final publication (1972, the year of her death) an edition of the *Catalogus Baronum*. (See the bibliography in her Festschrift, *Studies in Italian Medieval History*, ed. Philip Grierson and John Ward Perkins [Rome, 1956].)

3. Ferdinand Chalandon, *Histoire de la domination normande en Italie et en Sicile* (1907).

4. C. R. Beazley, *The Dawn of Modern Geography* (1897) I:130.

5. On this, see the apt comments of Herwig Wolfram, "The Shaping of the Early Medieval Principality and a Type of Non-Royal Rulership" (1971), pp. 50–51; as Wolfram notes, "The efforts and achievements of these bodies politic are unjustly overlooked by a 'king-centered' historiography interested too exclusively in [that] centralized. . . . Leviathan, the modern state."

6. For example, Michele Amari, true son of the Risorgimento, deplored southern Lombard resistance to the ninth-century attempts of the Emperor Louis II to create a united Italy (Amari, *Storia dei Musulmani di Sicilia*, 2d ed. [1933], 1:517–18, 530).

7. Vera von Falkenhausen (1967); rev. and trans. ed., cited hereafter, *La dominazione bizantina nell'Italia meridionale dal IX all'XI secolo* (1978). Guillou's articles have been collected in two Variorum volumes: *Studies on Byzantine Italy* (1970) and *Culture et société en Italie Byzantine, VI–XI s.* (1978).

8. Poupardin, *Inst.*, Introduction, page v.

9. Amatus of Monte Cassino, *Storia de' Normanni di Amato di Montecassino*, ed. Vincenzo de Bartholomaeis (1935), pp. 21–24. The eleventh-century Latin original of Amatus is long lost; we know it only through a fourteenth-century vernacular version and an apparent paraphrase in twelfth-century manuscripts of the chronicle of Leo Marsicanus. (For the latter, Bk. II, ch. 37, see not only the de Bartholomaeis

volume but also now the new *Monumenta* edition of Leo's chronicle, ed. Hartmut Hoffmann.) There are problems with this tale. The only recorded Arab-Salernitan confrontation (in this period) in fact came nearly twenty years later; and sending "local products" to Normandy too closely echoes Paul the Deacon's story (Bk. II, ch. 5) about Narses luring the Lombards to Italy.

10. William of Apulia, *La Geste de Robert Guiscard*, ed. and trans. Marguerite Mathieu (1961), pp. 98–101. Like Amatus, William of Apulia wrote in the late eleventh century. (A variation on his tale, too, appears in some Leo Marsicanus mss.) The date William gives for his Lombard-Norman encounter, 1016, is plausible; and Normans might well have visited the celebrated shrine of St. Michael because of their own devotion to that saint. Thus some historians have accepted William's narrative (or an interweaving of William and Amatus, as in the later Leo Marsicanus mss.).

11. The third possibility, that Pope Benedict VIII prodded Norman adventurers south to counter increasing Byzantine strength there, was proposed by Einar Joranson ("The Inception of the Career of the Normans in Italy: Legend and History" [1948], pp. 353–96). Joranson rested his theory on somewhat problematic northern reports; nonetheless, given what we know about Benedict VIII, Joranson's theory at least warrants consideration.

12. Present-day Campania is larger than classical Campania, but notably smaller than Paul the Deacon's Campania, which apparently stretched all the way north to the outskirts of the city of Rome. (See William Smith, *A Dictionary of Greek and Roman Geography* [London, 1872], 1:490–96; and Paul the Deacon, Bk. II, ch. 17.) Calabria, as a geographical term, migrated in the early medieval period. In the classical era, "Calabria" denoted the heel of the boot, while the toe was "Brutium." By the ninth century, however, Apulia, as a term, had stretched down to encompass the heel, as it does today; and Calabria had its modern meaning (Falkenhausen, *Dominazione*, pp. 6–8). Present-day Basilicata had no exact classical equivalent, but it does include much of what the tenth century knew as "Lucania"; see Guillou, "La Lucanie byzantine" (1965).

13. I am echoing here Nicola Cilento, in his *Italia meridionale longobarda* (1966), p. 175; Cilento, surely more than anyone, repositioned non-Byzantine southern Italy in the thinking of contemporary Italian historians. This study owes much to his work.

14. Cilento, "Il falsario della storia del longobardi meridionali: Francesco Maria Pratilli," *Italia meridionale longobarda*, pp. 24–39.

15. On the edition of the Salernitan charters (*Codex Diplomaticus Cavensis*), see Chapter 3, note 69.

16. The Westerbergh edition of the *Chronicon Salernitanum* includes a comprehensive analysis of its orthography and phonology (pp. 223–83) and, as is indicated there, the idiosyncratic usage in the *Chronicon* is similar to that of most ninth- and tenth-century south Italian documents. Usually, however, the meaning can be sensed, and I have therefore inserted "sic" only when some such alert seems vital. (In the case of obscure words, Du Cange, who plainly was familiar with south Italian material, remains much the best dictionary resource—but even he does not solve all problems.)

Chapter 1

1. Gay, *Ital. byz.*, viii.

2. Strabo described the Greek roots and the continuing Greek flavor of Naples in his day: *Geography*, Bk. V, sect. 4, ch. 7. The legend concerning St. Paul was still proudly repeated in the early tenth century, as the *Vita Athanasii* (p. 440) illustrates. On this legend, see Michelangelo Schipa, "Il ducato di Napoli," *ASPN* 17 (1892): 117–18.

3. One indication of prompt accommodation with Odoacer was that Romulus Augustulus was sent to end his days imprisoned in the castle of Lucullus on the Bay of Naples.

4. Cassiodorus, *Variae*, Bk. VI, Formula 23 (sample letter appointing Count of Naples, first quarter of the sixth century).

5. For a vivid description of Naples' suffering during the Byzantine reconquest, see E. A. Thompson, *Romans and Barbarians* (1982), p. 101.

6. See Schipa ("Napoli," *ASPN* 17 [1892]: 127ff.) on the vicissitudes of Naples and the infusion of new Byzantine settlers in the seventh century to repopulate its rural areas.

7. Thomas Hodgkin speculated that the Lombards found particularly congenial the upland, interior setting of Benevento (*Italy and her Invaders* [1880–99] 6: 67–68). Keeping away from the coasts would also have avoided the likeliest areas of confrontation with Byzantium.

8. Paul the Deacon, Bk. II, ch. 32. On the history of Monte Cassino, see Herbert Bloch, *Monte Cassino in the Middle Ages* (1986) 1: 3–14; or Bloch, "Monte Cassino, Byzantium and the West in the Earlier Middle Ages" (1946), pp. 163–224.

9. Paul the Deacon, Bk. V, ch. 29. Paul's many references to plague and pestilence should be remembered in relation to these "loca deserta"; the population had suffered not only at the hands of the Lombards.

10. Paul the Deacon, Bk. V, ch. 7.

11. After describing the Italian provinces, Constantine observed regretfully: "They used to remit annually to the emperor the sums due to the treasury" (*De admin. imp.*, ch. 27, pp. 112, 114). André Guillou noted this fiscal concern in "L'Italia bizantina" (1967), p. 2.

12. Bernard the Monk, *Itinerarium Bernardi Monachi*, p. 319. Bernard reports, astounded, that if a man goes on a journey there and his camel or ass dies, stranding his goods by the roadside, he can safely leave the goods while he goes off for help.

13. *Vita S. Nili Abbatis*, sects. 60–62.

14. Paul the Deacon, Bk. VI, ch. 1.

15. Ibid., ch. 27. The towns included Sora, Arce, and Arpino.

16. Evidence for the varying extent of Lombard/Byzantine/papal control in eighth-century southern Italy is fragmentary, but historians are roughly agreed on the division; for the territorial and political situation in the areas nearest Rome, see Thomas F. X. Noble, *The Republic of St. Peter* (1984), pp. 161–66, 179.

17. The ninth-century chronicler (and Monte Cassino monk) Erchempert looked back on Arichis II as "vir christianissimus et valde illustris atque in rebus

bellicis strenuissimus," presiding over a Beneventan golden age (Erchempert, pp. 235–36). Modern scholars seem inclined to agree; see, on the cultural goals and achievements of Arichis, Hans Belting, "Studien zum Beneventanischen Hof im 8. Jahrhundert" (1962), pp. 143–93. For Lombard involvement with Monte Cassino in this period, see the excellent study of Armand O. Citarella and Henry M. Willard, *The Ninth-Century Treasure of Monte Cassino in the Context of Political and Economic Development in South Italy* (1983). On San Vincenzo al Volturno, which "at its height in the early ninth century . . . may have rivalled its near neighbor Monte Cassino," see Chris Wickham, "The *terra* of San Vincenzo al Volturno in the 8th to 12th Centuries: the Historical Framework," in *San Vincenzo al Volturno: The Archaeology, Art and Territory of an Early Medieval Monastery*, ed. Richard Hodges and John Mitchell (1985), p. 227ff. See also the excavation reports by Hodges, Wickham, and Mitchell on the scale, complexity, and richness of the ninth-century buildings in *Archeologia Medievale* 8 (1981) and 10 (1983).

18. Hodgkin, *Italy and Her Invaders*, 8:63; Gay, *Ital. byz.*, pp. 33–34. In either case, a seat of Lombard power on the coast would obviously be an asset; "quod propter mare conticuum," said Erchempert (ch. 3, p. 235) of the move to Salerno.

19. Hodgkin, *Italy and Her Invaders*, 8:60.

20. *Cod. Carol.*, no. 80, pp. 612–13. On the question of Arichis's new title, it should be noted that in the ninth and tenth centuries Carolingian and papal documents continued to refer to Benevento's ruler only as *dux* (Poupardin, *Inst.*, pp. 6–7).

21. Erchempert, ch. 4, p. 236: "eum sacramento huiusmodi vinxit, ut Langobardorum mentum tonderi faceret, cartas nummosque sui nominis caracteribus superscribi semper iuberet."

22. We learn of Arichis sending only hostages and a promise of tribute from Einhard, *Vita Karoli*, ch. 10.

23. *Cod. Carol.*, no. 83, p. 617: "promittens ei, tam in tonsura quam in vestibus usu Graecorum perfrui sub eiusdem, imperatoris dicione."

24. See Hodgkin, *Italy and Her Invaders*, 8: 81–82, for a good discussion of the evidence concerning these events.

25. Erchempert said that recognition of Charlemagne on coins and in indictions continued for a while; however, "reliqua autem pro nihilo duxit observanda; mox rebellionis iurgium initiavit" (Erchempert, ch. 4, p. 236).

26. *Cod. Carol.*, no. 83, p. 618.

27. Pope Hadrian had learned early that the Lombards formed unlikely partnerships when it served their purposes; in 778, Hadrian indignantly wrote Charlemagne that Arichis was urging subjects of the pope ("nostrum populum") near Terracina to ally themselves with the Byzantine *patricius* of Sicily (*Cod. Carol.*, no. 61, p. 588).

28. "Liber et ingenuous sum natus utroque parente; semper ero liber, credo, tuente Deo!" (Erchempert, ch. 6, p. 237).

29. See, on this, and on the southern Lombard position in general in relation to Charlemagne, Ottorino Bertolini, "Carlomagno e Benevento" (1967), pp. 609–71; for the 812 agreement in particular, p. 669.

30. In 801, writing to Count Chrodogar: "Audivi vos ituros esse ad vastandam

Beneventam patriam. Scis optime, quale periculum ibi imminet tibi propter pestilentem illius terrae aerem." From this same year, there are two additional gloomy references to Benevento and Pippin's expedition against Grimoald and, in the same decade, another mention of Italy's "escas noxias" (*Alcuini Epistolae*, nos. 224, 211, 218, 281).

31. Noble, *Republic of St. Peter*, p. 179. Noble's analysis of the *Ludovicianum* controversy, and particularly of its territorial implications, is exemplary.

32. "Les territoires byzantins . . . [by this time] . . . ne sont que des morceaux épars, envelopées par les domaines . . . des Lombards de Benevent" (Gay, *Ital. byz.*, p. 3).

33. On the still visible stretches of the Appian Way, see D. J. Hamblin and M. J. Grunsfeld, *The Appian Way* (1974); since the topography of Lombard southern Italy echoed that of classical Rome, following the Appian Way leads past the remains of many Lombard sites.

34. *Chron. S. Ben Casin.*, ch. 4, p. 471. These baths long continued to draw visitors. Peter of Eboli's *De Balneis Puteolanis* notes thirty-five baths at Puteoli in Frederick II's time; Boccaccio talks of cures combined with amorous dalliance there. Apparently many of the baths survived more or less intact until a 1538 earthquake (C. M. Kauffmann, *The Baths of Pozzuoli* [1959], pp. 3–5).

35. The transformation of southern Italy's urban geography deserves its own study. Significant change apparently began only in the Norman period (and accelerated thereafter). If we draw a map based on towns mentioned in ninth-century sources, we find, for example, Roman Compsa and Aceruntia still important, functioning (as "Conza" and "Acerenza") as centers of Lombard gastaldates. But neither place appears on most maps depicting fifteenth-century southern Italy; presumably by then they had already become what they are today: small, isolated settlements well off the beaten track.

36. Paul the Deacon, Bk. IV, chs. 44, 46; Bk. VI, ch. 2.

37. The Emperor Leo's decree is not in question; see, for example, George Ostrogorsky, *History of the Byzantine State* (1957), p. 146. But on the issue of actual ecclesiastical control, especially in the more remote areas, see Noble, *Republic of St. Peter*, pp. 241–43.

38. On this tenth-century battling over jurisdiction, see the studies cited in Chapter 7, note 38.

39. This is a controversial question. Ostrogorsky (*Byzantine State*, p. 155), echoing once traditional opinion, stated that in the period of the zealous iconoclast Constantine V (741–75) "refugee monks fled, particularly to southern Italy, where they founded monasteries and schools and so created new centres of Greek culture." Lynn White and others objected that any such refugee monks could hardly have created *permanent* "centres of Greek culture," monks being by definition non-reproductive (White, *Latin Monasticism in Norman Sicily* [1938], p. 28). Nonetheless, if there indeed was an influx, this surely could have had some effect. Guillou objected that iconodule monks would not have fled to an area claimed by Constantinople ("Grecs d'Italie du Sud et de Sicile au Moyen Age: Les moines" [1963], pp. 83–84). However, that assumes far more stringent control than was ever exercised in the more remote areas of southern Italy.

40. Peter Charanis, applying linguistic evidence, asserted that the Greek-speaking population of pre-Norman southern Italy was almost entirely Byzantine Greek ("On the Question of the Hellenization of Sicily and Southern Italy During the Middle Ages" [1946], pp. 74–75). But exactly when, and from where, Byzantine Greeks came to southern Italy remains somewhat controversial. L. R. Ménager insisted that the major influx came only in the ninth and tenth centuries, when Byzantine Greeks fled from the Muslims now occupying Sicily ("La byzantinisation réligieuse de l'Italie méridionale (IX–XII siècles) et la politique monastique des Normands d'Italie" [1958], p. 759); Guillou disagreed, but not quite convincingly ("Grecs d'Italie du Sud," pp. 83–84). Silvano Borsari tended to share Ménager's view and also agreed with him that in any case there were never large numbers of Greek-speaking people (*Il monachesimo bizantino nella Sicilia e nell'Italia meridionale prenormanna* [1963], pp. 10–12).

41. The letter from Gregory the Great is quoted, apparently verbatim, by Paul the Deacon (Bk. IV, ch. 19). On substantial deforestation not taking place until the nineteenth century, see Russell Meiggs, *Trees and Timber in the Ancient Mediterranean World* (1983), esp. 382–83.

42. Ibn 'Abd al-Hakam, *La Conquête de l'Afrique du Nord et de l'Espagne* (1947), p. 47: "The *Rūm* have no olive trees in their own lands, and so they come to us to buy oil." (Written in the first half of the ninth century. "*Rūm*" [Romans] was the term for south Italians as well as Byzantines.) And Augusto Lizier, in a comprehensive survey of south Italian land contracts from the ninth to the eleventh centuries, found virtually no mention of olive trees in southern Italy (Lizier, *L'economia rurale dell'età prenormanna nell'Italia meridionale* [1907], p. 122).

43. *Cod. Carol.*, no. 59, p. 585: "famis inopia eos constringebat; qui alii ex eisdem Langobardis propria virtutae in navigia Grecorum ascendebant, dum nullum habebant spem vivendi." Gay speculated that these "Greek" slavers were from then-Byzantine-connected Amalfi or Naples; but Giuseppe Galasso, surely correctly, dismissed this notion ("Le città campane nell'alto medioevo" [1965], p. 111). Pope Hadrian knew Amalfitans and Neapolitans all too well and in his letters always clearly identified them. Amalfitans and Neapolitans were undoubtedly not averse to slave trading, but in this case the slavers do seem more likely to have been from elsewhere.

44. As Galasso has noted, agricultural decline appears to have begun in southern Italy in the last centuries of the Roman Empire ("Città campane," p. 64); the grim developments of the sixth and seventh centuries thus merely worsened an already deteriorating situation, and the eighth century had provided no opportunity for improvement.

45. Gay, *Ital. byz.*, p. 4; Gay undoubtedly meant not only wealth but well-being, but he notes (pp. 30–32) Arichis's lavish expenditures, to which there were many contemporary references. For example, when St. Mercury's body was brought from Cappadocia to Benevento, Arichis "oblatione munerum bone mentis nitorem pretenderet, ut de pupureis gausapis taceam et telis Phocaico stagmine textis et vasis argento aurove celatis, quibus etiam plurimum decoris extrinsecus margaritae electro variante polita clusione rutilantes addiderant . . . [and so forth] (*Translatio Sancti Mercuri*, p. 577).

46. Robert S. Lopez, "East and West in the Early Middle Ages" (1955), pp. 118–

26; Lopez's picture of conditions in northern Italy surely applies equally well to the south.

47. J. Lestocquoy, "The Tenth Century" (1947), p. 5; although focused on northern Europe, this article has relevance—and wise reminders—for the early medieval scene in general.

48. For a full description of Abbot Gisulf's new basilica, see Citarella and Willard, *Ninth-Century Monte Cassino*, pp. 39–41; for the ninth-century building program at San Vincenzo al Volturno, see the studies cited in note 17, above.

49. Galasso, "Città campane," p. 83; according to Galasso's calculations, Naples' walls (at least in the twelfth century) measured 4.5 kilometers around. At both cities, although we cannot be sure, it appears that the twelfth-century walls were identical with those of the tenth century, when at least at Salerno the city walls had been expanded.

50. Early medieval Bari and Taranto were both situated on small projections (in Taranto's case, a barely separated island) alongside the ancient harbors; the early medieval boundaries, confirmed by both contemporary sources and recent archaeology, present a marked contrast to the sprawling modern cities.

51. Galasso, "Città campane," p. 63.

52. In 778, Hadrian wrote to Charlemagne that the Byzantine *patricius* of Sicily was visiting Gaeta (*Cod. Carol.*, no. 61, p. 588); and in 812, although Naples apparently refused, Gaeta (with Amalfi) responded to a plea from a later *patricius* for naval help against Arab raiders attacking islands all along the Tyrrhenian coast (*MGH Epist.* V: 96). On Gaeta and Naples as attached to the Sicilian patriciate, see Gay, *Ital. byz.*, p. 17. Nonetheless, in the 812 instance Gaeta's response hardly seemed that of a dependency; the choice was clearly Gaeta's to make.

53. During a mid-eighth-century controversy over the selection of a new bishop, the pope was said to be powerless because "tunc Parthenopensis [Neapolitan] populus potestati Graecorum favebat" (John the Deacon, p. 424). Gay, however, noted that though Naples' aristocracy may then have been strongly pro-Byzantine, the clergy in the main stayed loyal to Rome (Gay, *Ital. byz.*, pp. 17–18). And in matters ecclesiastic, even the aristocracy seems increasingly to have tilted toward Rome; Duke Stephen II (755–800), who in 766 also assumed the office of bishop, sent his clergy to Rome for training and insisted that they adhere to a Latin/Roman liturgy (John the Deacon, p. 425). See, on this period, Schipa, "Napoli," *ASPN* 17 (1892): 377–84. (And on all issues relating to the duchy of Naples, see Giovanni Cassandro, "Il ducato bizantino," in *Storia di Napoli*, ed. Ernesto Pontieri [1967–74], Vol. 2, Part 1.)

54. *Vita Athanasii*, pp. 440, 441.

55. Evidence for the midcentury gastaldates comes primarily from the 849 division of the principality of Benevento, with half becoming the new principality of Salerno (*Radelgisi et Siginulfi Divisio Ducatus Beneventani*, known as the *Divisio*). The *Divisio* document lists Taranto among the gastaldates transferred to Salerno; the gastaldates that Benevento retained were not named, but their identities have been deduced from circumstantial evidence and they clearly included Bari and Brindisi (Gay, *Ital. byz.*, p. 63). Ibn al-Athīr, describing the Arab capture of Bari in the 840s, said that it was then held by Christians who were not "*Rūm*" (i.e., not

Greek-speaking): *Annales du Maghreb et de l'Espagne* (1898), p. 214. There is ample evidence that the Lombards were in control all along southern Italy's Adriatic coast in the early decades of the ninth century.

56. On Naples minting its own coinage by the latter eighth century, with first Naples' duke, and later St. Januarius, replacing the Byzantine emperor on the coins, see Arthur Sambon, *Recueil de monnaies médiévales du Sud de l'Italie avant la domination normande* (1919), p. 74.

Chapter 2

1. The document formally splitting Lombard southern Italy into the two principalities of Benevento and Salerno—the *Divisio*—may actually have been signed not in 849 but late in 848 (Cilento, *Sign. cap.*, p. 93). Lacking sure proof, however, in this study I will hold to the traditional 849.

2. "Beneventanorum princeps" is the term usually employed in contemporary south Italian sources, but in formal documents we sometimes find instead the assertive "Langobardorum gentis princeps"; see, for example, the *Pactum Sicardi*, *MGH Leges* IV: 217. On the embellishment of Benevento, see Belting, "Studien zum Benventanischen Hof"; on the fortification and embellishment of Salerno, see Paolo Delogu, *Mito di una città meridionale* (1977), pp. 36–37.

3. In 717, Pope Gregory II tried to help Naples regain from the Lombards the *castrum* of Cuma (Roman Cumae), just above the Bay of Naples (Jaffé-Loew., nos. 2154, 2155). In the eighth century the Lombards also took from Naples the town of Nola (inland, to the northeast) and part of the adjoining Terra di Lavoro (Schipa, "Napoli," *ASPN* 17 [1892]: 589–90).

4. Sico was not only gastald of Acerenza but apparently a bastard son of Arichis II; see Michelangelo Schipa, "Storia del principato longobardo di Salerno" (1887, republished 1968), p. 97. Possibly Grimoald was thought weak because in 814 he had agreed to resume paying tribute to the Carolingians (*Annal. Reg. Franc*, p. 141).

5. *Chron. Salern.*, ch. 60, p. 60; ch. 68, p. 65.

6. "Vir omnibus vitiis carnalibus circumsessus, ac super omnia avarissimus" (Leo Marsicanus, Bk. I, ch. 22, p. 67).

7. Arichis II had set new standards for Benevento's gold coinage; his *solidus* had a value roughly half that of the contemporary Byzantine *solidus*. His coins, particularly his *tremisses*, were frequently specified at Salerno even a century later. Plainly, Sicard's gold coinage was also highly valued, since it was still stipulated in the 850s, nearly two decades after his death (*CDC* I, nos. 42, 44, 47, 54, 556). See, on both, Sambon, *Monnaies du Sud*, pp. 12–14, 19–21.

8. *Chron. Salern.*, ch. 57, p. 58.

9. John the Deacon, ch. 57, p. 431: "Contra hunc etenim Andream [the new Duke of Naples] Sichardus Beneventanorum princeps, filius Siconis, innumerabilies molitus est irruptiones. Pro quibus commotus Andreas dux, directo apocrisario, validissimam Saracenorum hostem ascivit." ("Directo apocrisario," in con-

temporary south Italian usage, indicated ecclesiastical approval at a high level; possibly here the bishop of Naples.)

10. Letter from Pope Leo III to Charlemagne, August 26, 812 (*MGH Epist.* V: 96.) See, on this raid, Chapter 1, note 52.

11. At the time of the Ischia raid, this splinter group of Ommayids was a menace in the central Mediterranean; Stanley Lane-Poole, certainly overgenerous, described them as "supporting themselves as best they could by sea commerce" (*A History of Egypt in the Middle Ages* [1936], p. 36).

12. John the Deacon (note 9, above) described these new mercenaries only as "Saracens," but Amari guessed them to be Aghlabids and from Sicily (Amari, *Storia*, 1: 446).

13. The complete text of the *Pactum Sicardi* is given in *MGH Leges* IV: 216–21. For an excerpt in translation, and commentary, see Robert S. Lopez and Irving W. Raymond, *Medieval Trade in the Mediterranean World* (1961), pp. 33–35.

14. On the "Greek" slavers, see Chapter 1, note 43.

15. *MGH Epist.* V: 96, no. 6. (This episode was cited in Chapter 1, note 52, and in note 10, above.) At Lampedusa, all of the raiders were reportedly captured or killed.

16. Ibid., p. 97: "familia et peculia Neapolitanorum non parva invenerunt."

17. See Chapter 1, note 56.

18. At Naples in the previous century this had happened in reverse. Stephen II, *dux* from 755 to 800, had become bishop as well in 766 and in his dual role defended Naples against both Pope Hadrian and the Lombards. See Schipa, "Napoli," *ASPN* 17 (1892): 381–84. (On Duke Stephen II and his policies, see also Chapter 1, note 53.)

19. In the 780s, Arichis had tried to seize Amalfi but was thwarted by Naples (*Cod. Carol.*, no. 78, p. 610). For the reports of Sicard's success in 838, see the *Chronicon Amalfitanum*, in Ulrich Schwarz, *Amalfi im frühen Mittelalter* (1978), chs. 3–4, pp. 197–98; and see also *Chron. Salern.*, chs. 72–74, pp. 71–73. (The version in the *Chronicon Salernitanum* largely derives from the ninth-century *Historia inventionis* of St. Trophimena; Trophimena was Amalfi's patron saint, and her remains went off to Salerno too.)

20. *Chron. Salern.*, chs. 79–80b, pp. 75–79. Taranto, like most of southern Italy, had been under Sicard's control, and Sikenolf had initially been imprisoned because he had rebelled against his brother. Presumably he continued to be held after Sicard's death because he was still thought a threat, as indeed he was.

21. There is ample evidence of a pulling apart at this point; see M. Berza, "Amalfi preducale: 596–957" (1938), pp. 363–67; and Carmine Noschese, "Coincidenze e contrasti nei rapporti tra Amalfi e Salerno nell'età prenormanna," p. 160.

22. *Annal. Reg. Franc.*, p. 153; for the 813 raid at Civitavecchia, p. 139.

23. Both Amari and Schipa speculated that Naples encouraged Sicilian Arabs to attack Brindisi, in order to keep Sicard too busy to harass Naples; on this and the assaults on Bari and Taranto, and on the ill-fated Venetian expeditions, see Giosue Musca, *L'Emirato di Bari* (1964), pp. 15–20.

24. John the Deacon, ch. 60, p. 432. Waitz, the *Monumenta* editor of John the Deacon's narrative, dated the Ponza episode to 846, but John the Deacon clearly reported it taking place just as Michael III assumed the Byzantine throne, in 842.

25. *LP* II: 81–82 (Life of Gregory IV).

26. For the Arab conquest of Sicily, one should still turn first to Amari's *Storia dei Musulmani di Sicilia* (in the 1933 annotated edition of C.A. Nallino); no major new sources have been discovered since Amari's day. But for mainland Italy as well, and for cultural as well as politico-military developments, there is now a large, superbly illustrated volume by Francesco Gabrieli and Umberto Scerrato: *Gli Arabi in Italia* (1979, rpt. 1985).

27. Ibn al-Athīr, *Annales du Maghreb*, p. 216. There has been disagreement about the translation of Ibn al-Athīr's sentence reporting this; some have thought the Arabic to imply an actual force sent from Naples. Fagnon's translation suggests, as seems more likely, that there were some individuals from Naples (merchants?) in Messina when the siege began: "Les habitants de Messina de Naples [i.e., who were from Naples] lui [the Muslim leader] demanderent quartier et firent cause commune avec lui."

28. Benevento was the first, apparently hiring some North African Berbers ("Agarenos Libicos") who had been raiding around Bari; Salerno then promptly hired "Hismaelitas Hispanos," Spanish Muslims found marauding in the Taranto region (Erchempert, ch. 17, p. 241; see also *Chron. Salern.*, ch. 81, and *Chron. S. Ben. Casin.*, ch. 5, p. 471). It is thought that the Spanish Muslims had come from that colony now occupying Crete—but once again restless.

29. *LP* II: 99 (Life of Sergius II). According to this narrative, a warning, giving these numbers, was sent by the Carolingian governor of Corsica two weeks before the raiders landed at Ostia, but the warning had not been taken seriously. (Doubtless the numbers were exaggerated but this force does appear to have been very large.)

30. John the Deacon, ch. 60, pp. 432–33.

31. *LP* II: 100.

32. In the *Liber Pontificalis*, the thirty-three pages of the Life of Leo III (795–816), *LP* II, are almost entirely devoted to donations of solid silver liturgical vessels, jeweled vestments, and other such rich embellishments. The Life of Hadrian I (772–98) and the Life of Gregory IV (827–44) also contain impressive listings. (On the new splendors of Rome's churches in this period, see Richard Krautheimer, *Rome: Profile of a City, 312–1308* [1980], chapter 5.)

33. For example, the *Annales Bertiniani* reports them desecrating St. Peter's high altar and then moving on to St. Paul's, where they were met by a force rushed in from south of Rome (*Annal. Bertin.*, pp. 52–53). It is not clear whether the raiders had time also to strip St. Paul's before they were driven from Rome.

34. See Philarète Lauer, "Le poème de 'La Destruction de Rome' et les origines de la cité Léonine" (1899), for the best analysis of all relevant facts and fictions, including those involving the raiders' activities after leaving Rome (for this, see esp. pp. 348–49). See also Duchesne's analysis in *LP* II: 104, n. 38.

35. *Cap. Reg. Franc.* II: 65–68, no. 203. On the building of the wall (and the 846 sack), see Peter Llewellyn, *Rome in the Dark Ages* (1971), pp. 262–65.

36. *LP* II: 118 (Life of Leo IV).

37. The design is attributed to Raphael, the execution to Giulio Romano; this and the other frescoes in the Stanza dell'Incendio were commissioned by Pope Leo

X. The Battle of Ostia seems actually to have taken place off Gaeta, quite far down the coast, but the aim was the protection of Ostia.

38. John the Deacon, ch. 60, p. 433. John the Deacon wrote his *Gesta Episcoporum Neapolitanorum* in the latter ninth century; it is not always possible to reconcile his chronology of the 846–49 events with that of the *Liber Pontificalis*, but his narrative is invaluable for its south Italian detail.

39. *Chron. Salern.*, ch. 81, p. 80; *Chron. S. Ben. Casin.*, ch. 7, p. 473; Leo Marsicanus, Bk. I, ch. 26, pp. 74–75. The two latter reports, the first nearly contemporary and the second compiled in the late eleventh century, describe in detail the staggering array of treasures taken by Sikenolf to pay his Arabs. (For these reports, with translations, see Citarella and Willard, *Ninth-Century Monte Cassino*, pp. 86–89.)

40. *Cap. Reg. Franc.* II: 65–68, no. 203.

41. Erchempert, ch. 18, p. 241. We can be no more precise today than was Du Cange in translating *nummis* (*Glossarium* V: 623: "minutior moneta"). In this case, however, the small gold pieces may well have largely been *tremisses*, worth one-third of a *solidus*; *tremisses* constituted the most common gold coinage of both Arichis and Sicard.

42. *LP* II: 90 (Life of Sergius II).

43. This seems implied by the report that 2,000 gold *solidi* were extorted from Monte Cassino by Sikenolf's "cognatus" to take on a mission to Spoleto; shortly thereafter Sikenolf himself, on his way to Rome for the coronation, took away a gold and emerald crown that Sico had presented to the monastery (Leo Marsicanus, Bk. I, ch. 26, pp. 75–76).

44. *Chron. Salern.*, ch. 82, p. 82.

45. *Chron. S. Ben. Casin.*, ch. 7, p. 473. It is roughly fifty-five miles from Telese to Isernia, and another fifty-five miles or so on from Isernia, past Monte Cassino, to Aquino; Arab raiders thus covered a considerable area on each sweep.

46. *Chron. Salern.*, ch. 83, p. 84.

47. There are several references to Sikenolf campaigning with his mercenaries, including one colorful anecdote in the *Chronicon Salernitanum* (ch. 81, p. 81). According to the *Chronicon*, Apolaffar had begun his mercenary career not with Radelchis but with Sikenolf, but had stormed off from Salerno in a rage one day because Sikenolf insulted him as they were returning together from a military foray. As the *Chronicon* describes it, the two were clambering up the outer stairs of the palace when Sikenolf, exuberant over their success, impulsively grabbed Apolaffar, a small man, and hoisted him up to the next step. Apolaffar, very sensitive about his size, found this an unpardonable humiliation.

48. Erchempert, ch. 17, p. 241. Little remains today of Siponto; by the thirteenth century it had suffered so many vicissitudes, including earthquake, that its inhabitants were moved nearby to the newly created town of Manfredonia. But in our period Siponto had special importance for Lombards as the gateway to their great shrine of St. Michael.

49. Ibid. If Erchempert's narrative is accurate, the whole affair was artfully staged by Guy, who was Sikenolf's brother-in-law. Learning of Radelchis's fear and sensing the possibilities, Guy told Sikenolf there might be more profit in *not* taking

territory; Guy then asked Radelchis for 70,000 gold *nummis* and divided the take with Sikenolf.

50. On this emirate, see the excellent study by Giosue Musca cited in note 23, above.

51. Leo Marsicanus, Bk. I, ch. 29, p. 84. Hartmut Hoffmann, editor of this new edition of Leo's Monte Cassino chronicle, dates this action to May 848.

52. Two Monte Cassino chroniclers (Erchempert, ch. 19, pp. 241–42; and Leo Marsicanus, Bk. I, ch. 29, p. 84) describe Louis as present along with "omnibus Langobardis." The *Chronicon Salernitanum* (ch. 84, pp. 84–85) credits Guy of Spoleto with the agreement and makes no mention of Louis. John the Deacon (ch. 61, p. 433) says of the division only that Louis ordered it.

53. *MGH Leges* IV: 221–25. See note 1, above, on the date.

54. Gay, *Ital. byz.*, p. 63; Cilento, *Sign. Cap.*, p. 93.

55. Gay, *Ital. byz.*, p. 63.

56. "Generatione" (generation of vipers) frequently appears in south Italian sources of this period as a general term for Muslims or Arabs; no doubt it was included here lest some clever south Italians claim that their Arabs were not "Saraceni" (typically, a term for North African or Sicilian Arabs) but "Mauri."

57. "Et praesentaliter, antequam domnus Ludovicus rex cum suo exercitu exeat de ista terra" (*Divisio*, clause 24, p. 224).

Chapter 3

1. Erchempert, ch. 20, p. 242. Musca (*Bari*, pp. 42–43) notes errors in the northern reports concerning this 852 expedition.

2. *Chron. Salern.*, ch. 94, p. 95.

3. "Sarraceni de Benevento Neapolim fraude adeuntes vastant, diripiunt et funditus evertunt" (*Annal. Bertin.* [856], p. 73). No southern source mentions this raid, but presumably territory claimed by the duchy was indeed raided. Yet the connection with Benevento is puzzling. Perhaps the distant annalist confused Benevento with Bari; otherwise, this suggests that, despite Louis' hard work three or four years before, there still were Arab bands around Benevento.

4. *Chron. S. Ben. Casin.*, ch. 16, p. 476; ch. 18, p. 477; ch. 19, pp. 477–78; also (for 861) *Annal. Ben.*, p. 174. The first source here is confusing in its chronology, but Musca (*Bari*, pp. 62–65) sorts it out.

5. Gay, (*Ital. byz.*, p. 71) accepted also a north Italian report that Louis came south in 863, but Musca sensed confusion with a later trip (Musca, *Bari*, p. 62, and p. 67, n. 13).

6. Taranto, first held briefly by an Arab force in 839, was taken for the second time in 846 and thereafter remained almost continuously in Arab hands until 880, when a resurgent Byzantium reclaimed it. Sources for Muslim Taranto are even more meager than for Muslim Bari, but Musca incorporates within his *L'Emirato di Bari* what little Taranto information there is.

7. Erchempert, ch. 29, p. 245. Waitz, in editing this chronicle for the *Monu-*

menta, gave 860 as the date for these raids, but 862 accords better with all other information.

8. Gay, *Ital. byz.*, p. 49; in Sicily, by this time, the Muslims controlled all but the easternmost end of the island.

9. Al-Balādhurī, *The Origins of the Islamic State*, ed. and trans. P. K. Hitti (1916; rpt. 1966), pp. 371–72; al-Balādhurī's narrative was written in Baghdad in the late ninth century.

10. Ibid., p. 372. Musca noted that designation as emir would have had religious as well as political significance, and that the request was sent to orthodox Baghdad, not to North Africa, the Bari Muslims' homeland (*Bari*, pp. 48–51, 68–69).

11. Bernard (*Itinerarium Bernardi*), p. 310. In fact, the letters proved only moderately useful in Egypt, where Bernard found he had to pay all manner of fees and buy new letters; the bureaucracy and costly paperwork in the highly organized Islamic world astonished Bernard, as did the requirement that one carry identification.

12. Ibid., p. 311.

13. *The Chronicle of Ahimaaz*, ed. and trans. Marcus Salzman (1924); the preferred edition now is apparently that of B. Klar (Jerusalem, 1944) but it provides the text only in Hebrew.

14. Erchempert, ch. 29, p. 245. His name was variously spelled in Christian sources, sometimes with a play on "Satan"; but "Sawdan," a frequent variant, does seem to have been close to his Arabic name (Musca, *Bari*, p. 59).

15. *Chronicle of Ahimaaz*, p. 76.

16. *Chron. S. Ben. Casin.*, ch. 13, p. 475. Waitz, the *Monumenta* editor, dated the episode tentatively to 852; Musca (*Bari*, p. 62) found better evidence for 860.

17. *Chron. Salern.*, ch. 99, pp. 99–100.

18. *Cap. Reg. Franc.* II: 94–96, no. 218. The indiction dates the capitulary to 866, but other evidence convinced Gay (*Ital. byz.*, p. 72) that it had actually been issued in 865; since we have the capitulary only by way of the notoriously haphazard *Chron. S. Ben. Casin.*, miscopying does seem likely.

19. Erchempert, chs. 30 and 32, p. 246; Erchempert indicates, however, that Salerno was only "minime" enthusiastic.

20. Erchempert, ch. 32, pp. 246–47; *Chron. S. Ben Casin.*, ch. 4, p. 471. For an interpretation more sympathetic to Landolf's position, see Cilento, *Sign. Cap.*, pp. 106–7.

21. On Guaifer's early assurance of loyalty, see Schipa ("Salerno," p. 125); on the fate of Ademar, Guaifer's predecessor, Schipa accepted the grim tale related in the *Chronicon Salernitanum* (ch. 105, p. 105). We cannot be sure how quickly Guaifer demonstrated his newly declared allegiance because no Salernitan charters from February 866 to September 868 survive. But from September 868 through July 871, all Salernitan charters included Louis in the indiction (*CDCI*, nos. 64–70).

22. See Chapter 1, note 34.

23. Five years later Louis was to give vent to his frustration at Naples' collusion with the Arabs, and he may first have sensed the dimensions of the problem during this stay nearby.

24. *Chron. S. Ben. Casin.*, ch. 4, p. 471, provides the most complete report of the tour. Louis now made Benevento his headquarters for the taking of Bari: "Hludouvicus Italiae imperator una cum uxore sua Ingilberga in Beneventum contra Sarracenos movit" (*Annal. Bertin.* [866], p. 126).

25. Ch. 6 of the capitulary (see note 18, above).

26. Erchempert, ch. 33, p. 247; *Chron. S. Ben. Casin.*, ch. 4, p. 471; Lupus Proto. [867], p. 52. In the *Chronicle of Ahimaaz*, Oria is pictured as a thriving center before the Arabs came; perhaps the inhabitants of Oria thus helped Louis to retake it, whereas Matera resisted. Or perhaps Matera, more strategically located, was burned in order to render it useless to the Muslims in future.

27. Musca, *Bari*, p. 92.

28. The proposed Byzantine marriage is referred to in the 853 entry of the *Annal. Bertin.* (p. 68): "Greci . . . contra Ludouuicum, filium Lotharii, regem Italiae, concitantur propter filiam imperatoris Constantinopolitani ab eo desponsatam, sed ad eius nuptias uenire differentem." Some scholars have therefore dated the marriage negotiations, too, to 853. But we know that Louis married Engelberga in 851, since the traditional *morgencap* payment had been made in October of that year; see Charles E. Odegaard, "The Empress Engelberge" (1951), p. 96, n. 2. The annalist must therefore have simply been referring to continuing "Greci" resentment; see, on all of the abortive Byzantine overtures of the 840s, Werner Ohnsorge, "Das Kaiserbündnis von 842–844 gegen die Sarazenen" (1955), pp. 88–131.

29. This is not the place to retrace the "Photian schism." This issue, however, dominates the Hadrian II section of the *Liber Pontificalis* (*LP*II: 173–86), indicating that, far from abating with the death of Pope Nicholas, concern intensified in the five years (867–72) of Hadrian II's papacy.

30. That Louis was at Benevento in March we know because of an awkward situation he then faced. In February, Hadrian II had urged widespread prayers on Louis' behalf: "oretis pro christianissimo filio nostro Hlodowico imperatore Augusto, ut ei Deus omnipotens ad nostram perpetuam pacem Sarracenorum faciat subditam nationem" (*LP* II: 176). But the very next month Louis became the uncomfortable host at Benevento of one Arsenius, whose son had just abducted and forcibly married (or raped?) Pope Hadrian's daughter; Arsenius fled to Louis for safety. (In the wake of the ensuing scandal, both the unfortunate girl and her mother were killed, and Anastasius Bibliothecarius was temporarily banished from Rome; see *Annal. Bertin.* [868], pp. 144ff.)

31. *Chron. Salern.*, ch. 107, p. 107: "Sed ut cognovisset ille imperator [Louis] ut minime Varim [Bari] expugnare valeret, eo quod non haberet marinos hostes, statim Constantinopolim Basilio imperatori legacionem misit, quatenus sine mora navalis exercitus micteret, ut Varim una cum ipso posset attribuere."

32. Louis and Engelberga had only two children, both daughters. One, Gisela, died in this same year, 868, and the other, Ermengard, later married Boso of Provence; we do not know when in 868 Gisela died, so possibly either could have been the proposed bride. The only reports of this marriage alliance come after the fact; see notes 38 and 42, below.

33. See note 31, above, and *Chron. Salern.*, ch. 103, p. 104; see also *De admin. imp.*, ch. 29, p. 128.

34. In *De administrando imperio*, ch. 29, the history of Byzantium's connection with the peoples of the Dalmatian coast is told as preamble to Basil's overture to Louis II.

35. For example, Louis' reference in the letter to "populis Sclavenie nostre" (*Chron. Salern.*, ch. 107, p. 117), with its firm possessive, can serve to remind us—as it doubtless was meant to remind Basil—of understandings concerning part of the Dalmatian coast dating back to Charlemagne's day. (This celebrated letter is known to us only because it was copied within the *Chronicon Salernitanum*; see note 47, below.)

36. *Annal. Bertin.* [869], pp. 153–54. Pope Nicholas's severe punishment of the German bishops for granting the divorce had so enraged them that they had been in touch with Photius (who hoped to see Nicholas deposed). Moreover, for nearly ten years Lothar's marital problems had kept Lotharingia in ferment and had entangled not only the papacy but also Lothar's uncles, Louis the German and Charles the Bald; for a recent discussion, see Rosamond McKitterick, *The Frankish Kingdoms under the Carolingians* (1983), pp. 178–79.

37. Engelberga, who had once made peace between Louis and Pope Nicholas, may actually have been the better choice but it was not easy even to lure her from Benevento; she had to be begged and amply rewarded. With gifts to Pope Hadrian as well, however, the reconciliation was finally achieved (*Annal. Bertin.* [869], pp. 153–54; Jaffé-Loew., nos. 2915, 2916). Less than two months later, Lothar died of a fever, at Piacenza.

38. *Annal. Bertin.* [869], pp. 164–65: "Qui [Basil] patricium suum ad Bairam [Bari] cum CCCC navibus miserat, ut et Hludovvico contra Sarracenos ferret suffragium et filiam ipsius Hludovvici a se desponsatam de eodem Hludovvico susciperet et illi in coniugio sibi copulandam duceret. Sed quadam occasione interveniente, displicuit Hludovvico dare filiam suam, unde idem patricius molestus Corinthum rediit."

39. *Chron. Salern.*, ch. 107, p. 117.

40. Werner Ohnsorge theorized that Basil tied recognition of Louis' title to the marriage, whereas Louis wished it understood that the title was his by right ("Die Entwicklung der Kaiseridee im 9. Jahrhundert und Süditalien" [1963], pp. 220–22). Yet it is hard to believe that Basil would ever have agreed to Louis calling himself "Emperor of the Romans."

41. *Chron. Salern.*, ch. 107, p. 116.

42. *Anastasii Biblio. Epistolae*, p. 410, no. 5.

43. *Annal. Bertin.* [869], p. 165.

44. On this, see Musca, *Bari*, pp. 107–9.

45. On the dating of the fall of Bari, see Musca, *Bari*, p. 109, n. 49. The author of the *Chronicon Salernitanum* (ch. 108, p. 121) mentions only a land army of Franks and Lombards, but Louis' letter to Basil also refers to "eisdem Sclavenis nostris cum navibus suis" (*Chron. Salern.*, ch. 107, p. 118). Constantine Porphyrogenitus reported a major Byzantine role as well (*De admin. imp.*, ch. 29, p. 128) but there is no evidence for that; see *De administrando imperio*, II: *Commentary*, ed. Jenkins (1962), pp. 104–5, n. 29/108–12.

46. *De admin. imp.*, ch. 29, pp. 128–30.

47. Both date and authorship of the letter were much debated earlier in this century, but there now seems general consensus that it was written in the spring or early summer of 871, with Anastasius Bibliothecarius playing a major role in its composition.

48. Romilly J. H. Jenkins, *Byzantium: The Imperial Centuries, A. D. 610–1071* (1966), p. 180.

49. On the unresolved question of Engelberga's parentage, see Odegaard, "The Empress Engelberge," p. 77 and p. 96, n. 3; she was once erroneously thought to have been the sister-in-law of Charles the Fat.

50. *Annal. Bertin.* [872], p. 188.

51. *Chron. Salern.*, ch. 109, p. 121: "Cumque Beneventani hostiliter insequeretur sua coniuge, atque mulieres illorum omnimodis nimirum fedaret, idipsum Beneventanis variis iniuriis afficeret, asserens ad suos quia 'Minime se sciunt communire Beneventani clippeis'."

52. Erchempert, ch. 34, p. 247.

53. *Annal. Bertin.* [871], pp. 182–84.

54. Ibid., p. 183; *Chron. Salern.*, ch. 109, p. 122. For an excellent recent discussion of Louis' imprisonment and its literary echoes, see Carmela Russo Mailler, "La politica meridionale di Ludovico II e il 'Rythmus de captivitate Ludovici imperatoris'" (1982), pp. 6–27.

55. *Chron. Salern.*, ch. 109, p. 122.

56. *De admin. imp.*, ch. 29, p. 130. That Louis (urged by Engelberga) had planned to exile at least Adelchis was reported in the *Annal. Bertin.* [871], p. 183.

57. Musca, *Bari*, pp. 123–24; Sawdan apparently then joined the Taranto Muslims.

58. Gay, *Ital. byz.*, p. 102; John the Deacon, p. 435.

59. *Andreae Bergomatis Historia*, MGH SSrL, p. 229.

60. See Musca, *Bari*, pp. 34–35.

61. See Chapter 2, note 28.

62. *MGH Epist.* V: 98, no. 7.

63. Only a century or so earlier, the bishop of Stabia (modern Castellammare di Stabia) had been accused of going up into the mountains to perform animal sacrifices (*Vita S. Antonini Abbatis Surrenti*, p. 789).

64. For contemporary opinion that Islam represented only another form of heresy, see Marie Thérèse d'Alverny, "La connaissance de l'Islam en Occident du IXᵉ au milieu du XIIᵉ siècle" (1965), pp. 577–602. Ekkehart Rotter has contended that accurate knowledge was in fact widespread, but his proof is grounded solely in ecclesiastical writings (*Abendland und Sarazenen: Das okzidentale Araberbild und seine Enstehung im Frühmittelalter* [1986]).

65. See Chapter 1, note 42.

66. Willibald (*Hodoeporicon S. Willibaldi*), p. 256.

67. For the "Greek" slavers, see Chapter 1, note 43; the *Pactum Sicardi* reference to Naples' slave trade was discussed in Chapter 2.

68. Clause 24 of the *Divisio* (for which see Chapter 2, note 53).

69. The *CDC* includes nearly 1,400 miscellaneous acts (792–1065) from a hoard of charter rolls discovered in the early nineteenth century behind an old wall

within the Benedictine abbey of Ssa. Trinità di Cava dei Tirreni, in the mountains northwest of the city of Salerno. Since many were only partly legible, their subsequent editing was not without problems; see Jean-Marie Martin, "Notes sur la chronologie des actes de Lucera édités dans le *Codex Diplomaticus Cavensis*" (1972), pp. 7–11; and for the (dominant) Salerno charters, Maria Galante, *La datazione dei documenti del* Codex Diplomaticus Cavensis (1980). Working with the *CDC* one must of course heed this redating, but otherwise, fortunately, the errors seem relatively few in number; and my own sampling check of significant charters cited in this study revealed no problems. (For further discussion of the *CDC* as evidence, see Chapter 6.)

70. *CDC* I, no. 8 (April 819).

71. *CDC* I, nos. 20 (March 842) and 24 (January 844). In the ninth-century *CDC* charters, Lombard witnesses do not invariably give their fathers' names, but those who are clearly "outsiders" or foreigners never do.

72. *CDC* I, nos. 54 (April 858) and 65 (September 868). These obviously are not Lombard names, nor are they Greek or Romanic. Moreover, as in the case of "Saracino," no father is mentioned.

73. *CDC* I, no. 74 (April 872); eccentric spellings (and a casual approach toward case and syntax) are characteristic of these ninth-century charters.

74. Cilento, *Sign. cap.*, p. 184.

75. *Annal. Bertin.* [869], pp. 165–66. Commenting on the *Chronicon Salernitanum* as a mirror of southern Lombard values, Delogu noted *sagacitas* (shrewdness) and *audacia* (boldness) as preeminent virtues (*Mito di una città*, pp. 82–84).

76. *Chron. S. Ben. Casin.*, p. 474.

77. Bernard, *Itinerarium Bernardi*, pp. 310–11.

78. *Chron. Salern.*, ch. 80b, p. 79; Erchempert, ch. 16, p. 240.

79. Erchempert, ch. 20, p. 242: "pedentim Salernum ac Beneventum depopulare initiarunt."

80. Erchempert, ch. 35, p. 248.

81. For example, in 872 a widow named Walfreda, making her will, refers to her brother as "comprehensum . . . per is mali saracenis" (*CDC* I, no. 75). And in 882, one Rodelanda, selling property, speaks of a son "predatus a saraceni" (*CDC* I, no. 86).

82. *Chron. S. Ben. Casin.*, p. 472.

83. Non-Arabs, too, found Capua's amphitheatre a fine makeshift *castrum*; Guaifer of Salerno based a Salernitan force there in the 880s when he was attacking Capua, and later Aio of Benevento made similar use of it (Erchempert, ch. 71, p. 261). But Arab bands were the most frequent users; Cilento (*Civiltà napoletana del medioevo nel secolo VI–XII* [1969], p. 64) noted Arabs also using the Roman amphitheater at Minturno.

84. For Odoacer, see Chapter 1, note 3. Destruction of the castle of Lucullus is described in a letter reporting the transfer of the remains of St. Severinus, which had been enshrined within that "castrum" (Capasso, *Mon.* II, Part 2: p. 1, letter of 907). On the site, the Castel dell'Ovo later rose.

85. Cilento, *Italia meridionale longobarda*, p. 184.

Chapter 4

1. *Chron. Salern.*, chs. 110, 111, pp. 122–23.

2. *Chron. Salern.*, ch. 111, p. 123; Erchempert, ch. 35, p. 248; *Vita Athanasii*, p. 448.

3. According to Erchempert (ch. 35, pp. 247–48), there were thirty thousand invaders; according to the *Chronicon Salernitanum*, seventy-two thousand! Obviously it was at least a massive force. For the siege, see *Chron. Salern.* chs.111–15, pp. 124–28; see also Schipa, "Salerno," pp. 127 ff.

4. The exact date is uncertain: late fall 871 or early winter 872. See Musca, *Bari*, p. 122, on the circumstances and dating from the Aghlabid perspective.

5. *Chron. Salern.*, ch. 116, pp. 128–29.

6. Erchempert, ch. 35, p. 248: "Cuius advento cognito, Saraceni Salernum reliquentes, Calabriam adeunt eamque intra se divisam repperientes, funditus depopularunt, ita ut deserta sit veluti in diluvio." Among the colorful anecdotes about the last weeks of the siege is one with a familiar ring; the rescue force, we are told, marched toward Salerno carrying branches as camouflage, causing the besiegers to exclaim in fright "Mons est, et quasi contros nos venit!" (*Chron. Salern.*, ch. 118, p. 132).

7. Taormina, high above the northeastern Sicilian coast, resisted until 902 (and was not permanently held by the Muslims until the latter tenth century); but Taormina was far smaller and not a major administrative center.

8. Erchempert, ch. 38, p. 249.

9. Ibid., ch. 39, p. 249: "pacem habentes cum Saracenis."

10. Fred R. Engreen, "Pope John the Eighth and the Arabs" (1945), p. 318; although Engreen's article reveals insufficient understanding of the internal situation in southern Italy, it is valuable for placing John's efforts within a broad papal and European context. On the "crusade" aspect of John's efforts, see Raoul Manselli, "La 'Res publica Christiana' e l'Islam nell'alto medioevo" (1965), pp. 128–30.

11. Engreen, "Pope John," p. 227.

12. *MGH Epist*. VII: 276, no. 5.

13. Erchempert, ch. 39, p. 249: "navalibus [the Saracens] Romam graviter angustiabant."

14. On the Traietto meeting, see Berza, "Amalfi preducale," pp. 394–95; also *MGH Epist*. VII: 48–49, nos. 51, 52, 53. "Traietto" may have meant either a settlement adjacent to the ruins of Roman Minturnae or that general region, also then called "Traiectum" in some sources. Ironically, this very area was later to be the site of the notorious Garigliano Arab encampment.

15. *MGH Epist*. VII: 75, no. 79.

16. Ibid., 73, no. 77.

17. On this trip, see Engreen, "Pope John," p. 325.

18. *MGH Epist*. VII: 75, no. 79; 81, no. 86.

19. Ibid., 194, no. 217.

20. Ibid., 204, no. 230.

21. Ibid., 214–15, no. 246; 246, no. 279. In his letter of excommunication to Naples, John seemed particularly bitter since Athanasius had been favored with "multis argenti ponderibus" from the papal treasury.

22. Ibid., 218–19, no. 250: "Quodsi in tali impio scelere diabolo suadente amplius permanere presumpseritis . . . omnium terrarum aditus, in quibus negotiari soliti estis, vobis omnino claudemus, ut illie nulla possitis exercere negotia."

23. Ibid., 264–65, no. 305; the implication is that at least some "Saraceni maiores" were actually resident at Naples.

24. John first asked for Byzantine naval help in 877 (Ibid., 45, no. 47); he wrote again early in 879 (Ibid., 214, no. 245). On the welcome opportunity this provided for Constantinople, see Gay, *Ital. byz.*, pp. 120, 124, 126.

25. Gay, *Ital. byz.*, p. 123; this was also in 879.

26. On scholarly debates concerning this development, see A. A. Vasiliev, *History of the Byzantine Empire*, 2d ed. (1952), pp. 331–32.

27. On this (and other depredations), see *Chron. Vulturn.*, I: 362–65.

28. For the sack of Monte Cassino, with translations of the contemporary descriptions, see Citarella and Willard, *Ninth-Century Monte Cassino*, pp. 119–21. Fearing an attack, the abbot had already sent many of the monks to Teano, and they had carried with them manuscripts and other treasures; tragically, a fire at Teano subsequently destroyed most of these.

29. Erchempert, ch. 49, p. 255.

30. *Chron. Salern.*, ch. 126, p. 139.

31. Erchempert, ch. 44, p. 251; and Gay, *Ital. byz.*, p. 130. Gay cites Erchempert (ch. 79) for evidence of an advance base at Sepino.

32. *CDC* I, no. 86.

33. *CDC* I, no. 97.

34. *CDC* I, nos. 88, 91, 95, 96, 97. The land prices and leasing rates in the presbyters' transactions differ markedly from those in charters of a year or two earlier or later.

35. Erchempert, ch. 49, and ch. 51, pp. 255–56.

36. *Chron. Salern.*, ch. 139, p. 146.

37. For the campaign of Nicephorus Phocas, see Gay, *Ital. byz.*, pp. 132–36. Calabrian towns now freed from Arab control included Amantea, Tropea, and Santa Severina; Taranto, in Apulia, had already been retaken.

38. See Chapter 1, note 56; and Sambon, *Monnaies du Sud*, p. 77.

39. Erchempert, ch. 67, p. 260.

40. Gay, *Ital. byz.*, p. 139.

41. From the period between Guaimar's 887 trip to Constantinople and his death in 900, only seven Salernitan charters survive (*CDC* I, nos. 102, 104–6, 108, 109, 111), but in all these he is so identified.

42. Vasiliev, *Byzantine Empire*, p. 327.

43. As Vera von Falkenhausen has noted, from this point on many south Italian rulers acquired Byzantine titles, but this constituted only "nominal submission"; no tribute was paid and governance was unaffected. In the case of Salerno, Guaimar's title did not even prevent hostile actions on both sides (Falkenhausen, *Dominazione*, pp. 15, 36–37).

44. Erchempert, ch. 54, p. 257.

45. Ibid., ch. 56, p. 257.

46. Ibid., chs. 56 and 57, pp. 257–58; ch. 73, p. 262.

47. Poupardin, *Inst.*, p. 11.

48. On this, see Gay, *Ital. byz.*, p. 142, which pieces the story together from some confusing reports by Erchempert.

49. This Aghlabid assault on Calabria, in 888–89, was both massive and extremely threatening. Erchempert (ch. 81, p. 264) said the attackers came from both "Africa" and Sicily, and that the Agropoli and Garigliano Arabs also rushed down to Calabria to support their fellow Muslims (ch. 51, p. 256).

50. Not surprisingly, this action was widely reported in south Italian sources; on it, see Falkenhausen, *Dominazione*, p. 24.

51. *Chron. Salern.*, ch. 145, p. 151.

52. On this and its implications, see Falkenhausen, *Dominazione*, pp. 24–25, 31–33.

53. For the Emperor Guy of Spoleto, his place in the turbulent politics of the late ninth century, and his other son, Lambert (also briefly emperor), see Chris Wickham, *Early Medieval Italy* (1981), pp. 169–70; and McKitterick, *Frankish Kingdoms Under the Carolingians*, p. 263.

54. On "Radelchis the Foolish" (grandson of that Radelchis who had lost half of Benevento's territory in the midcentury *Divisio*), see *Chron. Salern.* chs. 148, 152. During his brief rule, Beneventan indictions recognized the Emperor Lambert (Poupardin, *Inst.*, no. 69 [898]). The dowager empress Ageltruda, whose unfortunate suggestion Radelchis had been, is best known for enthusiastic participation in the exhumation of Pope Formosus; see Llewellyn, *Rome in the Dark Ages*, p. 292.

55. Three years before, he very likely had been involved in the seizing of Guaimar when the latter was en route to Benevento; Guaimar had been caught in Capuan territory: *Chron. Salern.*, ch. 147*, p. 155.

56. *Chron. Salern.*, ch. 154, p. 161; the chronicler goes on to define "proceres" as "principes vel maiores." Cilento (*Sign. cap.*, pp. 146–48) discusses this coup and its dating.

57. Cilento, *Sign. cap.*, p. 60 (including n. 40).

58. As Cilento (*Sign. cap.*, p. 70) observed, only gastalds with significant territorial jurisdiction (and considerable autonomy in exercising jurisdiction) seem to have had the added title of *comes*. Poupardin (*Inst.*, pp. 39–41) had reached a similar conclusion; he also noted that *comes*, as an administrative title, had long been used by the Lombards (obviously adopted from late Roman practice), and was not to become hereditary until after the ninth century.

59. *Chron. Salern.*, ch. 58, p. 58.

60. This was in addition to "Rebelopolis." The ruins of the old city of Capua eventually became the nucleus of a new settlement, known today as Santa Maria Capua Vetere; there one can still see the great Roman amphitheater in which, in the ninth century, Arab bands encamped (see Chapter 3).

61. Erchempert, ch. 22, p. 243.

62. See Chapter 3, including note 20.

63. *Annal. Bertin.* [873], p. 192; Erchempert, ch. 36, p. 248; Gay, *Ital. byz.*, pp. 105–8. While keeping a wary eye on Carolingian power struggles in the north, Louis was now trying to gain papal absolution from his oath not to return to Benevento.

64. The rewards grew more generous as John grew more desperate. Shortly

after Landolf's death, Pope John, despite the scandal it caused, agreed to confirm as bishop of Capua a youthful, lay, and married nephew of Landolf. Later, to encourage Capua to attack pro-Arab Gaeta, he apparently offered Capua papal territory (Cilento, *Sign. cap.*, pp. 118–21, 125). Capua, in turn, for a time recognized Pope John on its coinage (Nicola Cilento, "Le condizioni della vita nella contea longobarda di Capua: seconda metà del IX secolo" [1951], p. 459).

65. "Ego sum ex regali stegmate orta, et cum subdito meo consanguinitatem annecto?" (*Chron. Salern.*, ch. 153, p. 160).

66. See notes 41 and 43, above.

67. See on this and on Gaeta's precarious balance between the papacy and Naples, Falkenhausen, *Dominazione*, p. 13. The standard work on medieval Gaeta is Margareta Merores, *Gaeta im frühen Mittelalter, 8–12 Jahrhundert* (1911). For another perspective, stressing Gaeta's essential independence from both Byzantium and Naples (despite Gaeta's Byzantinesque flavor), see Agate Leccese, *Le origine del ducato di Gaeta e le sue relazioni coi ducati di Napoli e di Roma* (1941).

68. See Chapter 1, note 52.

69. The Byzantine-derived *hypatus*, for example, was the title used by Gaeta's rulers through the ninth and halfway through the tenth century (*Codex Diplomaticus Cajetanus* I, no. 50 [949], p. 84).

70. Ibid., no. 36, p. 61.

71. Falkenhausen, *Dominazione*, pp. 13–14, 39.

72. In the dating of its charters and other documents, and in local chronicles, Naples continued to employ Byzantine-imperial chronology until the twelfth century (Falkenhausen, *Dominazione*, p. 12). And not only the Naples charters published by Capasso but also two Cava charters from Naples (*CDC* I, nos. 142 [924] and 178 [950]) have witness signatures in Greek letters or include Greek phrases.

73. Schipa, "Napoli," *ASPN* 17 (1892): 392.

74. For a half-century thereafter, the formality of Byzantine confirmation of new dukes had apparently continued, but it was a token gesture (Falkenhausen, *Dominazione*, pp. 10–11).

75. John the Deacon (ch. 50, p. 428) reports the appeal to Sicily for arbitration; Naples' unwillingness to supply ships was discussed in Chapter 1.

76. Chapter 1, note 56.

77. For Amalfi in particular, see Chapter 2, note 21. In both cases, evidence of the break comes in 839 (Falkenhausen, *Dominazione*, pp. 13–14).

78. *Chron. Salern.*, ch. 107, pp. 119–20; Louis goes on to describe Sicilian Arab "latrunculi" finding supplies and a safe refuge at Naples.

79. The Aghlabid attempt to take Ponza (John the Deacon, ch. 60, p. 432) had been a preamble to their assault on Rome.

80. *Vita Athanasii*, ch. 7, p. 446; Athansius I died a few months later, on his way home from begging Louis II's help against the Arabs besieging Salerno.

81. Schipa, "Napoli," *ASPN* 17 (1892): 789. Caesar was ill repaid for three decades of service; he had been Naples' preeminent military leader, not only commanding the fleet at the Battle of Ostia but also leading the duchy's forces in a major confrontation with Capua in 859 (Cilento, *Sign. cap.*, p. 103).

82. *Vita Athanasii*, ch. 7, p. 447; Schipa, "Napoli," *ASPN* 17 (1892): 792.

83. Cilento, *Sign. cap.*, p. 132.

84. John the Deacon, ch. 63, p. 434: "Ordinavit autem lectorum et cantorum scolas. . . . Praeterea [in the church of St. Januarius] nobilium doctorum effigies in ea depinxit [and he also had constructed a marble altar embellished with silver and covered with a cloth] in quo martyrium sancti Januarii eiusque sociorum acu pictili opere digessit." Another church was beautified with hundreds of pounds of silver and with pictorial hangings "multo auro multisque gemmis decorata."

85. Cilento, *Civiltà napoletana*, pp. 33, 42–50. Even Naples' coinage seems to have become more elegant under Athanasius II; see Schipa, "Napoli," *ASPN* 18 (1893): 636.

86. See Cilento, *Civiltà napoletana*, pp. 71–72, on the many manuscript transmissions we owe to Naples in this period. In effect, this represented continuation of a tradition that had earlier enriched Bede's Britain. Hadrian, the traveling companion there of Theodore of Tarsus, had been the abbot of a monastery at Naples. And not only was he "proficient in both Greek and Latin," according to Bede, but he presented to Lindisfarne an Evangelary brought from Naples, which then was extensively copied (ibid., pp. 14–16).

Chapter 5

1. See Chapter 4, note 7.

2. On the Aghlabids and Ibrāhīm II, see Michael Brett, "Aghlabids" (1982), pp. 70–72. The fullest Muslim report of the 902 campaign is that of Nuwairī, in Vasiliev, *Byzance et les Arabes* II, Part 2 (1958), pp. 233–35. The major Christian account, with fearsome anecdotes about Ibrāhīm ("tyrannus insatiabilis," "infestissimus"), is in the contemporary *Translatio S. Severini*, pp. 452–59.

3. Gabrieli has observed that the ease with which Ibrāhīm swept through Calabria suggests that Byzantine defenses must have been almost nonexistent ("Storia, cultura e civiltà degli Arabi in Italia," p. 115).

4. See Chapter 3, note 84.

5. Nuwairī (note 2, above) said that Ibrāhīm died of dysentery. For St. Elias and Ibrāhīm's invasion, see the *Vita di Sant'Elia il Giovane*, pp. 79–83. The prophetic visions of Elias the Younger (also known as Elias of Enna) were always dramatic; in this case, returning briefly to Taormina in the spring of 902, he had been walking through the city when he suddenly lifted his robe in horror, saying the streets were running with blood.

6. Leo Marsicanus, Bk. I, ch. 50, pp. 130–31.

7. Although the Amalfitans are best known as sea traders, the importance of land-based trading was recognized in the *Pactum Sicardi* in 836. And we know that the Amalfitans traded at Rome because Pope John VIII had threatened to cancel their privileges there. The Garigliano Arabs could block both the coastal route north, with its river crossing at Roman Minturnae, and the inland route up the valley of the Liri beneath Monte Cassino. Moreover, positioned as they apparently were near the mouth of the Garigliano, they could also threaten coastal shipping.

8. On this embassy to Constantinople, see Leo Marsicanus, Bk.I, ch. 52, p.

133. Hartmut Hoffmann, in his new edition of Leo Marsicanus, dates the trip to 910; others have suggested 909 or even earlier. The indiction of a Beneventan charter of 912 (*CDC* I, no. 131) shows Landolf now a *patricius*.

9. As Cilento observed (*Sign. cap.*, p. 183), these two embassies to Constantinople very likely led to the glowing description of Capuan preeminence in chapter 27 of the *De administrando imperio*.

10. Leo Marsicanus, Bk. I, ch. 52, p. 134.

11. Liutprand, *Antapodosis*, Bk. II, chs. 47–54.

12. Other Roman magnates are also listed; see Otto Vehse, "Das Bündnis gegen die Sarazenen vom Jahre 915" (1927), p. 185. There once was some question about this grant since it was known only through mention in a 1014 Gaetan *placitum* (*Codex Diplomaticus Cajetanus*, no.130). Vehse resolved all doubts with a fourteenth-century text that included John X's complete document.

13. See, for example, *Cod. Carol.* no. 61.

14. Vehse, "Das Bündnis," pp. 187–99, 202–4. The territory was granted "cum omnibus castellis et villis et casalibus et ecclesiis et monasteriis sibi pertinentibus tam de regimine apostolorum quam de ecclesiis . . . quam et de proprietatibus de Romanis populis." (This last phrase suggests that Rome's leading families did also make some sacrifice.) Later in 915, when Berengar came to Rome to be crowned, John X tried to undo the effect of his grant through gaining Berengar's support for the old papal claim to Gaeta itself (ibid., p. 192); the 1014 *placitum* (note 12, above) indicates that this maneuver failed.

15. It has sometimes been erroneously stated that Berengar was involved as well. And the location of the raiders' base has long been argued. Liutprand (*Antapodosis*, Bk. II, ch. 44) referred to "montem Garelianum," but he was doubtless confusing the Garigliano River with Monte Gargano on the Adriatic coast. Certainly all other sources refer to the base only as on ("apud") the river, and Muslim raiders in southern Italy favored river sites. Pietro Fedele, whose analysis of the battle remains invaluable, suggested a site on the Garigliano within the ruins of Roman Minturnae, and this would fit other known facts. ("La battaglia del Garigliano dell'anno 915 ed i monumenti che la ricordano" [1898], pp. 190–92). True, archaeologists have found no trace of a Muslim presence there (no Islamic coins or pottery fragments): see S. Dominic Ruegg, "The Underwater Excavation in the Garigliano River: The Roman Port and Bridge at Minturnae" (1983), p. 217. But raiders would surely arrive with few possessions, and live off local plunder. (On this area, see Chapter 4, note 14.)

16. Jaffé-Loew., no. 3556 (papal letter to the archbishop of Cologne).

17. Vehse accepted Liutprand's statement that John X had sent an embassy to Constantinople to obtain Byzantine participation. But Liutprand is demonstrably wrong here on many points, and Fedele rejected this report. John had become pope only in the spring of 914, and the Byzantine *strategos* was already in Campania before the end of that year. Leo Marsicanus (note 10, above) described the pope as involved only after learning of the impending Byzantine-Capuan attack. No doubt representatives did then go back and forth, but merely between Rome and the Byzantine *strategos* and his Capuan allies, to discuss the Gaetan problem and agree on an assault strategy.

18. Already in 911, Naples had signed a pact with Capua that included a promise of help against Arabs: *MGH Leges* IV: 215. Doubtless both Salernitans and Neapolitans were suffering in many ways. In 912, for example, a small landowner in the principality of Salerno referred to a son captured by the "Sarraceni" (*CDC* I, no. 129).

19. Matteo Camera, *Memorie storico-diplomatiche dell'antica città e ducato di Amalfi*, 2 vols. (1876).

20. Beazley, *Dawn of Modern Geography* 1: 170.

21. Wilhelm Heyd, *Histoire du commerce du Levant au Moyen Age* (1885), 1: 98–108; Adolf Schaube, *Händelsgeschichte der Romanischen Völker des Mittelmeergebiets bis zum Ende der Kreuzzuge* (1906), pp. 30–34.

22. Adolf Hofmeister, "Zur Geschichte Amalfis in der byzantinischen Zeit" (1920), p. 97: "Trotzdem ist die Abhängigkeit von Byzanz unbestreitbar."

23. Armand O. Citarella, "The Relations of Amalfi with the Arab World Before the Crusades" (1967), pp. 299–312.

24. *Chron. Salern.*, chs. 88, 89; pp. 88–90. Other early narratives of Amalfi's founding tell essentially the same story.

25. *MGH Epist.* I: 400.

26. *Cod. Carol.*, no. 78, p. 610.

27. *Cod. Carol.*, no. 83, p. 618; see Chapter 1 for the full story of this plot.

28. *MGH Epist.* V: 96; this episode was noted in Chapters 1 and 2.

29. See Chapter 2, note 13.

30. Nicetas Paphlagonis, Oratio X: "In praise of the sainted apostle Bartholomew," *PG* 105: 218. Nicetas described Lipari as already then in Arab hands but this is doubted.

31. See Chapter 2, including note 20.

32. See Chapter 2, notes 19 and 21; and Francesco Forcellini, "L'impresa di Sicardo contra Amalfi e l'emancipazione politica di questo città del ducato di Napoli" (1945), pp. 1–48.

33. Letter from Nicholas Mysticus, *PG* III: 371; Nicholas contributed a pound of gold toward this good work.

34. Ibn Hayyan, *Al-Muqtabis (V)* (1981), pp. 358–59.

35. In 978, one Leo the Amalfitan reconfirmed an exchange of property arranged by his wife while he was voyaging to Cairo ("quando ego eram Babilonia ad navigandum"): *CDC* II, no. 300. ("Babylon" was the old Roman fortress at Cairo's site.) On the 996 massacre, see Claude Cahen, "Un texte peu connu relatif au commerce oriental d'Amalfi au Xe siècle" (1955), pp. 61–67. Cahen's Arab sources speak of 107 or 160 "Rūm malāfita"; Cahen suggests the numbers may have been exaggerated and that certainly not all may have actually been Amalfitans.

36. Few early Amalfitan charters have survived, but in the first with prices we find *tari*: *CDA* I, no. 2 (922) and no.3 (931). The first tenth-century Salernitan sale contract, in 908 (*CDC* I, no. 124), also gives the price in *tari*. From then on, prices are always cited in *tari* at Amalfi, and almost always at Salerno.

37. S. D. Goitein, "The Mediterranean Mind in the High Middle Ages, 950–1150" (1977), p. 186. This interpretation of *Rūm* now seems standard among those working with Arab sources; see, for example, Alauddin Samarrai, "Medieval Commerce and Diplomacy: Islam and Europe, A.D. 850–1300" (1980), p. 3, n.7.

38. Liutprand, *Rel. Const.*, ch. 55.

39. Franz Dölger, *Corpus der griechischen Urkunden des Mittelalters und der neueren Zeit* 1: 100; also cited in the prohibition were Bari Lombards and (presumably Italian) Jews.

40. Liutprand, *Rel. Const.*, ch. 45; Liutprand cited this recruiting of Amalfitans as proof of Byzantium's military feebleness. In any case, the Amalfitans must have been already present in Constantinople, since the force was hastily assembled. Earlier, in 945, Amalfitans were reported involved in the flurry when the throne passed to Constantine Porphyrogenitus (Liutprand, *Antapodosis*, ch. 21). On Amalfi's (Latin-rite) Mount Athos community, see Agostino Pertusi, "Nuovi documenti sui Benedittini amalfitani dell'Athos" (1953), pp. 407–9.

41. By 922, we find Amalfi's current ruler an *imperialis patricius* and his son a *protospatarius* (*CDA*, no. 2). Constantine Porphyrogenitus confidently listed Amalfi (together with Naples and Sorrento) as "always subject to the Empire of the Romans" (*De admin. imp.*, ch. 29) but, as Vera von Falkenhausen noted, in actuality "Nulla indica una dipendenza da Bisancio, neanche formale" (*Dominazione*, p. 14).

42. Eventually there were three Amalfitan hostels or hospices, all in Jerusalem; one was later turned over to the Knights of St. John. The first seems to have been founded in the early or middle eleventh century. See, for slightly different opinions on the timing, Jonathan Riley-Smith, *The Knights of St. John in Jerusalem and Cyprus, 1050–1310* (1967), pp. 34–37; and Timothy Miller, "The Knights of St. John and the Hospitals of the Latin West" (1978), pp. 727–28. It appears that these establishments were for pilgrims; the Amalfitans, whose trading base would surely have been not inland but on the coast, seemingly diversified into hostelries.

43. The Institute of Nautical Archaeology (Texas A&M University) is currently preparing formal publication of this wreck, known as the Serçe Liman ship or "the glass wreck." The surviving cargo and personal possessions include glass cullet and fine glassware (presumably Islamic); Byzantine amphoras; spears, javelins, and swords of mixed Byzantine and Islamic provenance; Islamic gaming pieces; both Fatimid and Byzantine coins; and Fatimid glass coin weights (Frederick Van Doorninck et al., "The Glass Wreck: An 11th-Century Merchantman" [1988]).

44. Fatimid control was not uniformly established in North Africa for some years after 909, largely because of problems with the Berbers, but 909 marked the first major step.

45. For an excellent brief account of the Fatimid period (and of its relative openness to non-Muslims, whether Christian or Jew), see Paula Sanders, "Fatimids" (1985), pp. 24–30.

46. Archibald R. Lewis, *Naval Power and Trade in the Mediterranean: A.D. 500–1100* (1951); Lewis titled his chapter on this period "The Islamic Imperium."

47. Al-Balādhurī, *Origins of the Islamic State*, pp. 383–84, 199.

48. See note 35, above; and also Claude Cahen, "Amalfi en Orient à la veille, au moment at au lendemain de la Première Croisade" (1977), p. 272.

49. In the tenth-century Maghreb, Ibn Hawqal noted "special levies on Jews" only at the port of Gabes (Ibn Hawqal *Configuration de la terre*, 1: 66). H. Z. [J. W.] Hirschberg concluded that in North Africa there was usually no distinction between Jew and Muslim in relation to customs fees, although Islamic law theoret-

ically provided for it (*A History of the Jews in North Africa* [1974] 1: 256). We do not know the situation for foreign Christian merchants like the Amalfitans, but for an extensive discussion of the customs duty issue, although primarily for the eleventh century and later, see S. D. Goitein, *A Mediterranean Society*, vol. 1: *Economic Foundations* (1967), pp. 339–46.

50. Ibn Hawqal, *Configuration de la terre*, 1: 129–30.

51. Ibid., 197; this was apparently in the 970s.

52. Reportedly, the sister of a Christian bishop in North Africa even married an emir (*Vita S. Nili*, sect. 53). On converted Jews rising to powerful positions in North Africa (and on Ahimaaz's story concerning one of his relatives), see Hirschberg, *Jews in North Africa*, pp. 103–5. See also Sanders, "Fatimids."

53. See note 49, above; there are five volumes in all. Goitein's studies of the Cairo Geniza documents have immeasurably enhanced our knowledge of the medieval Mediterranean as a whole; regrettably, however, these documents provide no information concerning south Italian trade before the eleventh century.

54. For North African bishops, see note 52, above, and the *Vita di Sant'Elia il Giovane*, pp. 15, 25. Bernard the Monk spoke of a patriarch at Alexandria in the ninth century (*Itinerarium Bernardi*, pp. 311–12). For patriarchs in Palestine, see Romilly J. H. Jenkins, "The Emperor Alexander and the Saracen Prisoners" (1953), pp. 389–90.

55. For members of the Jewish communities adopting customs and fashions of the Muslim society around them, see S. D. Goitein, "Changes in the Middle East (950–1150) as Illustrated by the Documents of the Cairo Geniza" (1973), pp. 18–19.

56. *Vita di Sant'Elia*, pp. 15, 43.

57. *Chronicle of Ahimaaz*, p. 93; unfortunately, read in its entirety this anecdote does not inspire confidence.

58. See the sections relating to southern Italy by Cecil Roth, J. Schirmann, and H. J. Zimmels in *The World History of the Jewish People*, ser. 2, vol. 2: *The Dark Ages*, ed. Cecil Roth (1966). For specific individuals and topics, see also Salo W. Baron, *A Social and Religious History of the Jews* (1952–83), vols. 3–8. The most famous figure was the tenth-century scholar-physician known as Donnolo, born in Oria, in Apulia.

59. On evidence for the Apulian communities, see Cesare Colafemmina, "Insediamenti e condizione degli Ebrei nell'Italia meridionale e insulare" (1980), pp. 197–227 (with discussion, 230–35); and idem., "Archaeologia ed epigrafia nell'Italia meridionale" (1983), pp. 199–210. See also Roberto Bonfil, "Tra due mondi: Prospettive di ricerca sulla storia culturale degli Ebrei dell'Italia meridionale nell'alto medioevo" (1983), pp. 135–58.

60. It is risky to use names as proof of anything. Nonetheless, most individuals figuring in or witnessing Salernitan charters bear Lombard names, so these exceptions stand out (particularly since the principals in these charters were all Lombards). In the 840s, a Jacob witnessed three charters, *CDC* I, nos. 23 (843), 31 (848), 32 (848); and in 859 (*CDC* I, no. 58) we encounter Joseph, son of Jacob. Two of these charters were drafted "at the baking ovens in the marketplace," and internal evidence suggests that the others were as well. Next, in 848, 854, and 856, a "Josep medicus" bought exceptionally large tracts of land involving large sums of money

(*CDC* I, nos. 29, 39, 47); and in 865 (*CDC* I, no. 61) land was given to St. Maximus, a foundation of Salerno's ruling house, by "Josueb medico." And then in *CDC* I, no. 74 (872), a piece of land is described as "next to [the land of] Rebecca" ("propio ad Rebecca").

61. Ahimaaz, who told of many Jews moving into Lombard territory, said that his grandfather Samuel became supervisor of the treasury at Capua and his father held an even loftier post (*Chronicle of Ahimaaz*, p. 100); there is no other documentation to prove or disprove this, but Nicola Ferorelli felt that, at most, Ahimaaz had perhaps exaggerated the importance of the positions (*Gli Ebrei nell'Italia meridionale dall'età romana al secolo XVIII* [1915], p. 27. See also ibid., pp. 24–25, on the charter references from Naples.) The first mention at Salerno comes in 936 (*CDC* I, no. 159); some land is said to border that of "Josepi ebrei." And then in *CDC* II, no. 442 (991), a member of Salerno's ruling family exchanges plots of land with a local presbyter, with some wooden houses ("case lingnitie") to be moved elsewhere; on one plot, the house owners are described as Jews, and the other plot is next to the land of "Leonti hebrey."

62. *CDC* IV, no. 651 ("ad ipsa judaica"). Also, by the mid-eleventh century we find Jews at Capua treated as part of the royal fisc (Schipa, "Salerno," pp. 262, no. 45).

63. See note 60, above. They were co-witnessing with Lombards.

64. Benjamin of Tudela, *The Travels of Rabbi Benjamin of Tudela, 1160–1173*, p. 260.

65. Theodosius monachus, "De expugnatione Syracusarum," *PG* 135: col. 59, footnote.

66. *MGH Epist.* II: 160, 393–94.

67. Ibn Hawqal, *Configuration de la terre*, 1:197.

68. Michelangelo Schipa once suggested a somewhat similar explanation ("Napoli," *ASPN* 18 (1893): 635–36).

69. See the *Vita S. Antonini Abbatis Surrenti* (p. 788, sect.4), written in the late ninth century.

70. *CDC* II, nos. 296, 299 (977). Both involved large tracts of undeveloped land on the Cilento peninsula below the Gulf of Salerno, bought from the bishop of Paestum for 1,010 and 1,050 pounds of silver respectively. (Amalfitan purchase of Salernitan land will be further discussed in Chapters 6 and 7; on some of the revealing provisions in these two charters, see Chapter 7, n. 3.)

71. Mario Del Treppo and Alfonso Leone, *Amalfi medioevale* (1977), Chapter 5 ("La società senza mercanti").

72. Ibid., pp. 96–101.

73. Camera, *Memorie*, 1: 89.

74. See Del Treppo and Leone, *Amalfi medioevale*, pp. 6, 66–70; the key document here is the sea code known as the "tavola amalfitana" (*Tabula de Amalphae*, ed. Vincenzo Giuffre [1965]).

75. For the proliferation of *comites*, see Del Treppo and Leone, *Amalfi medioevale*, pp. 101–9. On Amalfitan governance in the ninth and tenth centuries, see Schwarz, *Amulfi im frühen Mittelalter*, pp. 21–45. Schwarz perhaps attaches too much significance to the Byzantine titles of Amalfi's rulers. But his narrative is a

major contribution because it interweaves (and closely analyzes) Amalfitan sources; and he has also reconstructed a definitive text for the *Chronicon Amalfitanum*.

76. Ibn Hawqal, *Configuration de la terre*, 1: 197.

77. Robert P. Bergman, "'Amalfi sommersa': Myth or Reality?" (1979), pp. 23–30. Supposedly these impressive harbor works had been destroyed in the earthquake of 1343.

78. There are several suggestive references in the early charters; for example, in 947 we find "terra . . . foras porta de Atrano" (*CDA*, no. 6) and in 970 the sale, for a large sum, of a house with storage outbuildings along Atrani's sea wall (*CDA*, no. 8). There are no similar references to Amalfi's port area.

79. See note 43, above; the Serçe Liman vessel is some fifty feet long, broad of beam and with a large hold and flat bottom. It was thus barge-like in design, and otherwise, in length and tonnage, roughly half the size of a typical twelfth-century Genoese *navis*. (On the latter, see Hilmar C. Krueger, *Navi e proprietà navale a Genova* [1985], p. 24.)

80. On the *sagena*, see Barbara M. Kreutz, "Ships, Shipping and the Implications of Change" (1976), pp. 101–3; on indications that Amalfitan ships were small (and sometimes hybrid in design), see also Del Treppo and Leone, *Amalfi medioevale*, pp. 64–66. Interestingly, ship depictions on the sixteenth-century fresco maps of the Vatican's Galleria delle Carte Geografiche show, for the Gulf of Salerno off Amalfi, small, shallow, beamy boats with single large lateen sails and eight oars or sweeps.

81. On Amalfitan development of the lateen sail, see the 'Horologium' section of Giovanni Tortelli, *De orthographia dictionum e Graecis Tractarum*, in Alex Keller, "A Renaissance Humanist Looks at 'New' Inventions" (1970), p. 349. For the compass, see Flavio Biondo, *De Roma triumphante, Roma instaurata: Italia illustrata* (1531), p. 420.

82. For the lateen sail, see Kreutz, "Ships, Shipping," pp. 80–86, 103; for the evolution of the compass, Barbara M. Kreutz, "Mediterranean Contributions to the Medieval Mariner's Compass" (1973), pp. 367–83. The polarity principle, which underlay the maritime compass, had long been recognized; but the perfected instrument seems to have achieved widespread use (together with charts) only in the thirteenth century, no doubt because of the explosion then in commercial shipping, which meant an extended sailing season and large numbers of new, inexperienced mariners.

83. See, on wind conditions, Barbara M. Kreutz, "The Ecology of Maritime Success: The Puzzling Case of Amalfi" (1988), pp. 106–8; and W. M. Murray, "Do Modern Winds Equal Ancient Winds?" (1987), pp. 139–67.

84. A. L. Udovitch, "Time, the Sea and Society: Duration of Commercial Voyages on the Southern Shore of the Mediterranean During the High Middle Ages" (1978), pp. 510–14.

85. John H. Pryor, *Geography, Technology, and War* (1988), Ch. 3; and pp. 51–54, on the speed of voyages and the myth that "coasting" had been related to lack of a compass.

86. This was a ship from Alexandria with a Jewish merchant aboard; his letter was dated "probably eleventh-century" by Goitein. For commentary and an Italian

translation of the letter, see Armand Citarella, "Scambi commerciali fra l'Egitto e Amalfi in un documento inedito della Geniza del Cairo" (1977), pp. 99–117.

87. A Mediterranean Muslim world by now largely denuded of timber was proposed by Maurice Lombard, "Arsenaux et bois de marine dans la Méditeranée musulmane (VII–XI siècles)" (1958). This is at variance with the findings of Aly Mohamed Fahmy, *Muslim Naval Organization in the Eastern Mediterranean from the Seventh to the Tenth Century, A.D.* (1966), pp. 143–47. But in any case the varieties of trees would certainly have been different in the Muslim regions.

88. In 1959, Claude Cahen, in a review in the *Journal of the Economic and Social History of the Orient* 2: 340–41, suggested that Amalfitans were the "Rūm" from whom the Fatimids once purchased two ships. Armand Citarella ("Patterns in Medieval Trade: The Commerce of Amalfi Before the Crusades" [1968], pp. 539–43) attempted to make a case for a significant Amalfitan grain trade in this period, but his evidence was late and his assumption that grain was milled before shipment surely untenable.

89. Dietrich Lohrmann, *Das Register Papst Johannes' VIII* (1968), pp. 186–87.

90. Claude Cahen has suggested that this shift to the Red Sea, from the old Persian Gulf route, would have made Egypt even more attractive to Italian merchants ("Quelques problèmes concernant l'expansion économique musulmane au haut Moyen Age" [1965], pp. 428–29).

Chapter 6

1. Delogu, *Mito di una città*, ch. 2 ("Una società allo specchio"). See also Nicola Cilento's discussion of the *Chronicon* and its author (*Italia meridionale longobarda*, pp. 56–62, 65–72).

2. Belting, "Beneventanischen Hof," p. 152.

3. On the contents of this *Codex*, and their provenance and reliability, see Chapter 3, note 69.

4. Guaimar's ill-fated attempt in 897 to assume power at Benevento was discussed in Chapter 4.

5. *Chron. Salern.*, ch. 155, pp. 162–63. Later (ch. 169), the *Chronicon*'s author noted with some asperity that Berengar was not wise enough to step down in favor of *his* son.

6. Delogu, *Mito di una città*, pp. 99–100.

7. References in charters and the *Chronicon Salernitanum* (e.g., ch. 176) suggest that the gastaldates of Lauria, Marsico, Accrenza, Conza and Sarno formed the outer ring of the principality. In addition, Sorrento, at the southern tip of the Bay of Naples (and formerly attached to the duchy of Naples), had apparently by now come under Salernitan control (Jaffé-Loew. I, no. 3074; *Chron. Salern.*, ch. 150).

8. In the tenth century, within the city of Salerno ("at the sacred palace"), gastalds frequently presided over gifts or the amicable division of property (e.g., *CDC* I, no. 158, in 935; II, no. 283, in 975). And though *judices* now dealt with most

controversies, sometimes gastalds joined *judices* to consider a case (e.g., *CDC* I, no. 174, in 947; II, no. 220, in 963).

9. *CDC* I, no. 124.

10. *CDC* I, nos. 133 (917) through 141 (923).

11. Lupus Proto., p. 53.

12. *Annal. Ben.*, p. 175; the raid is also noted in the annals of Lupus Protospatarius (p. 53) but as occurring in 920.

13. *Annal. Ben.*, p. 175; Lupus Proto., p. 54.

14. *Annal. Baren.*, p. 52. This sack of Oria is also noted in the Sicilian "Cambridge Chronicle" (known to us in both Arabic and Greek versions): see translation in Vasiliev, *Byzance et les Arabes* II, Part 2, p. 104 (and on the chronicle, ibid., I: 342–44). This was the raid so devastating to Oria's Jewish community.

15. Gay (*Ital. byz.*, p. 208) dated this raid to 926, but the south Italian annals reported it as 927 or 929; the "Cambridge Chronicle" indicated 927–28, and said the Arab force was led by a Slav (Vasiliev, *Byzance et les Arabes* II, Part 2, p. 104).

16. "Cambridge Chronicle," in Vasiliev, *Byzance et les Arabes* II, Part 2: 103–4. On the duration of these payments, see Amari, *Storia*, 2: 202–4; and on maritime aspects of these confrontations, see Yaacov Lev, "The Fatimid Navy, Byzantium and the Mediterranean Sea, 909–1034," *Byzantion* 54 (1984): 230–32. Here again, Slav generals were reported leading the Muslim forces; on this apparent alliance between Simeon the Bulgarian and the North African Fatimids, see Vasiliev, *Byzance et les Arabes* I: 251–56; and Gay, pp. 206–8.

17. Lupus Proto., p. 54; *Chron. Salern.*, ch. 158, p. 166. The godson, born of Guaimar's first marriage, had died.

18. See note 10, above.

19. Lupus Proto., p. 54, reports the Matera attack as of 940. Two or three years earlier, a Beneventan force had taken Siponto, on the upper Apulian coast (*Annal. Ben.*, p. 175), but the movement southward to Matera was far more significant.

20. On the inducements for Capua-Benevento, see Gay, *Ital. byz.*, p. 233. The proposed marriage did then unite Hugh's daughter with the future Romanus II. (And Liutprand would later describe understandings on southern Italy supposedly linked to this marriage: *Relat. Const.*, ch. 7.)

21. *Chron. Salern.*, ch. 158, p. 163; ch. 159, p. 166.

22. Constantine Porphyrogenitus not only stated that Naples and Amalfi had "always" been subject to the emperor but claimed this had been true of the Lombard principalities as well ever since the Byzantine return to southern Italy in the late ninth century (*De admin. imp.*, ch. 29). See also his groupings in *De ceremoniis*, Bk. II, ch. 48; and in *De thematibus*, Bk. II (eleventh theme, "Longobardia"). At one time, most Byzantinists simply accepted Constantine's view, noting the titles awarded and forms of address used. Yet many now appear more tentative; for example, Karl Leyser refers to Capua-Benevento and Salerno as "satellite principalities" but grants that westerners did not attach equal significance to Byzantine ceremonial usage ("The Tenth Century in Byzantine-Western Relationships" [1973], reprinted in his *Medieval Germany and its Neighbors, 900–1250* [1982], pp. 110–11, 122).

23. In 935 Naples qualified its commitment to a Capuan alliance with "salve

fidelitate sanctorum imperatorum" (cited by Gay, *Ital. byz.*, p. 246). But this was surely disingenuous; despite preserving Byzantine regnal dating, Naples always had to be prodded to respond to Byzantine appeals and indeed often refused outright. Equally adroit was Guaimar I of Salerno; in 899, wishing to seize a Salernitan's property, he proclaimed that the Emperors Leo and Alexander had confirmed his authority "to do whatever I wish" within his principality (*CDC* I, no. 139).

24. The *Chronicon Salernitanum* begins with that event, as does the monastic history in the *Chronicon Vulturnense* (I: 347ff.); the Bari annals of Lupus Protospatarius (p. 55) make note of 966 as the four hundredth anniversary of the Lombard arrival.

25. Leo Marsicanus (Bk. I, ch. 59) reports this visit; it is notable that the *Chronicon Salernitanum* does not mention it.

26. A 947 indiction mentions only Capua-Benevento's co-rulers, but the next year two charters add the regnal dates of Constantine Porphyrogenitus (*Regesta delle Pergamene, Abbazia di Montevergine*, I, nos. 1–3).

27. Ibn 'Idhari, *Al-Bayano'l-Mogrib*, I: 277. According to this thirteenth-century (and perhaps embroidered) narrative, both cities paid off the raiders with money and rich textiles.

28. Leo Marsicanus, Bk. I, ch. 55, pp. 140–41. Sarno, one of the towns reported hit, is less than twenty miles from the city of Salerno.

29. *Chron. Salern.*, ch. 161.

30. Ibid., ch. 157. The author of the *Chronicon* (whose life surely overlapped Guaimar's) also described his splendid embellishing of Salerno's principal church and his extensive remodeling of the royal palace (ch. 159).

31. For example, *CDC* I, nos. 114 and 116 (902), 129 (912), 148 (928).

32. *CDC* I, nos. 131 (912), 152 (932), 167 and 169 (940). Here, as in the preceding examples, some of the references are to Atranesi, Amalfitans from the port adjacent to the city of Amalfi.

33. *Chron. Salern.*, ch. 161.

34. According to Leo Marsicanus (Bk. II, ch. 5), the body had been in Ethiopia and Brittany [sic], then had been brought to "Lucania" (thought here to mean the Paestum area), where Gisolf found it. In 1080, Pope Gregory VII would dedicate Robert Guiscard's new cathedral at Salerno, built to honor these remains. See, on all of this, the invaluable *Bibliotheca Sanctorum* (1961), 9: 125.

35. Typically, the two Bari annals differ in dating this raid, one saying 947, the other 949 (Lupus Proto., p. 54; *Annal. Baren.*, p. 53).

36. The Byzantines apparently now reclaimed Ascoli and Siponto from the Lombards (*Annal. Ben.*, p. 175; Lupus Proto., p. 54).

37. *Annal. Ben.*, p. 175.

38. On this truce and the fierce Arab attacks preceding it, and on the Byzantine and Arab sources, see Vasiliev, *Byzance et les Arabes*, II, Part 1, pp. 366–70.

39. The 964 offensive and other developments leading up to the pact of 967 are well covered in Gay, *Ital. byz.*, pp. 290–91; and Lev, "Fatimid Navy," pp. 236–37.

40. Charters displaying Gisolf's Byzantine title are *CDC* I, nos. 190, 191, 194 (March to July 956). On this Byzantine effort, see Amari, *Storia*, 2: 288–89 (including notes).

41. *Chron. Salern.*, ch. 166, p. 170. The papal army was supplemented by "Tuscans" and Spoletans.

42. Ibid., ch. 167, p. 171. The sources mention no results of this meeting beyond the enhancement of Gisolf's image.

43. *MGH Dipl. RIG* I, no. 235 (February 13, 962).

44. Leo Marsicanus, Bk. II, ch. 6. Hartmut Hoffmann, in his new edition of this chronicle, indicates the date of this gift as either 962 or 971; but 962 is the traditionally accepted date. Gisolf had apparently inherited these lands (in central Italy) from his grandmother, Idta of Spoleto; presumably Gemma participated in the gift because of her *morgencap* rights.

45. And indeed in 964, two years after his coronation, Otto issued an elaborate confirmation of all Monte Cassino's holdings (Leo Marsicanus Bk. II, ch. 4), echoing similar actions by his predecessors.

46. Liutprand, *Historia Ottonis*, ch. 6.

47. Schipa, "Salerno," p. 165; as Schipa observed, no doubt the gratifying Terracina meeting predisposed Gisolf to favor John XII.

48. Both the *Annales Beneventani* (p. 176) and Leo Marsicanus (Bk. II, ch. 9) report this, albeit with garbled dates; Gay (*Ital. byz.*, pp. 297–98) puts it in 966.

49. *MGH Dipl. RIG* I, no. 336 (January 11, 967). It was now that Pandolf began to be called "caput ferreum" (for which see Leo Marsicanus, Bk. I, ch. 61, p. 157; Bk. II, Prologue, p. 164).

50. *MGH Dipl. RIG* I, no. 338 (February 13, 967), at Benevento. The next diploma, showing Otto back in northern Italy, was not issued until March 23, so it is thought possible that Otto visited Capua after Benevento.

51. Ibid., no. 355 (January 18, 968), at Capua; and no. 356 (February 15, 968), at Benevento.

52. Leo Marsicanus, Bk. II, ch. 9. In 969, the same honor was granted to Benevento (Jaffé-Loew. I, no. 3738).

53. *Chron. Salern.*, ch. 169, pp. 172–73. The term is "soror"; describing the meeting of Adelaide and Gisolf, the *Chronicon Salernitanum* has her addressing him as "confrater."

54. Leo Marsicanus, Bk. I, ch. 61; Schipa, "Salerno," p. 166, n. 11. As Schipa observed, "soror" was often used loosely.

55. Liutprand, *Antapodosis*, Bk. IV, ch. 13. On "spiritual siblings" see Joseph H. Lynch, "*Spiritale Vinculum*: The Vocabulary of Spiritual Kinship in Early Medieval Europe" (1987), pp. 193–94.

56. *Chron. Salern.*, ch. 169, p. 173.

57. Ibid., ch. 170, p. 173: "Ipse imperator deinde Apulie finibus venit, et valide eam scilicet denudavit, et civitas Varim [sic] aliquantulum eam obsedit, et quantum valuit undique constrinxit." The *Chronicon* provides the fullest description of Otto's campaigns in southern Italy, but without dates. Gay sorts out the chronology, and his analysis overall is masterly (Gay, *Ital. byz.*, pp. 304–5, 310–15).

58. Otto had obviously abandoned the siege very quickly; it began only in March, and by June 4 Liutprand had already reached Constantinople. As for the embassies, Byzantine legates first sought out Otto, at Ravenna, in the spring of 967; Otto then sent a message to Nicephorus Phocas by way of a Venetian; and early in

968 Byzantine envoys apparently met with Otto again, probably at Capua. (On these embassies, see Gay, *Ital. byz.*, pp. 300–304.)

59. Liutprand, *Rel. Const.*, chs. 15, 27, 36.

60. For Nicephorus on Bari's resistance, see ibid., ch. 11. The ravaging of Byzantine territory (ibid., chs. 4, 6) particularly enraged Nicephorus because, he said, the Venetian envoy had insisted that Otto had no such intentions (ibid., ch. 31).

61. Ibid., ch. 31.

62. Gay rejected the notion that Byzantine legates sought out Otto at Ravenna in 967 because southern Italy already seemed threatened (Gay, *Ital. byz.*, pp. 300–303). Yet one wonders; word of Pandolf's close relationship with Otto must have reached Constantinople (even if Otto's own first trip south, in February, could hardly have been reported before the legates left). And if Pandolf had already conducted hostile actions, that would obviously have caused concern.

63. Liutprand, *Rel. Const.*, chs. 57, 7.

64. Ibid., ch. 27. To emphasize this, in mid-July (while Liutprand was still at Constantinople) Nicephorus Phocas dispatched to Bari a large fleet carrying forces meant to restore order and also to connect with a dissident north Italian army to be recruited by Adalbert (ibid., chs. 29–31).

65. *Chron. Salern.*, chs. 171, 172, pp. 173–75. In two diplomas in the spring of 969, Otto spoke of subduing Calabria: *MGH Dipl. RIG* I, no. 371 (April 18, 969, issued near Cassano, in Calabria) and no. 373 (May 1, 969, issued while besieging Bovino but noting Calabrian successes). For a northern perspective on all of this, see Widukind, *Res Gestae Saxonicae*, chs. 71, 72.

66. *Chron. Salern.*, ch. 172, p. 175. Avellino, midway between Benevento and Salerno, had been Salernitan in the latter ninth century but by now, charters indicate, was firmly Capuan (*CDC* I, no. 192, and II, nos. 227, 231, 255, 272 [956–72]).

67. *Chron. Salern.*, chs. 173–74, pp. 175–77. We are told that Naples, as punishment, was stripped of all animals.

68. For Otto in Capuan territory in May of 970, see *MGH Dipl. RIG* I, no. 396. As Jules Gay noted, no agreements linked to the marriage have survived so we can only guess at understandings concerning southern Italy (Gay, *Ital. byz.*, pp. 318–19).

69. Liutprand, *Rel. Const.*, ch. 36.

70. Benevento had lost much of its territory to Byzantine incursions. And when in the 920s Landolf I of Capua-Benevento had audaciously proposed that he be appointed *strategos* of Langobardia, the proposal had been treated with disdain; see Falkenhausen, *Dominazione*, pp. 34–35.

71. *Chron. Salern.*, ch. 170, p. 173; ch. 173, p. 176.

72. On the city of Salerno, see Delogu, *Mito di una città*, chs. 1 (esp. p. 36 on) and 3.

73. On gastalds and *judices*, see note 8, above. Only twice in tenth-century Salernitan charters do we encounter the old Lombard title of *sculdais*: *CDC* I, no. 132 (913), and II, no. 268 (972). And *comes* seems routinely to have been an official's title only in Capua-Benevento (*CDC* II, no. 227, in 964), where northern influence was far stronger. In Salerno, a close male relative of the ruler might bear the title (*CDC* I, no. 153, in 933; II, no. 368, in 984) and these *comites* plainly were powerful figures, but it does not appear that they had any administrative function.

74. The Salernitan charters include many *morgencap* bestowals (one-fourth of the bridegroom's property), many sale contracts noting the wife's *morgencap* interest, and many examples of wives or widows conveying their *morgencap* shares. Also, women figuring in transactions were always accompanied by male relatives in whose *mundium* they were.

75. In the 820s, charters show the notary Leo at both Nocera and Sarno (*CDC* I, nos. 14, 15). In the 840s and 850s, one Cumpert drafted charters in Nocera, Sarno, and Barbattiano (*CDC* I, nos. 20, 24, 30, 33, 37, 57). And Ursus, although chiefly at Nocera, appears once in a marketplace at Castellamare di Stabia (*CDC* I, nos. 34, 49, 50, 63).

76. Ten witnesses were not uncommon in the ninth century; four charters have fourteen or more (*CDC* I, nos. 54, 56, 58, 90). In the tenth century, three or four became standard. (By then, contracting had in general become more formal; a *judex* usually presided. See Maria Galante, "Il notaio e il documento notarile a Salerno in epoca longobarda" [1982], pp. 76–79.)

77. *CDC* I, no. 34 (850). Other ninth-century sellers of land promised compensatory property should "uxor mea [claiming *morgencap* rights] introierit in ista mea vinditione et . . . vobis exinde tulerit" (*CDC* I, nos. 84 [880] and 88 [882]).

78. *CDC* I, no. 106 (894).

79. When we first encounter an *advocator* (*CDC* I, no. 87, in 882), he is a gastald merely seconding an action by the bishop of Salerno. But in the tenth century the *advocator* becomes the key defender or spokesperson—and in 969 someone accused of trespass and theft protests that "nesciret quit inde respondere sine adbovactorem [sic]" (*CDC* II, no. 259).

80. *I documenti cassinesi del secolo X con formule in volgare* (1960). It is noteworthy that one of those losing here was a gastald.

81. Laymen, learning quickly, often now produced even more documents than the ecclesiastical institutions with which they contended (e.g., *CDC* I, nos. 135 [918], 161 [936], 177 [949]). In the 949 instance, a woman contesting the abbot of St. Maximus had fifteen documents to his two, and won her case.

82. "Foreigners" (other than Amalfitans, Neapolitans, and the occasional Capuan or Beneventan) begin to figure in Salernitan contracts only in the latter half of the tenth century; see Chapter 7.

83. Among the charters mentioning new residential building are *CDC* I, nos. 158 (935), 174 (947); II, nos. 249 (966), 258 (968); there are also many references to newly embellished houses. *CDC* II, no. 263 (970) concerns a major new church dedicated to St. Matthew; and the *Chronicon Salernitanum* (ch. 159) reports Guaimar II's additions to the royal palace.

84. No records of ninth-century transactions have survived from Naples, but examples of its ninth-century copper coinage feature either St. Januarius (San Gennaro) or the current duke. Briefly, in the 880s, a silver *denarius* recognized "Basil imperator." See Sambon, *Monnaies du Sud*, pp. 72–78.

85. Charters stipulating Arichis *tremisses* include *CDC* I, nos. 63, 66, 68, 69, 73 (866–72); Camera (*Memorie* I: 95) also cited an 860 charter, now lost. Earlier, from 843 to 860, several charters specified Sicard's *tremisses*, but thereafter what purported to be Sicard's coins apparently became suspect.

86. On this period, see Sambon, *Monnaies du Sud*, pp. 41–44 (for Salerno, where charters specified 12 *denarii* to the *solidus*); pp. 28–30 (for Benevento); pp. 64–65 (for Capua).

87. See Chapter 5, note 36, for the first appearance of *tari* in Salernitan and Amalfitan charters. In Naples' charters (those published by Capasso and also the few scattered through the *CDC*), we find mixed use of *tari* and Byzantine *solidi* in the first half of the tenth century, but thereafter only *tari*. If Sambon's tentative attribution of some silver *denarii* was correct, Capua-Benevento may have resisted this change (Sambon, *Monnaies du Sud*, pp. 66–68); yet we do find *tari* in one of the few surviving Capuan charters (*CDC* II, no.272, in 972).

88. On *tari* in Islamic Sicily and southern Italy, see Samuel M. Stern, "Tari: The Quarter-Dinar" (1970), esp. pp. 184–89. The chronology of the Salernitan and Amalfitan coinages is much debated; many of the tenth-century datings of Sambon and other Italian numismatists have been challenged, for the most part (if not always) persuasively, by Philip Grierson, in three articles reprinted in his *Later Medieval Numismatics* (1979). Grierson, however, does accept as tenth century some examples of local *tari* complete with mock-cufic lettering, and many such survive. Charters specifying genuine Fatimid-issue *tari* include *CDC* I, nos. 191 (956) and 195 (957), "auri tari boni cassimini" (a reference to the contemporary Sicilian emir al-Hasan or "al-Kasim").

89. There are also two sales with payment in Byzantine gold *solidi* ("auri solidos constantinos"); one, in 919 to Guaimar II, for 100 *solidi* (a huge estate including property in both Capua and Salerno: *CDC* I, no. 137), and a sale in 933 to Guaimar's brother or half-brother (*CDC* I, no. 153).

90. Most charters simply give the price in *tari*, but a few, at both Salerno and Amalfi, speak of *solidi* payable in tari (e.g., *CDC* II, no. 283, and *CDA* I, no. 7); and one Salernitan charter gives the rate as four *tari* to the *solidus* (*CDC* I, no. 156, in 934). Four Amalfitan charters say something like "auri solidi mancosi ana [payable in] tari quatuor per mancosum" (*CDA* I, nos. 2 [934], 4 [939], 6 [947], 8 [970]). "Solidi mancosi" here presumably meant dinars; we know that *tari* were four to the dinar, and *mancus* (in a Mediterranean context) is now generally conceded, even by Grierson, to mean an Arab coin. (Yet we might recall that Pope John VIII had paid off Campanian rulers in silver "mancusi"; *mancus*, as a term, must sometimes have been used loosely.)

91. These "loans" (*CDC* I, nos. 91 and 95) and also the eleven land sales during Guaimar I's reign were all lay transactions involving small plots. (Presbyters appear in some, but acting as individuals.) Before 880, there had been four other "loans" using land ingeniously (*CDC* I, nos. 56, 69, 70, 73).

92. The statistics here (and in note 91) reflect only *CDC* sale charters drafted within the principality of Salerno (and not redated by Gentile). I have assumed all sales to be genuine, not fictive (not disguised loans). Some do provide for reclaiming the property if the seller decides to return to the area (e.g., *CDC* I, no. 124, in 908). And many (for example, six of the eleven sales in Guaimar II's period) include a phrase calling for double the price and compensation for improvements should the seller want his land back or be unable to deliver clear title (e.g., *CDC* I, no. 162, in 936). In context, however, this phrase seems only a more realistic substitute for

the conventional penalty clause; if anything was disguised or hidden, more likely it was the pressure exerted on small landowners to sell.

93. For the *pastinum*, see Raymond Billiard, *La vigne dans l'antiquité* (1913), p. 293. On *pastenare* contracts as a distinctive phenomenon, see Augusto Lizier, *L'economia rurale dell'età prenormanna nell'Italia meridionale* (1907), pp. 84–86; and Del Treppo and Leone, *Amalfi medioevale*, pp. 22–23.

94. J. K. Hyde, *Society and Politics in Medieval Italy* (1973), pp. 25–26.

95. *CDC* I, no. 159. This, then, was actually a *pastenare ad partionem* contract, although that fuller phrase does not appear until later (e.g., *CDC* II, no. 224, in 963). "Inserte" or "insitetum" were the terms used for grafted trees in these charters; Lizier thought them chestnut trees, Filangieri (editor of the Amalfitan charters) fruit trees. Georges Duby speaks of division provisions ("méplant" or "complant") as commonplace from the Mâconnais to Trier in the eleventh and twelfth centuries, but only for viticulture (*Rural Economy and Country Life in the Medieval West*, trans. Cynthia Postan [1968], p. 139).

96. *CDC* I, no. 132. In addition to the output of the vineyard, any grain grown on the property would be divided half-and-half—provided St. Maximus supplied seed and oxen.

97. The first of these is *CDC* II, no. 313 (979).

98. *CDC* I, nos. 169 (940), 170 (942). The bishop of Salerno is the disposing principal in both charters. In the first, he leases a church and its land, including the former vineyard, to three Amalfitans who promise to restore the church and see that it has a priest. In the second, Arabs are referred to as "generationibus," that common local shorthand for them; see Chapter 2, note 56.

99. In 940 (*CDC* I, no. 165), a man moving to the Sarno area, some twenty miles away, disposed of half a house in the city of Salerno with the option of reclaiming it if Sarno suffered "perturbatio gentis" (typically, a reference to Arab depredations). In fact, however, Arabs thereafter threatened only occasionally, at most appearing by sea to demand tribute from some coastal city.

100. The first references to *pastenare* in Amalfitan charters come in 939 (*CDA* I, nos. 4 and 5). Tenth-century charters from Naples include several such references, and often (as in Amalfitan charters) land there is described as originally obtained through *pastenare in partionem* (e.g., Capasso, *Mon.* II, Part I, no. 219, in 978). See also *CDC* II, no. 336, a Naples *pastenare* charter.

101. Leo Marsicanus, Bk. II, ch. 1, p. 166.

102. On San Vincenzo's territory, see Mario Del Treppo, "La vita economica e sociale in una grande abbazia del Mezzogiorno: San Vincenzo al Volturno nell'alto medioevo" (1956), pp. 41–43. Del Treppo estimated a contiguous core holding (not counting isolated, remote possessions) of roughly four hundred square kilometers, about half the size of Monte Cassino's core holding.

103. *Chron. Vulturn.* II, nos. 87 (939), 92 (945), 95 (950).

104. Hyde, *Medieval Italy*, p. 24. Hyde saw as the key factor a rise in population (an issue to be considered in Chapter 7).

105. For example, Doreen Warriner, *Economics of Peasant Farming*, 2d ed.

(1964), pp. 23–27, 101. Others have devoted even more attention to the market factor but, for medievalists, Warriner's study of the impoverished peasant farms of prewar eastern Europe is particularly valuable because her types of holdings were in many respects "medieval."

106. For the period 900 to 983 (the richest period for agricultural contracts) we find in the Salernitan leases forty-six mentions of vines or vineyards and twenty-three of chestnut and hazelnut trees (not including references to grafted trees). Fruit trees, at seven mentions, come third; grain is seldom mentioned, or only incidentally.

107. *Ramage in South Italy*, ed. Edith Clay (1987), p. 82. (See also pp. 144–45, for the comments of this perceptive early nineteenth-century traveler on the disastrous local effect of limitations then on trade.)

108. In one three-year *pastenare* lease from Amalfi, the tenant must plant vines, employ three or four men to care for them, do all the improving at his own expense, yet still give half-shares throughout to the landowner (*CDA* I, no. 10, in 977). In another, the landlord's share is an exceptional two-thirds, and the tenant's compliance with cultivation instructions will be subject to scrutiny by *boni homines* (*CDC* II, no. 363, in 984).

109. In this same decade, which offers a particularly good range of Salernitan charters, Amalfitans (or Atranesi) also figured in three of the sixteen leases of Salernitan land. For one area of Amalfitan activity within the principality, see Bruno Figliuolo, "Gli Amalfitani a Cetara: Vicende patrimoniali e attività economiche (secc. X–XI)" (1979–80), pp. 31–46, 53–55, 60–66.

110. A term constantly encountered in local charters in relation to vines or vineyards is "arbustis vitatis": vines festooned between trees or otherwise held high, to be nearer the sun. For this Roman practice, see Billiard, *La Vigne*, p. 366.

111. No analysis has been done for twelfth-century Salerno, but for Amalfi in the twelfth century twenty-six of the surviving twenty-nine agricultural leases are *ad pastenandum* in type and phrasing (Del Treppo and Leone, *Amalfi medioevale*, p. 25).

112. The first "straight" lease in the Salernitan charters (*CDC* I, no. 182) comes in 952; it ran for eight years, with the tenant permitted to cut trees from the woods but also to plant grain and continuously share that.

113. In the Cava/Salerno charters, the phrase first appears in 957 (*CDC* I, no. 196); thereafter it continues to appear and by the end of the century has become commonplace.

114. *CDC* III, nos. 465–74. Figliuolo, assessing Amalfitan landowning and leasing at Cetara, found in the second half of the tenth century a similar Amalfitan shift toward "stirpi comitali" ("Gli Amalfitani a Cetara," p. 54).

115. These copper coins, also bearing the legend "Gisulfus princeps," date to the reign either of Gisolf I (946–77) or Gisolf II (1052–77); see Grierson's advocacy of the latter in "La cronologia della monetazione salernitane nei secoli XI e XII" (1972), pp. 162–65. But Grierson's view (as he grants) has not been universally accepted, and his argument for the eleventh century seems based on insufficient familiarity with the reign and predilections of Gisolf I.

Chapter 7

1. J. D. Gould, *Economic Growth in History* (1972), pp. 3–4.
2. For goldsmiths, *CDC* II, no. 226; for the shoemaker, no. 228.
3. *CDC* II, nos. 296, 299. In no. 296, it is stipulated that a consortial member wishing to sell his share must first offer it to fellow members (who will then have thirty days to buy it "ad iusto valiente pretium"). Further, if a member dies without heirs his share reverts to the group. For other evidence of Amalfitan entrepreneurship, see Del Treppo and Leone (*Amalfi medioevale*, pp. 46–51) on the buying and selling of mill shares at Amalfi.
4. These San Vincenzo leases were discussed in Chapter 6.
5. Del Treppo, "Vita in una grande abbazia," pp. 101–2.
6. See Chapter 5, note 39, and related text.
7. On the south Italian themes, see Falkenhausen, *Dominazione*, esp. pp. 23–25, 30–33, 40–41; in the latter tenth century, Longobardia (Apulia and part of Basilicata) was elevated to a catepanate (Vera von Falkenhausen, "I Bizantini in Italia" [1982], pp. 62–63).
8. Gay (*Ital. byz.*, pp. 331, 334) notes risings at Bari, Trani, and Ascoli. For the assassinations, see Lupus Proto., p. 56; these annals do not identify the perpetrators but do place one assassination at Bari.
9. This was described in Chapter 1.
10. Figliuolo, "Amalfitani a Cetara," pp. 54–55.
11. Siblings, and husbands and wives, provide most of the examples, but in one instance (*CDC* II, no. 288, in 976) a man whose wife had died while he was away is fighting for custody of his baby daughter Miranda; the wife's family had wished instead to raise the baby. (Property was not at issue.)
12. On the wicked Landolf, his sons, and the disastrous results of this generosity, see *Chron. Salern.*, chs. 175–83.
13. *Vita S. Lucae Abbatis*, p. 339.
14. The *Chronicon Salernitanum* ends, abruptly, with Pandolf's army restoring Gisolf in 974; what happened thereafter must be deduced from Salernitan charter indictions. In the fall of 974, shortly after the restoration, we find Gisolf, Gemma, and the young Pandolf ("optatus filius") all listed as co-rulers (*CDC* II, no. 280); this continued to be true until Gisolf's death.
15. In December 977, just after Gisolf's death, the co-rulers listed were Gemma and young Pandolf (*CDC* II, no. 299). But by August 978 Gemma's name had disappeared; Pandolf Ironhead and the young Pandolf appear as sole co-rulers (*CDC* II, nos. 300–303), and Gemma is never again mentioned.
16. It is impossible to fix with precision the dates of Manso's tenure at Salerno because (perhaps understandably) there are gaps in the charter sequence during the period in which he took over and also the period in which he was ousted. But September 981 to November 983 seems most likely.
17. Amalfi was made an archbishopric in 987. For the Amalfitan monastery at Mount Athos, see Pertusi, "Nuovi documenti sui Benedittini amalfitani."
18. Otto II's south Italian expedition is poorly documented, and his itinerary

can be tracked only through indictions in grants and confirmations issued along the way. These place Otto outside Lucera (in northern Apulia, nearly in Byzantine territory) from September 23 to October 1, 981, and then from October 10 to 18 back at Benevento, no doubt to learn more about Manso's coup. By November 4, Otto was at Naples (*MGH Dipl. RIG* II, nos. 258–65), perhaps mostly because of its proximity to Salerno, toward which he then moved.

19. The first Salerno indiction (December 5, 981) describes Otto as camped "super Salernitanam civitatem," where he "residebat cum suis honoratibus ostiliter" (ibid., no. 266). By January 6 of the new year, however, he had apparently entered the city ("actum Salerno," ibid., no. 267). We deduce that Manso's son was taken hostage from a passage in the *Life* of the hermit-saint Sabas, who later interceded to secure the youth's release: *Historia et Laudes SS. Sabae et Macarii*, ch. 46, pp. 63–64. The hagiographer, Orestes, Patriarch of Jerusalem, later speaks (confusingly) of a son of the Duke of Amalfi as also taken hostage, but we know—as Orestes plainly did not—that at this point the prince of Salerno and the duke of Amalfi were one and the same.

20. *MGH Dipl. RIG* II, no. 279 ("actum intra civitatem Salernam," August 18, 982); and no. 285, issued at Capaccio, in Salernitan territory near Paestum. (On the dating of no. 285, see Gay, *Ital. byz.*, p. 339, n. 4.)

21. For example, we find no charters like *CDC* II, no. 277 (974), during the regime of the wicked Landolf of Conza, when a husband and wife fled Salerno, deeding property to their daughters with the property to be reclaimed should they later find it possible to return.

22. In the ten years from 961 through 970, Amalfitans (or Atranesi) had figured in 22 percent of Salernitan charters. Under Manso's rule, it was 35 percent, and we also find an Amalfitan *comes* acquiring an impressive estate (for 50 gold *tari*) in what conceivably was a pressured sale (*CDC* II, no. 352). But St. Maximus, closely associated with the Guaimar/Gisolf line, continued very active in land transactions and seemed untroubled by Manso's takeover; and in judicial disputes during Manso's reign Amalfitans did not necessarily win.

23. The new prince was "John [son] of Lambert," and his son (and co-ruler) was named Guy; "Lambert" and "Guy" suggest connections with the old ducal line of Spoleto, from which had come Idta, the wife of Guaimar I. This presumably made John an appropriate (and properly eminent) choice. Prince John's grandson, Guaimar V (1027–52), was to ally himself with the elder brother of Robert Guiscard and thus secured for Salerno a privileged position through the first half-century of Norman conquest.

24. Leo Marsicanus Bk. II, chs. 9–11; Gay, *Ital. byz.*, p. 371.

25. *Thietmari Chronicon*, ch. 20.

26. Earlier, only the south Italian campaign of Ibrāhīm, in 902, had received much notice in Arab sources. But the raids of the 970s appear even in the narrative of Ibn al-Athīr, writing more than two hundred years later (Ibn al-Athīr, *Annales du Maghreb*, pp. 379–80). Similar details were recorded by one of Bari's annalists (Lupus Proto., p. 55).

27. Gay, *Ital. byz.*, pp. 328–30. As Gay noted, the monk of St. Gall stressed this motive: "Otto imperator non contentus finibus patris sui, dum esset Romae,

egressus est occupare Campaniam, Lucaniam, Galabriam [sic], Apuliam, et omnes ulteriores partes Italiae usque ad mare Siculum" (*Annales Sangallenses Maiores*, p. 80).

28. By late January, Otto was "circa Materiam civitatem" (*MGH Dipl. RIG* II, nos. 268–70); by mid-March, "iusta civitatem Tarentum," where he stayed at least until April 18 (ibid., nos. 272–75). For Otto's activities in the south to this point, largely as reported in German sources, see Karl Uhlirz, *Jahrbücher des Deutschen Reiches unter Otto II und Otto III* I (1902), pp. 169–77. The Uhlirz narrative is valuable for placing Otto's expedition within the context of German political developments (never far from Otto's mind, as diplomas issued en route demonstrate). But it contains some factual errors and unacceptable suppositions; as a corrective, see Gay, *Ital. byz.*, pp. 333–35.

29. *Historia et Laudes SS. Sabae et Macarii*, ch. 22, p. 37. In the event, the hagiographer tells us, the wicked Arabs invaded Calabria and Otto then fought them.

30. The battle of Stilo is described by Thietmar (*Thietmari Chronicon*, chs. 20–23) and also, if in garbled form, by Ibn al-Athīr (*Annales du Maghreb*, pp. 389–91); interestingly, both tell of the Jew who gave Otto a horse. It should be noted that some think the battle took place not near Stilo but at Cape Colonna, farther east along the coast. (Uhlirz, for example, favored Cape Colonna.) In any case, Uhlirz lists the Germans who fell in battle (*Jahrbücher* I: 177–80) and in an appendix provides most of the contemporary reports (ibid., pp. 254–57, 262–65). See also Gay, *Ital. byz.*, pp. 337–39.

31. On these incursions, see Lupus Proto., p. 56; Amari (*Storia* 2: 395–96), and Falkenhausen, "Bizantini in Italia," pp. 64–65. Early in this period of renewed hostilities, a Byzantine fleet attacked Sicily and the Byzantines briefly took Messina; however, they were unable to hold their ground, and in the end this operation only worsened matters for Byzantine Calabria.

32. Ibn Khaldūn, *The Muqaddimah*, 2: 41–42.

33. Cahen, "Un texte peu connu," pp. 61–67; this is the massacre reference mentioned in Chapter 5 (and its note 35).

34. This was reported by Amatus of Monte Cassino (on whose narrative see Introduction, note 9).

35. The fullest contemporary report of Capua's tribulations is in the untitled Capuan chronicle edited by Cilento in *Italia meridionale longobarda* ("La cronaca della dinastia capuana," pp. 132–34); see also Leo Marsicanus, Bk. II, chs. 10, 15. Gay (*Ital. byz.*, pp. 372–75) summarizes Otto's unpleasant relations with both Capua and Benevento; for a lengthier description (highly sympathetic to Otto), see Mathilde Uhlirz, *Jahrbücher des Deutschen Reiches unter Otto II und Otto III*, II (1954), pp. 289–306. The internecine battling within Capua and its effect on Monte Cassino apparently caused Otto's angry intervention in Capua; as for Naples, we can only hypothesize some Neapolitan connection with the anti-Otto Crescentius faction at Rome.

36. *Annal. Ben.*, p. 177. On the ruse, see Leo Marsicanus, Bk. II, ch. 24.

37. Contributing to the decline of Capua and Benevento had been the fecundity of its rulers. Landolf, founder of the dynasty (count-gastald of Capua, 815–43),

left four sons, and this became typical. Pandolf Ironhead had six sons as well as four nephews, sons of his brother and co-ruler. (See Cilento, *Italia meridionale longobarda*, Tables 1 and 2.) With no firm system of primogeniture, almost any of of these men could (and did) make claim to power in Capua and Benevento.

38. For perspectives on this jurisdictional conflict, its start reported by Liutprand, see the very full discussion in Gay, *Ital. byz.*, pp. 350–65. See also Ménager, "Byzantinisation réligieuse," part 2, pp. 5–7; and Falkenhausen, *Dominazione*, pp. 166–72.

39. St. Vitalis, St. Leo-Luke, and St. Elias the Speleote all made pilgrimages to Rome; St. Elias the Younger attempted to do so; and St. Sabas made several trips there and in fact died in Rome. For the careers of the major south Italian hermit-saints, see G. da Costa-Louillet, "Saints de Sicile et d'Italie méridionale aux VIII, IX et X siècles" (1959–60), pp. 89–173. In most cases, their *Vitae* were written almost contemporaneously and by close associates, so the *Vitae* give us much valuable contemporary detail.

40. For the description of St. Nilus at Monte Cassino (drawing on his *Vita*), see Bloch, *Monte Cassino in the Middle Ages* 1: 10–12; and also, a splendid article, Olivier Rousseau, "La visite de Nil de Rossano au Mont-Cassin" (1973).

41. Many Greek works flowed in through Naples and were translated there. But many came in other ways; for example, in the 870s Anastasius Bibliothecarius sent to the bishop of Benevento (where St. Bartholomew's body was enshrined) a Latin translation of a Theodore the Studite homily on St. Bartholomew (*MGH Epist.* VII: 441–42, no. 18).

42. Otto III visited Nilus when the latter was settled for a time in Gaetan territory; the visit apparently preceded Otto's pilgrimage to Monte Gargano (*Vita S. Nili*, sects. 92, 93).

43. Ibid., sects. 6, 14, 30, 70–71.

44. For obvious reasons, André Guillou gives in full this passage from the *Life* of St. Nilus, in "Production and Profits in the Byzantine Province of Italy: An Expanding Society" (1974), p. 92.

45. See Gay, *Ital. byz.*, p. 285, for the saints' dispersing into "Lucania." *CDC* II, no. 382, shows St. Sabas and a follower taking possession of a church at Vietri in 986.

46. One example is *CDC* I, no. 98 (now dated by Gentile to 899). Also, in *CDC* I, nos. 140 and 141 (923), we find property deeded to St. Maximus with the donors to receive half-shares of all produce during their lifetimes (a sort of life annuity).

47. Among the many examples of gastalds as *dominii* of foundations in the latter tenth century are *CDC* II, nos. 239, 240, 248 (966), 290 (976), 305 (978), 314 (979), 327 (980); III, no. 535 (1000). Even if one translates *dominus*, benignly, as "guardian," the position was surely a rewarding one.

48. Leo Marsicanus, Bk. II, ch. 29; this revealing episode took place at the very end of the tenth century, but the pragmatism reflected was evident throughout our period, and everywhere.

49. Figliuolo has suggested that lands may sometimes have been described as "vacua" or "inculta" only to circumvent strictures against selling ecclesiastical property ("Amalfitani a Cetara," pp. 36–37). Yet sometimes this must have been an

accurate description and the sale or trade of the land genuinely in everyone's best interest. Similarly, we cannot always doubt the statement that bishops and abbots have given careful consideration to a proposed transaction and have conferred at length with their colleagues.

50. On this general topic, see Cinzio Violante, "Le strutture organizzative della cura d'anime nelle campagne dell'Italia centrosettentrionale, secoli V–X" (1982) and (in the same conference volume) the discussion that followed Violante's paper. The situation in contemporary north-central Italy appears to have been more or less analogous to that in Campania. For the organization of parishes in Campania in the eleventh century, see Bruno Ruggiero, "Per una storia della pieve rurale nel Mezzogiorno medievale" (1977).

51. St. Maximus at Salerno was a notable example of a proprietary foundation, held by the Salernitan dynasty totally free from any "condicionem aut dationem aut serbitium aut imperationem aut excommunicationem" on the bishop's part, as well as from any "censu" (CDC I, no. 87, in 882). On St. Maximus, what it represented and its social environment, see Bruno Ruggiero, Principi, nobiltà e Chiesa nel Mezzogiorno longobarda: L'esempio di s. Massimo di Salerno (1973). But there are many other examples in the Salerno charters, some plainly only small funerary chapels or oratories, some more impressive.

52. CDC I, nos. 169, 242, 265, 276. Particularly useful on these proprietary churches (and their relation to Lombard tradition) is Cosimo Damiano Fonseca, "Particolarismo istituzionale e organizzazione ecclesiastica della campagna nell'alto medioevo nell'Italia meridionale" (1982).

53. CDC I, no. 64 (868).

54. On this Beneventan Lombard community, see Falkenhausen, Dominazione, p. 36. The [Latin-rite] Amalfitan community on Mount Athos also attracted south Italian Lombards; see Pertusi, "Nuovi documenti."

55. Ménager, "Byzantinisation réligieuse," pp. 747–48.

56. In the Salernitan Lombard charters, a woman involved in transactions (whether wife or widow) is always accompanied or represented by a male relative, and Lombard law on mundium is cited. At Amalfi, we find widows transacting freely (CDA I, no. 8 [970])—and seeming uncertainty about wives. When an Amalfitan wife exchanged some land while her husband was at sea, the transaction held, but on his return the husband had it reconfirmed (CDC II, nos. 292 [976], 300–301 [978]).

57. CDC III, nos. 501, 516. Salernitan Lombard women were always described in charters as acting with the consent of their husbands "in accordance with Lombard law"; the Salernitan notaries here were simply using that phrase and substituting "lex romanorum." (The economic implications of the legal position of southern Lombard women deserve attention, and I will explore this in a forthcoming article.)

58. Two good examples are CDC II, nos. 274 (973), 366 (984).

59. It was perhaps not surprising to find guadia and mediatores in contracts between Salernitans and Amalfitans, but in some instances, such as CDC II, nos. 307 and 315, both parties were Amalfitan. These two charters are also interesting because both show Amalfitans as entrepreneurial owners of urban property within the city of Salerno.

60. Falkenhausen, "Bizantini in Italia," p. 92.

61. *CDC* I, nos. 38 (854), 85 (881), 121 (905); II, nos. 332, 335 (981), 361 (983). Nos. 335 and 361 involved Amalfitans and were drafted at Amalfi.

62. *CDC* I, no. 47 (856).

63. *CDC* I, no. 152 (932); this was a Salernitan charter but the lender was from Atrani and thus an Amalfitan.

64. *CDC* II, nos. 337 (982), 363 (984). No. 337 was a Salernitan charter; but no. 363 ("adequate cultivation") was drafted at Amalfi by an Amalfitan scribe.

65. *CDC* I, nos. 135 (918) and 175 (947); II, no. 258 (968).

66. Wickham, *Early Medieval Italy*, p. 139.

67. Southern Lombard rulers' rights to port and entry fees and the like are best illustrated by royal charters in Poupardin, *Inst.*: no. 20, p. 74; no. 59, p. 86; no. IV, p. 139.

68. *CDC* I, nos. 101 (886), 202 (959); for confiscation, *CDC* I, no. 111 (899).

69. In the tenth century many charters document sales to Salerno's ruling family, but there were some earlier as well, such as *CDC* I, nos. 65 (868), 66 (869). Gifts of land also occur in both centuries: for example, *CDC* I, no. 36 (853), and II, no. 368 (984) in which section 4 cites a gift of some lands to Gisolf's wife, Gemma. Also, in 972 some politic Atranesi made a major land gift to a Salernitan gastald (*CDC* II, no. 267).

70. *CDC* II, no. 368; not only are extensive royal lands described here but also some are bordered by lands belonging to a gastald and a count.

71. See the southern Lombard royal charters in Poupardin, *Inst.*; and the tenth-century Capuan-Beneventan donations summarized in *Monte Cassino: I Registi dell'Archivio* II (1965), ed. Tommaso Leccisotti.

72. *CDC* III, nos. 500–514. Of the other six charters, one concerns urban property of a Salernitan *comes*, two involve Amalfitan holdings, one is a woman's modest will, one a minor (lay) trespass case, and one a lay transaction involving some distant land.

73. Discussion in *Christianizzazione ed organizzazione ecclesiastica delle campagne nell'alto medioevo* (Spoleto *Settimane*, 1982) 2: 1201–2.

74. See, for example, *CDC* I, nos. 60 (860), 137 ((919), 210 (960); II, nos. 294 (976), 476 (995). The term also appears in many grants and confirmations to Monte Cassino.

75. For a sampling in the tenth century, see *CDC* I, nos. 149 (928), 201 (959); II, nos. 225 (964), 235 (966), 334 (981); III, nos. 463 (993), 491 (996), 501 (997). These freed *servi* and *ancillae* provide a useful glimpse of domestic servitude, even though the names (Grusa, Petrus) often leave obscure their ethnic background. The *servus* in no. 225 was "ex genere francorum," however, and in 868 (I, no. 64) Prince Guaifer had been given, by "Leo of Alexandria," a slave named Palumbo; presumably most domestic *servi et ancillae* were non-Lombard.

76. Mario Del Treppo (and more recently Chris Wickham) have examined this question in connection with the lands of San Vincenzo al Volturno; in a carefully reasoned analysis, Del Treppo posited several forms of servitude in the ninth century ("Vita in una grande abbazia," pp. 52–55). Wickham has criticized Del Treppo's inclusion of "plantation slavery" ("*Terra* of San Vincenzo," p. 233), but Wickham focused on the tenth century, when indeed it may have disappeared.

77. *Leges Langobardorum*, *MGH Leges* IV: *Capitula Adelchis Principis*, ch. 1. Strictly speaking, this new edict only allowed for exceptions to the old law, but it soon came to be liberally interpreted.

78. Before 947, no "foreign nationals" from beyond Campania (other than "Graeci" and Arabs) had appeared in the Salerno charters. Between 947 and 1000, however, we find not only more Greeks but also six Franks, a Genoese, a Slav, a "filius quondam nordemanni" [an early Norman?] and, as owners of some city property, a group of men identified only as "foretani hominibus" (*CDC* I, no. 174; II, nos. 211, 225, 234, 287, 333, 353, 421, 452; III, 536). One Frank was a *servus* now being freed, and two others were pointedly called "liber homo"; several of these foreigners may thus have initially come as *servi*, but they were all now active in what had once been a closed (and totally Lombard) society.

79. Examples of this are two St. Maximus documents, *CDC* II, no. 383 (986); IV, no. 568 (1004). In both cases, St. Maximus will recognize the free status of the wife and children—but in return will take two-thirds of whatever they produce.

80. Falkenhausen, *Dominazione*, p. 157.

81. The first is in 965: *CDC* II, no. 230. Others (through the 990s) are ibid., nos. 232, 287, 313, 340, 413, 428, 452.

82. For example, Poupardin, *Inst.*, nos. 115 (965), 117 (966).

83. Del Treppo, "Vita in una grande abbazia," pp. 49, 54.

84. A good example is *CDC* III, no. 503 (997), a St. Maximus *pastenare* lease in which only one-third shares are owed, and not until after the first twelve years; also, if there should be renewed Arab ("generatione") problems, the tenant could be absent for up to *five* years and still reclaim his tenancy.

85. Del Treppo, "Vita in una grande abbazia," pp. 73–83; Chris Wickham, *Il problema dell'incastellamento nell'Italia centrale: L'esempio di San Vicenzo al Volturno* (1985), pp. 46–49, 65–66, and "*Terra* of San Vincenzo," pp. 228, 250–51.

86. These San Vincenzo leases were discussed in Chapter 6. Del Treppo's pathbreaking article ("Vita in una grande abbazia") was published in 1956 and, as Toubert has noted, influenced the latter's explorations of *incastellamento*.

87. Del Treppo, "Vita in una grande abbazia," p. 84.

88. *CDC* II, no. 369 (984); *civitas* implied a major city, a jurisdictional center and *urbs episcopalis*, somewhat too grand, one would have thought, for Avellino.

89. In Campania, we do find a few populations moving and rebuilding at a new site, as Capua had done in the ninth century, but the reasons for these moves are unclear and may well have differed in each instance.

90. See Falkenhausen, "Bizantini in Italia," pp. 90–91.

91. *CDC* II, no. 372; since "ista cartula" has survived, we can know that its width was thirty-five centimeters (a most ample foot).

92. Ibid., no. 379 (986).

93. *CDC* III, no. 495 (996). At other times now, it was often stipulated that the measurement be "in justo passi," the accuracy agreed to by both parties (e.g., ibid., no. 533).

94. The concept of a public standard might well have come from the Byzantine or Islamic world. Interestingly, however, the length specified in Salerno for the foot or *pes* (35 cm.) is close to that which Ronald Zupko gives as the old "Germanic" foot

(33.5 cm.); the Roman measure, which one might have expected to survive in Italy, was apparently 29.6 cm. (Zupko, *British Weights and Measures: A History from Antiquity to the Seventeenth Century* [1977], pp. 6, 10).

Chapter 8

1. For mills in Capua-Benevento, see Poupardin, *Inst.*, nos. 92 (944), 119 (966). Mills appear in four of the seventeen tenth-century Amalfitan charters (*CDA* I, nos. 1, 2, 3, 9) and in Salernitan charters from the late tenth century on (*CDC* II, nos. 354, 391, 413, 433, 458, 470).

2. For example, an Arab band operating northward from Benevento first took Telese, near the confluence of the Calore and Volturno rivers, and from there raided up the Volturno to Isernia (on a tributary) and then on to San Vincenzo, presumably floating their loot downstream, perhaps sometimes all the way to the coast.

3. The first of these is *CDC* II, no. 249 (966).

4. *CDC* II, no. 342 (982); surely one could only have left half the timbers (not half the house). In any case, the same provision appears in nos. 432 and 452, and in III, no. 508 (997).

5. The first stone house not associated with a gastald or a member of the ruling family appears in *CDC* II, no. 315 (979); subsequent examples include III, nos. 488 (995), 505 (997), 535 (1000). The two with domestic aqueducts (*sericidia*, nos. 315, 535) may both have been owned by merchants; the first belonged to some Atranesi and the second to the son of a man from Sorrento. (For a splendid overview of the city of Salerno in the tenth and eleventh centuries, including its buildings and public spaces, see Delogu, *Mito di una città*, ch. 3.)

6. *Chron. Salern.*, chs. 76, 180.

7. Poupardin, *Inst.*, nos. 35, 36, 46; *CDC* II, no. 226.

8. *CDC* II, nos. 344 (982), 292 (976); Poupardin, *Inst.*, no.124 (969).

9. *CDC* II, no. 257 (968); actually, since the tunic was of cotton (*bambace*) and this was very early for cotton in Italy, this man must indeed have been relatively prosperous.

10. *CDC* II, no. 324 (980); since this property was used for growing grain, the oxen would have been important for cultivation (and would also have helped to fertilize the land).

11. See Guglielmo Cavallo, "La trasmissione dei testi nell'area beneventano-cassinese" (1975), p. 367.

12. *Chron. Salern.*, ch. 122.

13. Ibid., ch. 155.

14. No one has quantified the autograph signatures in the Salernitan charters, but many have noted them. And in my own brief sampling of some of the original ninth-century rolls, I did find many autograph signatures, including (for some charters drafted "in the marketplace") autograph signatures by what were unquestionably female witnesses.

15. *Chron. Salern.*, ch. 94.

16. Agostino Pertusi, "Bisancio e l'irradiazone dells sua civiltà in Occidente nell'alto medioevo" (1964), pp. 105–6.

17. Hans Belting, *Studien zur Beneventanischen Malerei* (1968), pp. 3–4. Since his publication of two major studies in the late 1960s, Belting has been recognized as the preeminent authority on Beneventan art and his analyses are particularly valuable for their sensitivity to the sociohistorical context.

18. E. A. Loew published the definitive work on the Beneventan script and its manuscripts, and it has recently been republished in an exemplary new, two-volume edition prepared and enlarged by Virginia Brown: *The Beneventan Script*, 2d ed. (1980). The script continued in use, to some extent, until the fifteenth century.

19. Cavallo, "Trasmissione," p. 400.

20. Loew/Brown, *Beneventan Script* 1: 8–9; see also Herbert Bloch, "Monte Cassino's Teachers and Library in the High Middle Ages" (1972), esp. pp. 563–76.

21. Many small churches are simply described as having *codices* (unspecified), but we do have a list of those presented by Salerno's new ruler, in 990, to his new foundation in the city: two "libri comites," an antiphonary for day and one for night, an Ambrosian liturgy, a homily book for Lent and other sacred occasions, writings on the Apocalypse and Gregory the Great's *Moralia on the Book of Job*, a Heptateuch together with a "Solomon," and apparently a second copy of Gregory the Great's *Moralia* bound with two sets of *questiones* (*CDC* II, no. 425).

22. On the Exultet rolls (which vary in length from two to nine meters) the standard works are Myrtilla Avery, *The Exultet Rolls of South Italy* (1936), and Guglielmo Cavallo, *Rotoli di Exultet dell'Italia meridionale* (1973); the latter, however, though good on the liturgical background and possible derivation of these rolls, treats in depth only a select few. See then also the manuscripts section of Belting, *Malerei*.

23. We know this to have been true of the early ninth-century building programs at Monte Cassino and San Vincenzo al Volturno. And elsewhere we sometimes find pieced-together simulations; see Gino Chierici, "Note sull'architettura della contea Longobarda di Capua" (1933), pp. 543–53.

24. See the amply illustrated *San Vincenzo al Volturno e la cripta dell'abbate Epifanio* (1970); and also for San Vincenzo, and for other examples from the ninth or tenth century, Belting, *Malerei*, passim.

25. In earlier chapters, reference was made to the embellishing of the major churches in Naples in the ninth century, and of St. Maximus at Salerno by both Guaimar II and Gisolf; in 990, Salerno's new Prince John gave not only *codices* but also many other treasures to his new church: a silver chalice, two silver patens and a silver censer, four silk rugs to surround the altar and four silk altar covers, a large portable reliquary, and silk vestments (*CDC* II, no. 425).

26. These eleventh-century references were gathered together long ago by Adolf Schaube; see his citations in *Händlesgeschichte der Romanischen Völker*, p. 33. We may suspect, however, that some of silks and "pannos" given earlier (to Prince John's new church, for example) had reached southern Italy by way of Fatimid trade.

27. These fragmentary panels are now thought to have come from choir or

chancel screens. On their mythical beasts (winged griffins, hippocamps), see W. F. Volbach, "Oriental Influence in the Animal Sculpture of Campania" (1942), pp. 172–80. See also Hans Belting, "Beobachtungen an Vorromanischen Figurenreliefs aus Stein" (1969), pp. 47–63 and plates.

28. Presentation by Genevieve Fisher, University of Pennsylvania, at the Twenty-Fourth International Congress of Medieval Studies (1989), Western Michigan University, Kalamazoo, Michigan.

29. See André Grabar, "Le succès des arts orientaux à la cour Byzantine sous les Macédoniens" (1951), pp. 32–60.

30. Proof of this, in addition to the evidence noted by Grabar, is provided by the mixed Byzantine-Islamic cargo of the shipwreck mentioned in Chapter 5 (and its note 43).

31. See Richard Ettinghausen, "Muslim Decorative Arts and Painting: Their Nature and Impact on the Medieval West" (1975), pp. 14–15. For Campania we have no solid, documented proof of Muslim textiles wrapping relics, but in the Vatican collection there is a padded-silk reliquary cross (ca. tenth century) that provides a splendid regional example of this practice.

32. Janine Wettstein, *Sant'Angelo in Formis et la peinture médiévale en Campanie* (1960), p. 1.

33. Ernesto Pontieri, "La crisi di Amalfi medioevale" (1964), pp. 384, 333.

34. This mingling of cultures was noted long ago by Emile Bertaux, whose three-volume *L'art méridionale de la fin de l'empire romain à la conquête de Charles d'Anjou* (1903) remains indispensable for anyone interested in medieval south Italian art. It has now been reissued together with a three-volume *Aggiornamento*: 6 vols. (1978). For other recent studies, see Valentino Pace, "Quarant'anni di studi sull'arte medievale nell'Italia meridionale" (1985).

35. On these oliphants, see Ernst Kühnel, *Die islamischen Elfenbeinskulpturen, VIII–XIII Jahrhundert* (1971), pp. 6–53. Since there are also apparent oliphants in at least one of the Exultet rolls, serving as angels' trumpets, it may be that they adorned churches as well.

36. Jenkins, "Emperor Alexander and the Saracen Prisoners" (1953), pp. 389–93; Falkenhausen, "Bizantini in Italia," p. 95.

37. See Paul Oskar Kristeller, "The School of Salerno" (1945), esp. pp. 143–44; and idem, "La Scuola Medica di Salerno secondo ricerche e scoperte recenti" (1980). For other studies, see the excellent bibliography in Morris S. Saffron, ed., *Maurus of Salerno* (1972).

38. John F. Benton concluded that there *was* a Trotula (probably in the twelfth century), but that she was not the author of the works later attributed to her, her own *Practica* having been lost ("Trotula, Women's Problems, and the Professionalization of Medicine in the Middle Ages" [1985], esp. p. 44). For further analysis, and an edition and translation of the treaties, see Monica H. Green and John F. Benton, *The Gynecological and Cosmetic Treatises attributed to "Trotula" of Salerno* (forthcoming).

39. *Gesta Episcoporum Virdunensium*, p. 47; Richer of Rheims, *Richeri Historiarum Libri IV*, p. 600.

40. *CDC* II, no. 298; *Chron. Salern.*, ch. 163, p. 169.

41. Poupardin, *Inst.*, pp. 138, 140 (nos. III, V).

42. *CDC* I, nos. 29 (848), 40 (855), 47 (856); the prices paid were 65, 35, and 50 gold *solidi*.

43. *CDC* I, no. 61 (865); a Jew (or converted Jew) might particularly have considered such a gift politic.

44. *CDC* IV, no. 567; because only "local" fathers seemed typically noted in Salerno charters, we can assume that "Judah medicus" had practiced there.

45. *Vita S. Nili*, sects. 50, 51; Donnolo offered St. Nilus medicines for an ailment but St. Nilus, rejecting the medicine, tried to convert Donnolo to Christianity.

46. For Surano, see Cilento, *Sign. cap.*, p. 184; for the prince, *Vita S. Eliae Speleotae*, sects. 59, pp. 871–72. The "prince" seems suspect (or at least cannot be identified), but Palermo doubtless had celebrated doctors.

47. Poupardin, *Inst.*, nos. 53, 67.

48. Beneventan script always indicates south Italian provenance; on ninth- and tenth-century Beneventan medical mss., see Loew/Brown, *Beneventan Script*, 1: 18–19.

49. Albert Dietrich, "Islamic Sciences and the Medieval West: Pharmacology" (1980), p. 50.

50. John M. Riddle, "Theory and Practice in Medieval Medicine" (1974), p. 168.

51. *Chron. Vulturn.*, I: 231.

52. In 997, a lease was still providing for absences that might be caused by "ista generatione" (*CDC* III, no. 503); and in 1006 a marriage contract stipulated that the husband must pay a share of the ransom if the wife was captured and about to be carried off from Italy (*CDC* IV, no. 590).

53. *Chron. Salern.*, ch. 127.

54. Erchempert, ch. 39.

55. *Chron. Vulturn.*, II: 31, doc. 80 (892); the Byzantine *strategos* is here confirming rights and immunities associated with two of San Vincenzo's subordinate houses.

56. *MGH Dipl. RIG* II, no 273; from July 981 until just before his death in 983, Otto was also besieged with confirmation requests from both Monte Cassino and San Vincenzo.

Chapter 9

1. Gay, *Ital. byz.*, i–ii.

2. The tangled and violent history of eleventh-century southern Italy is described by Jules Gay, but in addition, for the Norman perspective, there is the first volume of Chalandon's classic study, *Histoire de la domination normande en Italie et en Sicile*, and there is also an eminently readable (and solid) treatment by John Julius Norwich, *The Other Conquest* (1967; published in England as *The Normans in the South, 1016–1130*).

3. There is considerable controversy over the dating of Byzantine monuments in southern Italy; some identified as eleventh century may in fact be later, some earlier. But on the Byzantine artistic thrust beginning in the eleventh century see Hans Belting, "Byzantine Art Among Greeks and Latins in Southern Italy" (1974); and Valentino Pace, "Pittura bizantina nell'Italia meridionale (secolo XI–XIV)" (1982), in *I Bizantini in Italia*. In the latter volume also see, specifically for the Byzantine regions, Raffaella Farioli Campanati, "La cultura artistica nelle regioni bizantine d'Italia dal V all'XI secolo."

4. Falkenhausen, *Dominazione*, p. 149.

5. Ibid., pp. 173–75.

6. The prime example came in the 1080s, when Monte Cassino's Abbot Desiderius and the archbishop of Salerno were both involved in major construction (the archbishop busy with Salerno's new cathedral). See on this Ernst Kitzinger, "The Gregorian Reform and the Visual Arts: A Problem of Method" (1972), esp. pp. 93–94.

7. Cilento, *Sign. cap.*, pp. 9–10.

8. Evelyn Jamison, "The Norman Administration of Apulia and Capua" (1913), passim.

9. Notably, this was not true at Salerno, but bishops there seem to have been exceptionally docile.

10. On the impact of Islamic art on southern Italy, including the rarity of examples from before the twelfth century, see the splendid (and splendidly illustrated) article by Umberto Scerrato, "Arte islamica in Italia" in *Gli Arabi in Italia* (1979).

11. See on this Kitzinger, "Gregorian Reform"; in the Monte Cassino-Salerno instance that Kitzinger discusses, Byzantine craftsmanship seemed the prime objective. But in many other instances Byzantine style was deliberately sought; see the articles cited in note 3, above.

12. Jamison, "Norman Administration," pp. 229–35, 248, 259–61. Jamison tracked this "anti-municipal" policy (as she rightly named it) and ended by observing, "Everywhere [in southern Italy] the same policy of breaking the effective power of the towns as centres of revolt was pursued."

13. On this pact, see Bartolommeo Capasso, "Il *pactum* dal Duca Sergio ai Napoletani (1030?)" (1884); Capasso prints the pact and discusses his reasons for believing it genuine. Since Capasso, its genuineness has not been contested, but Capasso's dating (to 1030, when an exiled duke was seeking to reclaim power) has proved highly controversial. Some scholars have opted instead for ca. 1130 (Duke Sergius VII), just before Naples' surrender to the Normans. See on this Giovanni Cassandro, "Il ducato bizantino," pp. 331–37.

14. L. R. Ménager, "La legislation sud-italienne sous la domination normande" (1969), p. 454, note 39. As Ménager notes in this article, Norman recognition of *consuetudines* became a common mainland feature in the twelfth century. (But this did not keep the Norman rulers from suppressing all liberties when it suited their purposes—as usually proved to be the case.)

Appendix: The Southern Lombard Rulers, 758–1000

758–900

Arichis II, Duke, then Prince, of Benevento,
   758–87 (includes Salerno and Capua)
Grimoald III, 787–806
Grimoald IV, 806–17
Sico, 817–32
Sicard, 832–39
   [civil war begins]

Benevento	*Salerno*
Radelchis, 839–49	Sikenolf, 839–49
[formal *Divisio*, 849]	
Radelgarius, 849–54	Peter, 853–56
Adelchis, 854–78	Ademar, 856–61
	[ca. 860, *Capua*, under its count-gastald, essentially separates from Salerno]
	Guaifer, 861–80
Gaideris, 878–81	
Radelchis II, 881–85	Guaimar I, 880–900
Aio, 885–91	
Byzantine *strategos*, 892–95	
Guy of Spoleto, 895–97	
Radelchis II, 897–99	
Atenolf, Count of *Capua*, takes Beneventan throne as well, 900	

900–999

Capua-Benevento	*Salerno*
Atenolf I [Capua from 887], 900–910	Guaimar II, 900–946
Landolf I + Atenolf II, 910–43	
Landolf II, 943–61	
	Gisolf I, 946–77

Pandolf I, "Ironhead," 961–81   [Landolf of Conza, 973–74]
Pandolf Ironhead, co-ruler with son
Pandolf, 977–81

Capua	Benevento	Salerno
Landenolf, 982–93	*Pandolf II, 981–1014	Manso, Duke of Amalfi, 981–83
Laidolf, 993–99		John, 983–99

*The Pandolf who had been adopted by Gisolf and Gemma, and was thus co-ruler of Salerno 977–81, was killed in the Battle of Stilo; Pandolf II, ruler of Benevento 981–1014, was a cousin.

Bibliography

SOURCES AND SOURCE COLLECTIONS CITED

Alcuin Epistolae. MGH Epist. IV.

Amari, Michele. *Biblioteca Arabo-Sicula.* 2 vols. Turin and Rome, 1880.

Amatus of Monte Cassino. *Storia de' Normanni di Amato di Montecassino*, ed. Vincenzo de Bartholomaeis. Rome, 1935.

Anastasii Bibliothecarii Epistolae. MGH Epist. VII.

Andreas Bergomatis Historia. MGH SSrL.

Annales Barenses. See "Abbreviations."

Annales Beneventani. See "Abbreviations."

Annales Bertiniani. See "Abbreviations."

Annales Regni Francorum. See "Abbreviations."

Annales Sangallenses Maiores. MGH SS I.

al-Balādhurī. *The Origins of the Islamic State*, ed. and trans. P. K. Hitti. Columbia Studies in History 68. New York, 1916. Reprint Beirut 1966.

Benjamin of Tudela. *The Travels of Rabbi Benjamin of Tudela, 1160–1173.* In *Contemporaries of Marco Polo*, ed. Manuel Komroff. New York, 1928.

Bernard the Monk. *Itinerarium Bernardi Monachi.* In *Itinera Hierosolymitana et Descriptiones Terrae Sanctae*, ed. T. Tobler and A. Molinier [1879]. Reprint Osnabrück, 1966.

Biondo, Flavio. *De Roma triumphante, Roma instaurata: Italia illustrata.* Basle, 1531.

"Cambridge Chronicle." Relevant portion in A. A. Vasiliev, *Byzance et les Arabes*, Vol. 2, Part 2: *Extraits des Sources Arabes*, ed. H. Gregoire and M. Canard, trans. M. Canard, pp. 99–106. Brussels, 1958.

Capasso, Bartolommeo. See "Abbreviations," and "Studies Cited."

Capitularia Regum Francorum II. See "Abbreviations."

Chronica Sancti Benedicti Casinensis. See "Abbreviations."

The Chronicle of Ahimaaz, ed. and trans. Marcus Salzman. Columbia University Oriental Studies 18. New York, 1924.

Chronicon Amalfitanum. New ed., superseding all others, in Ulrich Schwarz, *Amalfi im frühen Mittelalter, 9.–11. Jahrhundert*, pp. 195–236. Deutschen Historischen Institut (Rome) 49. Tübingen, 1978.

Chronicon Salernitanum. See "Abbreviations." (The old edition, *MGH SS* III, has the same chapter numbering.)

Chronicon Vulturnense. See "Abbreviations."

Codex Carolinus. See "Abbreviations."

Codex Diplomaticus Cajetanus, Part I. Tabularium Casinense I. Monte Cassino, 1887. Reprint 1969.

212   Bibliography

Codex Diplomaticus Cavensis. See "Abbreviations."
Codice Diplomatico Amalfitano. See "Abbreviations."
Constantine Porphyrogenitus. De administrando imperio. See "Abbreviations."
———. De ceremoniis aulai byzantinae, ed. Reiske. Bonn, 1829.
———. De thematibus, ed. Bekker. Bonn, 1840.
Divisio. See "Abbreviations." (Also, with slight variation, in Muratori, RIS, Vol. 2, 1: 260–62.)
I documenti cassinesi del secolo X con formule in volgare [facsimile ed.], ed. Ambrogio Mancone. Rome, 1960.
Dölger, Franz. Corpus der Grieschischen Urkunden des Mittelaters und der Neueren Zeit. Vol. 1. Munich and Berlin, 1924.
Einhard. Via Karoli Magni Imperatoris, ed. Louis Halphen. Paris, 1923.
Erchempert. See "Abbreviations."
Gesta Episcoporum Virdunensium. MGH SS IV.
Historia et Landes SS. Sabae et Macarii, ed. and trans. Joseph Cozza-Luzi. Rome, 1953.
Historia inventionis ac translationis et miracula de S. Trophima seu Trophimena: AS, July II: 231–40.
Ibn 'Abd al-Hakam. La Conquête de l'Afrique du Nord et de l'Espagne, ed. and trans. Albert Gateau. Algiers, 1947.
Ibn al-Athīr. Annales du Maghreb et de l'Espagne, ed. and trans. E. Fagnan. Algiers, 1898.
Ibn Hawqal. Configuration de la terre [The Book of the Routes and the Kingdom], ed. and trans. J. H. Kramer and G. Wiet. 2 vols. Paris, 1964.
Ibn Hayyān. Al-Muqtabis V, ed. and trans. J. Viguero and F. Corriente. Zaragoza, 1981.
Ibn 'Idhari. Al-Bayano'l-Mogrib, ed. and trans. E. Fagnan. 2 vols. Algiers, 1901–4.
Ibn Khaldūn. The Muqaddimah, trans. Franz Rosenthal. 3 vols. New York, 1958.
Ibn Khurradadhbih. Description du Maghreb et de l'Europe au IX siècle, ed. and trans. M. Hadj-Sadok. Algiers, 1949.
Jaffé, P. Regesta Pontificum Romanorum. See "Abbreviations."
John the Deacon. Gesta Episcoporum Neapolitanorum. See "Abbreviations."
Leges Langobardorum: MGH Leges IV. See also The Lombard Laws, trans., with Introduction, by Katherine Fischer Drew. Philadelphia, 1973. (The latter, however, does not include the southern Lombard additions.)
Leo Marsicanus [Leo of Ostia]. See "Abbreviations."
Le Liber Pontificalis. See "Abbreviations."
Liutprand. Antapodosis: MGH SSrG in usum scholarum, ed. J. Becker. Hanover and Leipzig, 1915.
———. Historia Ottonis. (With Antapodosis, as above.)
———. Relatio de legatione constantinopolitane. (With Antapodosis, as above.)
———. The Works of Liutprand of Cremona, trans. F. A. Wright. London, 1930. (Book and chapter numbering identical with MGH edition.)
Lupus Protospatarius. See "Abbreviations."
Monte Cassino: I registi dell'archivio II, ed. Tommaso Leccisotti. Rome, 1965.
Nicetas Paphlagonis. "Oratio X, In praise of the Sainted Apostle Bartholomew." PG 105, col. 218.

Nicholas Mysticus. "Dilecto, spectatissimo spirituali filio illustri principi Amalphiae." *PG* III, cols. 371–72.

Nuwairī. Segments translated in A. A. Vasiliev, *Byzance et les Arabes*, Vol. 2, Part 2: *Extraits des sources arabes*, ed. H. Gregoire and M. Canard, trans. M. Canard, pp. 229–35. Brussels, 1968.

Pactum Sicardi: *MGH Leges* IV: 216–21. (Also in G. Padelletti, *Fontes iuris italici medii aevi*, pp. 308–324.)

Paul the Deacon. *Historia Langobardorum*. See "Abbreviations." See also Paul the Deacon, *History of the Lombards*, trans. W. D. Foulke. Philadelphia, 1907. Reprint Philadelphia 1974. (Book and chapter numbering identical with *MGH* edition.)

Regesta delle Pergamene, Abbazia di Montevergine, ed. G. Mongelli. Rome, 1956.

Richer of Rheims. *Richeri historiarum libri IV*: *MGH SS* III.

Tabula de Amalpha, ed. Vincenzo Giuffre. Cava dei Tirreni, 1965.

Theodosius monachus. "Epistola ad Leonem archdiaconem de Syracusanae urbis expugnatione." *PG* 135, footnote 83 to cols. 52–60.

Thietmari Merseburgensis Episcopi Chronicon, ed. Kurze: *MGH SSrG in usum scholarum*. Hanover, 1889.

Translatio Sancti Mercuri: *MGH SSrL.*

Translatio S. Severini: *MGH SSrL.*

Vasiliev, A. A. *Byzance et les Arabes*. 2 vols. in 3. Vol. 2, Part 2: *La dynastie macédonienne: Extraits des sources arabes*, ed. H. Gregoire and M. Canard, trans. Canard. Brussels, 1958.

Vita Athanasii Episcopi Neapolitani. See "Abbreviations."

Vita di Sant'Elia il Giovane [Elias of Enna], ed. and trans. Giuseppe Rossi-Taibbi. Palermo, 1962.

Vita S. Antonini Abbatis Surrentini. *AS*, February II: 784–96.

Vita S. Eliae Speleotae Abbatis. *AS*, September III: 848–88.

Vita S. Lucae Abbatis. *AS*, October VI: 337–341.

Vita S. Nili Abbatis [Nilus of Rossano]. *AS*, September VII: 262–320.

Widukind, *Res Gestae Saxonicae*, ed. H.-E. Lohmann and P.Hirsch: *MGH SSrG in usum scholarum*. Hanover, 1935.

William of Apulia. *La Geste de Robert Guiscard*, ed. and trans. Marguerite Mathieu. Palermo, 1961.

Willibald. *Hodoeporicon S. Willibaldi*: *Itinera hierosolymitana et descriptiones Terrae Sanctae*, ed. T. Tobler and A. Molinier, 1879. Reprint Osnabrück, 1966.

STUDIES CITED

Amari, Michele. *Storia dei Musulmani di Sicilia*. 3 vols. 2d ed., annotated by C. A. Nallino. Catania, 1933.

Avery, Myrtilla. *The Exultet Rolls of South Italy*. 2 vols. Princeton, 1936.

Baron, Salo W. *A Social and Religious History of the Jews*. 18 vols. New York, 1952–83. Vols. 3–8: *The High Middle Ages, 500–1200*.

Beazley, C. R. *The Dawn of Modern Geography*. 2 vols. London, 1897.

Belting, Hans. "Beobachtungen an Vorromanischen Figurenreliefs aus Stein." In

Colloquium über Frühmittelalterische Skulptur (1968), ed. V. Milojcic, pp. 47–63 and plates. Mainz, 1969.

———. "Byzantine Art Among Greeks and Latins in Southern Italy." *Dumbarton Oaks Papers* 28 (1974): 3–29 and plates.

———. "Studien zum Beneventanischen Hof im 8. Jahrhundert." *Dumbarton Oaks Papers* 16 (1962): 143–93.

———. *Studien zur Beneventanischen Malerei.* Wiesbaden, 1968.

Benton, John F. "Trotula, Women's Problems, and the Professionalization of Medicine in the Middle Ages." *Bulletin of the History of Medicine* 59 (1985): 30–53.

Bergman, Robert P. "'Amalfi sommersa': Myth or Reality." *ASPN* 3d ser., 18 (1979): 23–38.

Bertaux, Emile. *L'art méridionale de la fin de l'empire romain à la conquête de Charles d'Anjou.* 3 vols. Paris, 1903. Reissued with 3 vol. *Aggiornamento*, Bari, 1978.

Bertolini, Ottorino. "Carlomagno e Benevento." In *Karl der Grosse: Personlichkeit und Geschichte,* ed. Helmut Beumann, pp. 609–71. Düsseldorf, 1967.

Berza, M. "Amalfi preducale: 596–957." *Ephemeria Dacoromana* 8 (1938): 349–444.

Biblioteca Sanctorum. 12 vols. Rome, 1961.

Billiard, Raymond. *La vigne dans l'antiquité.* Lyons, 1913.

Bloch, Herbert. "Monte Cassino, Byzantium and the West in the Earlier Middle Ages." *Dumbarton Oaks Papers* 3 (1946): 163–224.

———. *Monte Cassino in the Middle Ages.* 3 vols. Cambridge, Mass., 1986.

———. "Monte Cassino's Teachers and Library in the High Middle Ages." In *La scuola nell'Occidente latino dell'alto medioevo* (1971 *Settimane*) II: 563–605. Spoleto, 1972.

Bonfil, Roberto. "Tra due mondi: Prospettive di ricerca sulla storia culturale degli Ebrei dell'Italia meridionale nell'alto medioevo." In *Italia Judaica,* Atti del I Convegno internazionale (Bari, 1981), pp. 135–58. Rome, 1983.

Borsari, Silvano. *Il monachesimo bizantino nella Sicilia e nell'Italia meridionale prenormanna.* Naples, 1963.

Brett, Michael. "Aghlabids." *Dictionary of the Middle Ages* 1: 70–72. New York, 1982.

Cahen, Claude. "Amalfi en Orient à la veille, au moment et au lendemain de la Première Croisade." In *Amalfi nel Medioevo,* Convegno Internazionale 1973, pp. 271–83. Salerno, 1977.

———. "Quelques problèmes concernant l'expansion économique musulmane au haut Moyen Age." In *L'Occidente e l'Islam* (1964 *Settimane*), 2: 428–29. Spoleto, 1965.

———. [review article], *Journal of the Economic and Social History of the Orient* 2 (1959): 234–54.

———. "Un texte peu connu relatif au commerce oriental d'Amalfi au X siècle." *ASPN* n.s. 34 (1955): 61–67. Reprinted in his *Turcobyzantina et Oriens Christianus.* London, 1978.

Camera, Matteo. *Memorie storico-diplomatiche dell'antica città e ducato di Amalfi.* 2 vols. Salerno, 1876.

Campanati, Raffaella Farioli. "La cultura artistica nelle regioni bizantine d'Italia dal VI all'XI secolo." In Cavallo, von Falkenhausen, Campanati, Gigante, Pace, and Rosati, *I Bizantini in Italia.* Milan, 1982.

Capasso, Bartolommeo. "Il *pactum* dal Duca Sergio ai Napoletani (1030?)," *ASPN* 18 (1884): 319–33.

Cassandro, Giovanni. "Il ducato bizantino." In *Storia di Napoli*, ed. Ernesto Pontieri, 8 vols. in 12. Naples, 1967–74. Vol. 2, Part 1.

Cavallo, Guglielmo. *Rotoli di Exultet dell'Italia meridionale*. Bari, 1973.

———. "La trasmissione dei testi nell'area beneventano-cassinese." In *La cultura antica nell'Occidente latino dal VII all'XI secolo* (1974 *Settimane*) I: 357–414. Spoleto, 1975.

Chalandon, Ferdinand. *Histoire de la domination normande en Italie et en Sicile*. 2 vols. Paris, 1907.

Charanis, Peter. "On the Question of the Hellenization of Sicily and Southern Italy During the Middle Ages." *American Historical Review* 52 (1946): 74–86.

Chierici, Gino. "Note sull'architettura della contea Longobarda di Capua." *Bollettino d'Arte* 27 (1933): 543–53.

Cilento, Nicola. *Civiltà napoletana del medioevo nel secolo VI–XII*. Cava dei Tirreni, 1969. (Originally published [some variations] in Vol. 2, Part 2 of *Storia di Napoli*, ed. Ernesto Pontieri, 8 vols. in 12, Naples, 1967–74.)

———. "Le condizioni della vita nella contea longobarda di Capua: Seconda metà del IX secolo." *Rivista Storica Italiana* 63 (1951): 437–68.

———. *Italia meridionale longobarda*. Milan and Naples, 1966.

———. *Le origini della signoria capuana nella Longobardia minore*. See "Abbreviations."

Citarella, Armand O. "Patterns in Medieval Trade: The Commerce of Amalfi Before the Crusades." *Journal of Economic History* 28 (1968): 531–55.

———. "The Relations of Amalfi with the Arab World before the Crusades." *Speculum* 42 (1967): 299–312.

———. "Scambi commerciali fra l'Egitto e Amalfi in un documento inedito della Geniza del Cairo." In his *Commercio di Amalfi nell'alto medioevo*. Salerno, 1977.

Citarella, Armand, and Henry M. Willard. *The Ninth-Century Treasure of Monte Cassino in the Context of Political and Economic Development in South Italy*. Montecassino, 1983.

Colafemmina, Cesare. "Archaeologia ed epigrafia nell'Italia meridionale." In *Italia Judaica: Atti del I Convegno Internazionale (Bari, 1981)*, pp. 199–210. Rome, 1983.

———. "Insediamenti e condizioni degli Ebrei nell'Italia méridionale e insulare." In *Gli Ebrei nell'alto medioevo* (1979 *Settimane*), 1: 197–227. Spoleto, 1980.

Costa-Louillet, G. da. "Saints de Sicile et d'Italie meridionale aux VIII, IX, et X siècles." *Byzantion* 19–20 (1959–60): 89–173.

d'Alverny, Marie-Thérèse. "La connaissance de l'Islam en Occident du IX au milieu du XII siècle." In *L'Occidente e l'Islam* (1964 *Settimane*), 2: 577–602. Spoleto, 1965.

Delogu, Paolo. *Mito di una città meridionale*. Naples, 1977.

Del Treppo, Mario. "La vita economica e sociale in una grande abbazia del Mezzogiorno: San Vincenzo al Volturno nell'alto medioevo." *ASPN* n.s., 35 (1956): 31–110.

Del Treppo, Mario, and Alfonso Leone. *Amalfi medioevale*. Naples, 1977.

Dietrich, Albert. "Islamic Sciences and the Medieval West: Pharmacology." In *Islam and the Medieval West*, vol. 2, ed. Khalil I. Semaan, pp. 50–63. Albany, N.Y., 1980.

Duby, Georges. *Rural Economy and Country Life in the Medieval West*, trans. Cynthia Postan. Columbia, S.C., 1968.

Engreen, Fred R. "Pope John the Eighth and the Arabs." *Speculum* 20 (1945): 318–30.

Ettinghausen, Richard. "Muslim Decorative Arts and Painting: Their Nature and Impact on the Medieval West." In *Islam and the Medieval West*, vol. 2, ed. Stanley Ferber, pp. 5–26. Binghamton, N.Y., 1975.

Fahmy, Aly Mohamed. *Muslim Naval Organization in the Eastern Mediterranean from the Seventh to the Tenth Century A.D.* 2d ed. Cairo, 1966.

Falkenhausen, Vera von. "I Bizantini in Italia." In Cavallo, von Falkenhausen, Campanati, Gigante, Pace, and Rosati, *I Bizantini in Italia*. Milan, 1982.

———. *La dominazione bizantina nell'Italia meridionale dal IX all'XI secolo*. See "Abbreviations."

Fedele, Pietro. "La battaglia del Garigliano dell'anno 915 ed i monumenti che la ricordana." *Archivio della R. Societa Romana di Storia Patria* 22 (1898): 181–211. [Now *Deputazione Romana di Storia Patria*.]

Ferorelli, Nicola. *Gli Ebrei nell'Italia meridionale dall' età romana al secolo XVIII* [1915]. Reprint Bologna, 1966.

Figliuolo, Bruno. "Gli Amalfitani a Cetara: Vicende patrimoniali e attivita economiche (secc. X–XI)." *Annali dell'Istituto Italiano per gli Studi Storici* 6 (1979–80): 31–82.

Fonseca, Cosimo Damiano. "Particolarismo istituzionale e organizzazione ecclesiastica della compagna nell'alto medioevo nell'Italia meridionale." In *Christianizzazione ed organizzazione ecclesiastica della campagna nell'alto medioevo* (1980 *Settimane*), 2: 1163–1200. Spoleto, 1982.

Forcellini, Francesco. "L'impresa di Sicardo contra Amalfi e l'emancipazione politica di questo città del ducato di Napoli." *ASPN* n.s., 24 (1945): 1–48.

Gabrieli, Francesco. "Storia, cultura e civiltà degli Arabi in Italia." In Francesco Gabrieli and Umberto Scerrato, *Gli Arabi in Italia*. Milan, 1979. Reprint 1985.

Galante, Maria. *La datazione dei documenti del* Codex Diplomaticus Cavensis. Salerno, 1980.

———. "Il notaio e il documento notarile a Salerno in epoca longobarda." In *Per una storia del notariato meridionale*. Rome, 1982.

Galasso, Giuseppe. "Le città campane nell'alto medioevo." In his *Mezzogiorno medievale e moderno*. Turin, 1965.

Gay, Jules. See "Abbreviations."

Goitein, S. D. "Changes in the Middle East (950–1150) as Illustrated by the Documents of the Cairo Geniza." In *Islamic Civilization, 950–1150*, ed. D. S. Richards, pp. 17–32. Oxford, 1973.

———. "The Mediterranean Mind in the High Middle Ages, 950–1250." In *Amalfi nel Medioevo* (Convegno Internazionale 1973), pp. 177–92. Salerno, 1977.

———. *A Mediterranean Society*. Vol. 1: *Economic Foundations*. Berkeley and Los Angeles, 1967.

Gould, J. D. *Economic Growth in History*. London, 1972.

Grabar, André. "Le succès des arts orientaux à la cour Byzantine sous les Macédoniens." In *Münchner Jahrbuch der Bildenden Kunst*, 1951, pp. 32–60.

Grierson, Philip. "La cronologia della monetazione salernitane nei secoli XI e XII." *Rivista Italiana di Numismatica* 74 (1972): 153–65. Reprinted in his *Later Medieval Numismatics*. London, 1979.

Guillou, André. "Grecs d'Italie du Sud et de Sicile au Moyen Age: Les Moines." *Mélanges d'Archaeologie et d'Histoire* 75 (1963): 79–110. Reprinted in his *Studies on Byzantine Italy*. London, 1970.

———. "Inchiesta sulla popolazione greca della Sicilia e della Calabria nel Medio Evo." *Rivista Storica Italiana* 75 (1963): 53–68. Reprinted in his *Studies on Byzantine Italy*. London, 1970.

———. "L'Italia bizantina." *Bulletino dell'Istituto Storico Italiano per il Medioevo* 78 (1967): 1–20 and plates. Reprinted in his *Studies on Byzantine Italy*. London, 1970.

———. "La Lucanie byzantine." *Byzantion* 35 (1965):119–49. Reprinted in his *Studies on Byzantine Italy*. London, 1970.

———. "Production and Profits in the Byzantine Province of Italy: An Expanding Society." *Dumbarton Oaks Papers* 28 (1974): 92–112. Reprinted in his *Culture et Société en Italie Byzantine (VI–XI s.)*. London, 1978.

Hamblin, D. J., and M. J. Grunsfeld. *The Appian Way*. New York, 1974.

Heyd, Wilhelm. *Histoire du commerce du Levant au Moyen Age*, Vol 1. Leipzig, 1885.

Hirschberg, H. Z. [J. W.]. *A History of the Jews in North Africa*. 2d ed., rev., 2 vols. Leiden, 1974. Vol. 1.

Hodges, Richard, and John Mitchell. "The San Vincenzo Project, 1982." *Archeologia Medievale* 10 (1983): 363–80.

Hodges, Richard, and John Mitchell, eds. *San Vincenzo al Volturno: The Archaeology, Art and Territory of an Early Medieval Monastery*. BAR International series 252. Oxford, 1985.

Hodges, Richard, and Chris Wickham. "Excavations and Survey at San Vincenzo al Volturno." *Archeologia Medievale* 8 (1981): 483–502.

Hodgkin, Thomas. *Italy and her Invaders*. 8 vols. Oxford, 1880–99. Vols. 6, 7, 8.

Hofmeister, Adolf. "Zur Geschichte Amalfis in der byzantinischen Zeit." *Byzantinisch-Neugriechische Jahrbücher* 1 (1920): 94–127.

Hyde, J. K. *Society and Politics in Medieval Italy*. New York, 1973.

Jamison, Evelyn. "The Norman Administration of Apulia and Capua." *Papers of the British School at Rome* 6 (1913): 211–481.

Jenkins, Romilly J. H. *Byzantium: The Imperial Centuries, A.D. 610–1071*. New York, 1966.

———. "The Emperor Alexander and the Saracen Prisoners." *Atti del VIII Congresso Internationale di studi Byzantini* (Rome, 1953) 1: 389–93. Reprinted in his *Studies on Byzantine History of the 9th and 10th Centuries*. London, 1970.

Joranson, Einar. "The Inception of the Career of the Normans in Italy: Legend and History." *Speculum* 23 (1948): 353–96.

Kauffmann, C. M. *The Baths of Pozzuoli*. Oxford, 1959.

Keller, Alex. "A Renaissance Humanist Looks at 'New' Inventions." *Technology and Culture* 11 (1970): 345–65.

Kitzinger, Ernst. "The Gregorian Reform and the Visual Arts: A Problem of Method." *Transactions of the Royal Historical Society* 5th ser., 22 (1972): 87–102.

Krautheimer, Richard. *Rome: Profile of a City, 312–1308.* Princeton, 1980.

Kreutz, Barbara M. "The Ecology of Maritime Success: The Puzzling Case of Amalfi." *Mediterranean Historical Review* 3 (1988): 103–13.

———. "Mediterranean Contributions to the Medieval Mariner's Compass." *Technology and Culture* 14 (1973): 367–83.

———. "Ships, Shipping and the Implications of Change." *Viator* 7 (1976): 79–109.

Kristeller, Paul Oskar. "The School of Salerno." *Bulletin of the History of Medicine* 17 (1945): 138–94.

———. "La Scuola Medica di Salerno secondo ricerche e scoperte recenti." In *Quaderni del Centro studi e documentazione della Scuola Medica Salernitane* 5. Salerno, 1980.

Krueger, Hilmar C. *Navi e proprieta navale a Genova.* Genoa, 1985.

Kühnel, Ernst. *Die islamischen Elfenbeinskulpturen, VIII–XIII Jahrhundert.* Berlin, 1971.

Lane-Poole, Stanley. *A History of Egypt in the Middle Ages.* London, 1936.

Lauer, Philarète. "Le poème de 'La Destruction de Rome' et les origines de la cité Léonine." *Mélanges d'Archaeologie et d'Histoire* 19 (1899): 307–61.

Leccese, Agate. *Le origini del ducato di Gaeta e le sue relazioni coi ducati di Napoli e di Roma.* Collana minturnense no. 8. Gubbio, 1941.

Lestocquoy, J. "The Tenth Century." *Economic History Review* 27 (1947): 1–14.

Lev, Yaacov. "The Fatimid Navy, Byzantium and the Mediterranean Sea, 909–1034." *Byzantion* 54 (1984): 220–52.

Lewis, Archibald R. *Naval Power and Trade in the Mediterranean: A.D. 500–1100.* Princeton, 1951.

Leyser, Karl. "The Tenth Century in Byzantine-Western Relationships." In his *Medieval Germany and Its Neighbors, 900–1250,* pp. 103–37. London, 1982. Reprinted from *The Relations between East and West in the Middle Ages,* ed. Derek Baker. Edinburgh, 1973.

Lizier, Augusto. *L'economia rurale dell'età prenormanna nell'Italia meridionale.* Palermo, 1907.

Llewellyn, Peter. *Rome in the Dark Ages.* New York, 1971.

Loew, E. A. *The Beneventan Script.* 2d ed. prepared and enlarged by Virginia Brown. 2 vols. Rome, 1980.

Lohrmann, Dietrich. *Das Register Papst Johannes' VIII.* Tübingen, 1968.

Lombard, Maurice. "Arsenaux et bois de marine dans la Méditeranée musulmane (VII–XI siècles)." In *La navire et l'économie maritime,* Deuxième Colloque d'histoire maritime, 1957. Paris, 1958.

Lopez, Robert S. "East and West in the Early Middle Ages." In *Relazioni del X Congresso Internazionale di Scienze Storiche* (1955), 3:113–163.

Lopez, Robert S., and Irving W. Raymond. *Medieval Trade in the Mediterranean World.* New York, 1961.

Lynch, Joseph H. "*Spiritale Vinculum*: The Vocabulary of Spiritual Kinship in Early Medieval Europe." In *Religion, Culture and Society in the Early Middle Ages,* ed. Thomas F. X. Noble and John J. Contremi. Kalamazoo, Mich., 1987.

Mailler, Carmela Russo. "La politica meridionale di Ludovico II e il 'Rythmus de captivitate Ludovici imperatoris'." *Quaderni medievali* 14 (1982): 6–27.

Manselli, Raoul. "La 'Res publica Christiana' e l'Islam nell'alto medioevo." In *L'Occidente e l'Islam* (1964 *Settimane*) 1: 115–47. Spoleto, 1965.

Martin, Jean-Marie. "Notes sur la chronologie des actes de Lucera edités dans le *Codex Diplomaticus Cavensis*." *Mélanges de l'Ecole Française de Rome* 2d. ser., 84 (1972): 7–11.

McKitterick, Rosamond. *The Frankish Kingdoms Under the Carolingians.* London and New York, 1983.

Meiggs, Russell. *Trees and Timber in the Ancient Mediterranean.* Oxford, 1983.

Ménager, L. R. "La byzantinisation réligieuse de l'Italie méridionale (IX–XII siècles) et la politique monastique des Normands d'Italie." *Revue d'histoire ecclesiastique* 53 (1958): 747–74, and 54 (1959): 5–40. Reprinted in his *Hommes et institutions de l'Italie normand.* London, 1981.

———. "La legislation sud-italienne sous la domination normande." In *I normanni e la loro espansione in Europa nell'alto medioevo* (1968 *Settimane*), pp. 439–96. Spoleto, 1969. Reprinted in his *Hommes et institutions de l'Italie normande.* London, 1981.

Merores, Margareta. *Gaeta im frühen Mittelalter, 8–12 Jahrhundert.* Gotha, 1911.

Miller, Timothy. "The Knights of St. John and the Hospitals of the Latin West." *Speculum* 53 (1978): 709–33.

Murray, W. M. "Do Modern Winds Equal Ancient Winds?" *Mediterranean Historical Review* 2 (1987): 139–67.

Musca, Giosue. *L'Emirato di Bari.* Bari, 1964. (2d. ed. 1977, with plates, expanded bibliography, additional notes.)

Noble, Thomas F. X. *The Republic of St. Peter.* Philadelphia, 1984.

Norwich, John Julius. *The Other Conquest.* New York, 1967. [Published in England as *The Normans in the South, 1016–1130.*]

Noschese, Carmine. "Coincidenze e contrasti nei rapporti tra Amalfi e Salerno nell'età prenormanna." *Rassegna Storica Salernitana* 6 (1945): 157–198.

Odegaard, Charles E. "The Empress Engelberge." *Speculum* 26 (1951): 77–103.

Ohnsorge, Werner. "Die Entwicklung der Kaiseridee im 9. Jahrhundert und Süditalien." In his *Abendland und Byzanz*, pp. 184–226. Darmstadt, 1963. Originally published as "L'idea d'Impero nel secolo nono e l'Italia meridionale," in *Atti del III Congresso Internazionale di Studi sull'Alto Medioevo.* Spoleto, 1959.

———. "Das Kaiserbündnis von 842–844 gegen die Sarazenen." *Archiv fur Diplomatik* 1 (1955): 88–131.

Ostrogorsky, George. *History of the Byzantine State.* Trans. Joan Hussey. New Brunswick, N.J., 1957.

Pace, Valentino. "Pittura bizantina nell'Italia meridionale (secolo XI–XIV)." In Cavallo, von Falkenhausen, Campanati, Gigante, Pace, and Rosati, *I Bizantini in Italia.* Milan, 1982.

———. "Quarant'anni di studi sull'arte medievale nell'Italia meridionale." In *Il Mezzogiorno medievale nella storiografia del secondo dopoguerra.* Soveria Mannelli, 1985.

Pertusi, Agostino. "Bisanzio e l'irradiazione della sua civiltà in Occidente nell'alto medioevo." In *Centri e vie di irradiazione della civiltà nell alto medioevo* (1963 *Settimane*), pp. 75–133. Spoleto, 1964.

————. "Nuovi documenti sui Benedettini amalfitani dell'Athos." *Aevum* 17 (1953): 400–429.

Pontieri, Ernesto. "La crisi di Amalfi medioevale." In his *Tra i Normanni nell'Italia Meridionale*. Naples, 1964.

Poupardin, René. *Etude sur les institutions politiques et administratives des principautés lombardes*. See "Abbreviations."

————. "La lettre de Louis II à Basil le macédonien." *Moyen Age* 16 (1903): 185–202.

Pryor, John H. *Geography, Technology, and War*. Cambridge and New York, 1988.

Ramage in South Italy, ed. Edith Clay. Chicago, 1987.

Riddle, John M. "Theory and Practice in Medieval Medicine." *Viator* 5 (1974): 157–84.

Riley-Smith, Jonathan. *The Knights of St. John in Jerusalem and Cyprus, 1050–1310*. New York, 1967.

Roth, Cecil, ed. *The World History of the Jewish People*, ser. 2, vol. 2: *The Dark Ages*. New Brunswick, N.J., 1966.

Rotter, Ekkehart. *Abendland und Sarazenen: Das okzidentale Araberbild und seine Enstehung im Frühmittelalter*. Berlin and New York, 1986.

Rousseau, Olivier. "La visite de Nil de Rossano au Mont-Cassin." In *La Chiesa Greca in Italia dall'VIII al XVI Secolo*: Atti del Convegno Storico Internazionale (Bari, 1969), 3 vols., 3: 1111–37. Padua, 1973. [Published as vols. 20, 21, 22, *Italia Sacra*.]

Ruegg, S. Dominic. "The Underwater Excavation in the Garigliano River: The Roman Port and Bridge at Minturnae." *International Journal of Nautical Archaeology* 12 (1983): 203–18.

Ruggiero, Bruno. "Per una storia della pieve rurale nel Mezzogiorno medievale." In his *Potere, istituzioni, chiese locali*. Bologna, 1977.

————. *Principi, nobilità e chiesa nel Mezzogiorno longobardo: L'esempio di S. Massimo di Salerno*. Naples, 1973.

Saffron, Morris H., ed. *Maurus of Salerno*. Philadelphia, 1972.

Samarrai, Alauddin. "Medieval Commerce and Diplomacy: Islam and Europe, A.D. 850–1300." *Canadian Journal of History* 14 (1980): 1–21.

Sambon, Arthur. *Recueil des monnaies médiévales du Sud de l'Italie avant la domination normande*. Paris, 1919.

San Vincenzo al Volturno e la cripta dell'abbate Epifanio, ed. Abbazia di Montecassino. Cava dei Tirreni, 1970.

Sanders, Paula. "Fatimids." *Dictionary of the Middle Ages*, 5: 24–30. New York, 1985.

Scerrato, Umberto. "Arte Islamica in Italia." In Francesco Gabrieli and Umberto Scerrato, *Gli Arabi in Italia*. Milan, 1979. Reprint 1985.

Schaube, Adolf. *Händelsgeschichte der Romanischen Völker des Mittelmeergebiets bis zum Ende der Kreuzzuge*. Munich and Berlin, 1906.

Schipa, Michelangelo. "Il ducato di Napoli." *ASPN* 17 (1892): 103–42, 358–421, 587–644, 780–807; 27 (1893): 41–65, 247–77, 463–93, 621–51; 19 (1894): 3–36, 231–51, 445–81.

————. "Storia del principato longobardo di Salerno" [1887]. Reprinted in *La Longobardia meridionale*, ed. Nicola Acocella. Rome, 1968.

Schwarz, Ulrich. *Amalfi im frühen Mittelalter (9.–11. Jahrhundert)*. Tübingen, 1978.

Stern, Samuel M. "Tari: The Quarter-Dinar." *Studi Medievali* 3d ser., 11 (1970): 177–207.

Thompson, E. A. *Romans and Barbarians*. Madison, Wisc., 1982.

Udovitch, A. L. "Time, the Sea and Society: Duration of Commercial Voyages on the Southern Shore of the Mediterranean During the High Middle Ages." In *La navigazione mediterranea nell'alto medioevo* (1977 *Settimane*), 2: 503–46. Spoleto, 1978.

Uhlirz, Karl. *Jahrbücher des Deutschen Reiches unter Otto II und Otto III* I. Leipzig, 1902.

Uhlirz, Mathilde. *Jahrbücher des Deutschen Reiches unter Otto II und Otto III* II. Berlin, 1954.

Van Doorninck, Frederick, Jr. et al. "The Glass Wreck: an 11th-Century Merchantman." INA *Newsletter* 15, no. 3 (September 1988).

Vasiliev, A. A. *Byzance et les Arabes*. 2 vols. in 3. Vol. 1: *La dynastie Amorium*, ed. H. Gregoire and M. Canard. Brussels, 1935. Vol. 2, Part I: *La dynastie macédonienne*, ed. M. Canard. Brussels, 1968. [For Vol. 2, Part 2, see "Sources."]

———. *History of the Byzantine Empire*. 2d ed. Madison, Wisc., 1952.

Vehse, Otto. "Das Bündnis gegen die Sarazenen vom Jahre 915." *Quellen und Forschungen aus Italienischen Archiven und Bibliotheken*. Preussischen Historischen Institut 19 (Rome, 1927): 181–204.

Violante, Cinzio. "Le strutture organizzative della cura d'anime nelle campagne dell'Italia centrosettentrionale (secoli V–X)." In *Christianizzazione ed organizzazione ecclesiastica delle campagne nell'alto medioevo* (1980 *Settimane*), 2: 963–1155. Spoleto, 1982.

Volbach, W. F. "Oriental Influence in the Animal Sculpture of Campania." *Art Bulletin* 24 (1942): 172–80.

Warriner, Doreen. *Economics of Peasant Farming*. 2d ed. London and New York, 1964.

Wettstein, Janine. *Sant'Angelo in Formis et la peinture médiévale in Campanie*. Geneva, 1960.

White, Lynn, jr. *Latin Monasticism in Norman Sicily*. Cambridge, Mass., 1938.

Wickham, Chris. *Early Medieval Italy*. London, 1981.

———. *Il problema dell'incastellamento nell'Italia centrale: L'esempio di San Vincenzo al Volturno*. Florence, 1985.

———. "The *terra* of San Vincenzo al Volturno in the 8th to 12th Centuries: The Historical Framework." In *San Vincenzo al Volturno: The Archaeology, Art and Territory of an Early Medieval Monastery*, ed. Richard Hodges and John Mitchell. BAR International Series 252, pp. 227–58. Oxford, 1985.

Wolfram, Herwig. "The Shaping of the Early Medieval Principality and a Type of Non-Royal Rulership." *Viator* 2 (1971): 33–51.

Zupko, Ronald E. *British Weights and Measures: A History from Antiquity to the Seventeenth Century*. Madison, Wisc., 1977.

Index

University of Pennsylvania Press
MIDDLE AGES SERIES
Ruth Mazo Karras and Edward Peters, General Editors

F. R. P. Akehurst, trans. *The* Coutumes de Beauvaisis *of Philippe de Beaumanoir*. 1992
F. R. P. Akehurst, trans. *The* Etablissements de Saint Louis. 1996
Peter L. Allen. *The Art of Love: Amatory Fiction from Ovid to the* Romance of the Rose. 1992
David Anderson. *Before the Knight's Tale: Imitation of Classical Epic in Boccaccio's* Teseida. 1988
Benjamin Arnold. *Count and Bishop in Medieval Germany: A Study of Regional Power, 1100–1350*. 1991
Mark C. Bartusis. *The Late Byzantine Army: Arms and Society, 1204–1453*. 1992
Thomas N. Bisson, ed. *Cultures of Power: Lordship, Status, and Process in Twelfth-Century Europe*. 1995
Uta-Renate Blumenthal. *The Investiture Controversy: Church and Monarchy from the Ninth to the Twelfth Century*. 1988
Gerald A. Bond. *The Loving Subject: Desire, Eloquence, and Power in Romanesque France*. 1995
Daniel Bornstein, trans. *Dino Compagni's* Chronicle *of Florence*. 1986
Maureen Boulton. *The Song in the Story: Lyric Insertions in French Narrative Fiction, 1200–1400*. 1993
Betsy Bowden. *Chaucer Aloud: The Varieties of Textual Interpretation*. 1987
Charles R. Bowlus. *Franks, Moravians, and Magyars: The Struggle for the Middle Danube, 788–907*. 1995
James William Brodman. *Ransoming Captives in Crusader Spain: The Order of Merced on the Christian-Islamic Frontier*. 1986
Kevin Brownlee and Sylvia Huot, eds. *Rethinking the* Romance of the Rose*: Text, Image, Reception*. 1992
Matilda Tomaryn Bruckner. *Shaping Romance: Interpretation, Truth, and Closure in Twelfth-Century French Fictions*. 1993
Otto Brunner (Howard Kaminsky and James Van Horn Melton, eds. and trans.). Land *and Lordship: Structures of Governance in Medieval Austria*. 1992
Robert I. Burns, S.J., ed. *Emperor of Culture: Alfonso X the Learned of Castile and His Thirteenth-Century Renaissance*. 1990
David Burr. *Olivi and Franciscan Poverty: The Origins of the* Usus Pauper *Controversy*. 1989
David Burr. *Olivi's Peaceable Kingdom: A Reading of the Apocalypse Commentary*. 1993
Thomas Cable. *The English Alliterative Tradition*. 1991
Anthony K. Cassell and Victoria Kirkham, eds. and trans. *Diana's Hunt/Caccia di Diana: Boccaccio's First Fiction*. 1991

John C. Cavadini. *The Last Christology of the West: Adoptionism in Spain and Gaul, 785–820.* 1993

Brigitte Cazelles. *The Lady as Saint: A Collection of French Hagiographic Romances of the Thirteenth Century.* 1991

Karen Cherewatuk and Ulrike Wiethaus, eds. *Dear Sister: Medieval Women and the Epistolary Genre.* 1993

Anne L. Clark. *Elisabeth of Schönau: A Twelfth-Century Visionary.* 1992

Willene B. Clark and Meradith T. McMunn, eds. *Beasts and Birds of the Middle Ages: The Bestiary and Its Legacy.* 1989

Richard C. Dales. *The Scientific Achievement of the Middle Ages.* 1973

Charles T. Davis. *Dante's Italy and Other Essays.* 1984

William J. Dohar. *The Black Death and Pastoral Leadership: The Diocese of Hereford in the Fourteenth Century.* 1994

Katherine Fischer Drew, trans. *The Burgundian Code.* 1972

Katherine Fischer Drew, trans. *The Laws of the Salian Franks.* 1991

Katherine Fischer Drew, trans. *The Lombard Laws.* 1973

Nancy Edwards. *The Archaeology of Early Medieval Ireland.* 1990

Richard K. Emmerson and Ronald B. Herzman. *The Apocalyptic Imagination in Medieval Literature.* 1992

Theodore Evergates. *Feudal Society in Medieval France: Documents from the County of Champagne.* 1993

Felipe Fernández-Armesto. *Before Columbus: Exploration and Colonization from the Mediterranean to the Atlantic, 1229–1492.* 1987

Judith Ferster. *Fictions of Advice: The Literature and Politics of Counsel in Late Medieval England.* 1996

Pier Massimo Forni. *Adventures in Speech: Rhetoric and Narration in Boccaccio's Decameron.* 1996

Jerold C. Frakes. *Brides and Doom: Gender, Property, and Power in Medieval Women's Epic.* 1994

R. D. Fulk. *A History of Old English Meter.* 1992

Patrick J. Geary. *Aristocracy in Provence: The Rhône Basin at the Dawn of the Carolingian Age.* 1985

Peter Heath. *Allegory and Philosophy in Avicenna (Ibn Sînâ), with a Translation of the Book of the Prophet Muḥammad's Ascent to Heaven.* 1992

John Bell Henneman. *Olivier de Clisson and Political Society in France Under Charles V and Charles VI.* 1996

J. N. Hillgarth, ed. *Christianity and Paganism, 350–750: The Conversion of Western Europe.* 1986

Richard C. Hoffmann. *Land, Liberties, and Lordship in a Late Medieval Countryside: Agrarian Structures and Change in the Duchy of Wroclaw.* 1990

Robert Hollander. *Boccaccio's Last Fiction:* Il Corbaccio. 1988

John Y. B. Hood. *Aquinas and the Jews.* 1995

Edward B. Irving, Jr. *Rereading* Beowulf. 1989

Richard A. Jackson, ed. Ordines Coronationis Franciae: *Texts and Ordines for the Coronation of Frankish and French Kings and Queens in the Middle Ages, Vol. I.* 1995

C. Stephen Jaeger. *The Envy of Angels: Cathedral Schools and Social Ideals in Medieval Europe, 950–1200*. 1994

C. Stephen Jaeger. *The Origins of Courtliness: Civilizing Trends and the Formation of Courtly Ideals, 939–1210*. 1985

Jenny Jochens. *Old Norse Images of Women*. 1996

Richard W. Kaeuper and Elspeth Kennedy, trans. *The* Book of Chivalry *of Geoffroi de Charny: Text, Context, and Translation*. 1996

Donald J. Kagay, trans. *The Usatges of Barcelona: The Fundamental Law of Catalonia*. 1994

Richard Kay. *Dante's Christian Astrology*. 1994

Ellen E. Kittell. *From* Ad Hoc *to Routine: A Case Study in Medieval Bureaucracy*. 1991

Alan C. Kors and Edward Peters, eds. *Witchcraft in Europe, 1100–1700: A Documentary History*. 1972

Barbara M. Kreutz. *Before the Normans: Southern Italy in the Ninth and Tenth Centuries*. 1992

Michael P. Kuczynski. *Prophetic Song: The Psalms as Moral Discourse in Late Medieval England*. 1995

E. Ann Matter. *The Voice of My Beloved: The Song of Songs in Western Medieval Christianity*. 1990

Shannon McSheffrey. *Gender and Heresy: Women and Men in Lollard Communities, 1420–1530*. 1995

A. J. Minnis. *Medieval Theory of Authorship*. 1988

Lawrence Nees. *A Tainted Mantle: Hercules and the Classical Tradition at the Carolingian Court*. 1991

Lynn H. Nelson, trans. *The Chronicle of San Juan de la Peña: A Fourteenth-Century Official History of the Crown of Aragon*. 1991

Barbara Newman. *From Virile Woman to WomanChrist: Studies in Medieval Religion and Literature*. 1995

Thomas F. X. Noble. *The Republic of St. Peter: The Birth of the Papal State, 680–825*. 1984

Joseph F. O'Callaghan. *The Learned King: The Reign of Alfonso X of Castile*. 1993

Odo of Tournai (Irven M. Resnick, trans.). On Original Sin *and* A Disputation with the Jew, Leo, Concerning the Advent of Christ, the Son of God: *Two Theological Treatises*. 1994

David M. Olster. *Roman Defeat, Christian Response, and the Literary Construction of the Jew*. 1994

William D. Paden, ed. *The Voice of the Trobairitz: Perspectives on the Women Troubadours*. 1989

Edward Peters. *The Magician, the Witch, and the Law*. 1982

Edward Peters, ed. *Christian Society and the Crusades, 1198-1229: Sources in Translation, including* The Capture of Damietta *by Oliver of Paderborn*. 1971

Edward Peters, ed. *The First Crusade: The* Chronicle of Fulcher of Chartres *and Other Source Materials*. 1971

Edward Peters, ed. *Heresy and Authority in Medieval Europe*. 1980

James M. Powell. *Albertanus of Brescia: The Pursuit of Happiness in the Early Thirteenth Century*. 1992

James M. Powell. *Anatomy of a Crusade, 1213–1221*. 1986

Susan A. Rabe. *Faith, Art, and Politics at Saint-Riquier: The Symbolic Vision of Angilbert*. 1995

Jean Renart (Patricia Terry and Nancy Vine Durling, trans.). *The Romance of the Rose or Guillaume de Dole*. 1993

Michael Resler, trans. Erec *by Hartmann von Aue*. 1987

Pierre Riché (Michael Idomir Allen, trans.). *The Carolingians: A Family Who Forged Europe*. 1993

Pierre Riché (Jo Ann McNamara, trans.). *Daily Life in the World of Charlemagne*. 1978

Jonathan Riley-Smith. *The First Crusade and the Idea of Crusading*. 1986

Joel T. Rosenthal. *Old Age in Medieval England: The Search for Lived Experience*. 1996

Joel T. Rosenthal. *Patriarchy and Families of Privilege in Fifteenth-Century England*. 1991

Teofilo F. Ruiz. *Crisis and Continuity: Land and Town in Late Medieval Castile*. 1994

James A. Rushing, Jr. *Images of Adventure: Ywain in the Visual Arts*. 1995

James A. Schultz. *The Knowledge of Childhood in the German Middle Ages, 1100–1350*. 1995

John A. Scott. *Dante's Political Purgatory*. 1996

Pamela Sheingorn, ed. and trans. *The Book of Sainte Foy*. 1995

Robin Chapman Stacey. *The Road to Judgment: From Custom to Court in Medieval Ireland and Wales*. 1994

Sarah Stanbury. *Seeing the* Gawain-*Poet: Description and the Act of Perception*. 1992

Robert D. Stevick. *The Earliest Irish and English Bookarts: Visual and Poetic Forms Before A.D. 1000*. 1994

Thomas C. Stillinger. *The Song of Troilus: Lyric Authority in the Medieval Book*. 1992

Susan Mosher Stuard. *A State of Deference: Ragusa/Dubrovnik in the Medieval Centuries*. 1992

Susan Mosher Stuard, ed. *Women in Medieval History and Historiography*. 1987

Susan Mosher Stuard, ed. *Women in Medieval Society*. 1976

Jonathan Sumption. *The Hundred Years War: Trial by Battle*. 1992

Ronald E. Surtz. *The Guitar of God: Gender, Power, and Authority in the Visionary World of Mother Juana de la Cruz (1481–1534)*. 1990

Ronald E. Surtz. *Writing Women in Late Medieval and Early Modern Spain: The Mothers of Saint Teresa of Avila*. 1995

Del Sweeney, ed. *Agriculture in the Middle Ages: Technology, Practice, and Representation*. 1995

William H. TeBrake. *A Plague of Insurrection: Popular Politics and Peasant Revolt in Flanders, 1323–1328*. 1993

Patricia Terry, trans. *Poems of the Elder Edda*. 1990

Hugh M. Thomas. *Vassals, Heiresses, Crusaders, and Thugs: The Gentry of Angevin Yorkshire, 1154–1216*. 1993

Mary F. Wack. *Lovesickness in the Middle Ages: The* Viaticum *and Its Commentaries*. 1990

Benedicta Ward. *Miracles and the Medieval Mind: Theory, Record, and Event, 1000–1215*. 1982

Suzanne Fonay Wemple. *Women in Frankish Society: Marriage and the Cloister, 500–900.* 1981

Kenneth Baxter Wolf. *Making History: The Normans and Their Historians in Eleventh-Century Italy.* 1995

Jan M. Ziolkowski. *Talking Animals: Medieval Latin Beast Poetry, 750–1150.* 1993